Reading Galatians, Philippians, and 1 Thessalonians

A Literary and Theological Commentary

Charles B. Cousar

SMYTH&HELWYS
PUBLISHING INCORPORATED   MACON GEORGIA
WWW.HELWYS.COM

Smyth & Helwys Publishing, Inc.
6316 Peake Road
Macon, Georgia 31210-3960
1-800-747-3016

Charles B. Cousar

The paper used in this publication meets the minimum
requirements of American National Standard for Information
Sciences—Permanence of Paper for Printed Library Materials.
ANSI Z39.48–1984   (alk. paper)

Library of Congress Cataloging-in-Publication Data

Cousar, Charles B.
Reading Galatians, Philippians, and 1 Thessalonians :
a literary and theological commentary / Charles B. Cousar.
        p. cm.
    Includes bibliographical references.
    ISBN 1-57312-323-4 (pbk.)
        1. Bible. N.T. Galatians—Commentaries.
2. Bible. N.T. Philippians—Commentaries.
3. Bible. N.T. Thessalonians, 1st—Commentaries.
I. Title: Reading Galatians, Philippians, and First Thessalonians. II. Title.

BS2685.3 .C65 2001
227'.077—dc21   2001018381

Contents

Philippians

1 Thessalonians

for
Davis and Elizabeth
Rachel and William

Editor's Foreword

"Reading the New Testament" is a commentary series that aims to present cutting-edge research in popular form that is accessible to upper-level under-graduates, seminarians, seminary educated pastors, and educated laypersons, as well as to graduate students and professors. The volumes in this series do not follow the word-by-word, phrase-by-phrase, verse-by-verse method of traditional commentaries. Rather, they are concerned to understand large thought units and their relationship to an author's thought as a whole. The focus is on a close reading of the final form of the text. The aim is to make one feel at home in the biblical text itself. The approach of these volumes involves a concern both for *how* an author communicates and *what* the religious point of the text is. Care is taken to relate both the *how* and the *what* of the text to its milieu: Christian (NT and noncanonical), Jewish (scriptural and postbiblical), and Greco-Roman. This enables both the communication strategies and the religious message of the text to be clarified over against a range of historical and cultural possibilities. Moreover, a section of commentary on a large thought unit will often contain a brief excursus on some topic raised by the material in the unit, sometimes sketching OT, postbiblical Jewish, Greco-Roman, NT, and noncanonical Christian views on the subject. Throughout, the basic concern is to treat the NT texts as religious documents whose religious message needs to be set forth with compelling clarity. All other concerns are subordinated to this. It is the hope of all participants in this project that our efforts at exposition will enable the NT to be understood better and communicated more competently.

—Charles H. Talbert
General Editor

Author's Preface

This commentary has been a long time in the writing and production process. Other institutional responsibilities necessitated my putting the manuscript aside on two different occasions, and too many months went by without its completion. The shift in publishers for the series meant a further delay. I am grateful for the patience of Charles Talbert, who has continued to nudge me along the way. And yet the delay, I trust, has resulted in a stronger volume. In the intervening time, several classes of students have worked through the exegesis of these three letters with me and have opened doors on the text that might otherwise have remained closed. I am indebted to them for their insights.

I owe a huge debt to Columbia Theological Seminary for the opportunity to teach the New Testament, for its generous sabbatical leave policy, and for colleagues and administrators who have been supportive through the long process.

Unfortunately, I completed the material on Galatians before the appearance of J. Louis Martyn's important commentary on Galatians in the Anchor Bible. As will be obvious, I am indebted to him at a number of points, but my sources were limited to his essays. Beverly R. Gaventa graciously gave me access to her typed manuscript on 1 and 2 Thessalonians, which has subsequently appeared as an excellent volume in the *Interpretation* series. Shirley Guthrie has gone beyond the call of duty in reading much of the manuscript and has given helpful advice at a number of critical points. Rick Olson has ably assisted in reading the final copy. Betty, my wife, has patiently listened to my frustrations in writing and throughout has offered constant support.

Throughout the commentary I have made my own translations from the Greek text. When published translations have been used, they are identical.

Works Cited

Alexander, Loveday
   1989   "Hellenistic Letter-Forms and the Structure of Philippians." *JSNT* 37: 87-101.
Aune, David E.
   1981   "Review of *Galatians.*" *RSR* 7: 323-328.
   1987   *The New Testament in Its Literary Environment.* Philadelphia: Westminster.
Barclay, John M. G.
   1987   "Mirror-Reading a Polemical Letter: Galatians as a Test Case." *NTS* 31: 73-83.
   1988   *Obeying the Truth: Paul's Ethic on Galatians.* Minneapolis: Fortress.
Barth, Karl
   1962   *The Epistle to the Philippians.* London: SCM.
Baur, F. C.
   1987   *Paulus, der Apostle Jesu Christi: Sein Leben und Wirken, Seine Briefe und Seine Lehre.* Leipzig: Fues's Verlag.
Beare, F. W.
   1959   *The Epistle to the Philippians.* BNTC. London: A & C Black.
Beardslee, William
   1975   "Narrative Form in the New Testament and Process Theology." *Encounter* 36: 301-315.
Becker, Jürgen
   1993   *Paul: Apostle to the Gentiles.* Louisville: Westminster/John Knox.

Best, Ernest
    1968   *Paul and His Converts.* Edinburgh: T & T Clark.
    1972   *The First and Second Epistles to the Thessalonians.* BNTC.
                  London: Adam & Charles Black

Betz, Hans Dieter
    1979   *Galatians.* Hermeneia. Philadelphia: Fortress.

Bligh, John Bligh
    1969   *Galatians: A Discussion of Paul's Epistle.* London: St. Paul
                  Publications.

Bruce, F. F.
    1982   *Commentary on Galatians.* NIGTC. Grand Rapids:
                  Eerdmans.

Bultmann, Rudolf
    1952   *Theology of the New Testament.* London: SCM.

Burton, E. D.
    1928   *A Critical and Exegetical Commentary on the Epistle to the
                  Galatians.* ICC. Edinburgh: T & T Clark.

Caird, George B.
    1976   *Paul's Letters from Prison.* NCB. Oxford: Oxford University
                  Press.

Calvin, John
    1965   *The Epistles of Paul the Apostle to the Galatians, Ephesians,
                  Philippians, and Colossians.* Grand Rapids: Eerdmans.

Castelli, Elizabeth A.
    1991   *Imitating Paul: A Discourse of Power.* Louisville:
                  Westminster/John Knox.

Collange, Jean-Francois
    1979   *The Epistle of Paul to the Philippians.* London: Epworth.

Collins, Raymond F.
    1984   *Studies on the First Letter to the Thessalonians.* Leuven:
                  University Press.

Cousar, Charles B.
    1990   *A Theology of the Cross: The Death of Jesus in the Pauline
                  Letters.* Minneapolis: Fortress.

Croy, N. Clayton
    1996   " 'To Die is Gain' [Phil 1:19-26]: Does Paul Contemplate
                  Suicide?" Unpublished Paper read at the Annual Meeting of
                  the Society of Biblical Literature.

Cullmann, Oscar
1962   *Peter: Disciple, Apostle, Martyr.* Philadelphia: Westminster.
Dahl, Nils A.
1977   *Studies in Paul: Theology for the Early Christian Mission.*
            Minneapolis: Augsburg.
De Boer, W. P.
1962   *The Imitation of Paul: An Exegeical Study.* Kampen: J. H.
            Kok.
Deissmann, Adolf
1912   *St. Paul: A Study in Social and Religious History* . London:
            Hodder & Stoughton.
Donfried, Karl Paul
1984   "Paul and Judaism: 1 Thess 2:13-16 as a Test Case." *Interp*
            38: 242-253.
Dunn, J. D. G.
1980   *Christology in the Making: A New Testament Inquiry into the
            Origins of the Doctrine of the Incarnation.* Philadelphia:
            Westminster.
1990   *Jesus, Paul, and the Law: Studies in Mark and Galatians.*
            Louisville: Westminster/John Knox.
1993   *The Epistle to the Galatians.* BNTC. Peabody MA:
            Hendrickson.
Esler, Philip F.
1994   *The First Christians in Their Social Worlds: Social-Scientific
            Approaches to New Testament Interpretation.* London:
            Rutledge.
Fee, Gordon D.
1995   *Paul's Letter to the Philippians.* NICNT. Grand Rapids:
            Eerdmans.
Fiore, Benjamin
1986   *The Function of Personal Example in the Socratic and
            Pastoral Epistles.* Rome: Pontifical Institute Press.
Fitzgerald, John T., ed.
1996   *Friendship, Flattery, & Frankness of Speech: Studies on
            Friendship in the New Testament World.* Leiden: E. J. Brill.
Fowl, Stephen
1990   *The Story of Christ in the Ethics of Paul: An Analysis of the
            Function of the Hymnic Material in the Pauline Corpus.*
            JSNTSup. Sheffield: JSOT Press.

Frame, J. E.
    1912   *A Critical and Exegetical Commentary on the Epistles of Paul to the Thessalonians.* New York: Charles Scribner's Sons.
Fredrickson, David E.
    1996   "*Parresia* in the Pauline Letters." In *Friendship, Flattery, & Frankness of Speech: Studies on Friendship in the New Testament.* Edited by John T. Fitzgerald. Leiden: Brill, 163-183.
Furnish, V. P.
    1963–1964   "The Place and Purpose of Philippians III." *NTS* 10: 80-88.
    1972   *The Love Command in the New Testament.* Nashville: Abingdon.
Garland, David E.
    1985   "The Composition and Unity of Philippians: Some Neglected Factors." *NovT* 27: 141-173
Gaventa, Beverly R.
    1985   *From Darkness to Light: Aspects of Conversion in the New Testament.* Philadelphia: Fortress.
    1990   "The Maternity of Paul." In *The Conversation Continues: Studies in Paul and John in Honor of J. Louis Martyn.* Edited by R T. Fortna and B. R. Gaventa. Nashville: Abingdon.
    1991   "The Singularity of the Gospel." In *Pauline Theology, Vol. I: Thessalonians, Philippians, Galatians, Philemon.* Edited by J. M. Bassler. Minneapolis: Fortress, 147-159.
    1991   "Apostles as Babes and Nurses in 1 Thessalonians 2:7." In *Faith and History: Essays in Honor of Paul W. Meyer.* Edited by J. T. Carroll, C. H. Cosgrove, E. E. Johnson. Atlanta: Scholars, 193-207.
    1998   *First and Second Thessalonians.* Interpretation. Louisville: John Knox.
Geoffrion, Timothy C.
    1993   *The Rhetorical Purpose and the Political and Military Character of Philippians: A Call to Stand Firm.* Lewiston NY: Mellen.
Grundmann, Walter
    1972   "*tapeinos*, etc." In *TDNT*, 8:1-26.
Hall, Robert G.
    1887   "The Rhetorical Outline for Galatians: A Reconsideration." *JBL* 106: 277-287.

Hays, Richard B.

1983   *The Faith of Jesus Christ: An Investigation of the Narrative
            Substructure of Galatians 3:1–4:11.* Chico CA: Scholars.

1989   *Echoes of Scripture in the Letters of Paul.* New Haven: Yale
            University Press.

Hendrix, Holland L.

1992   "Philippi." In *ABD*: 5: 313-317.

Hengel, Martin

1989   *The Zealots: Investigations into the Jewish Freedom Movement
            in the Period from Herod until 70 A.D.* Edinburgh: T & T
            Clark.

Holladay, Carl R.

1969   "Paul's Opponents in Philippians 3." *ResQ* 3: 77-90.

Hooker, Morna D.

1990   *From Adam to Christ: Essays on Paul.* Cambridge:
            Cambridge University Press.

1990   "*Pistis Christou.*" In *From Adam to Christ: Essays on Paul.*
            Cambridge: Cambridge University Press.

Howard, George

1990   *Paul: Crisis in Galatia: A Study in Early Christian Theology.*
            Cambridge: Cambridge University Press.

Hultgren, Arland J.

1987   *Christ and His Benefits: Christology and Redemption in the
            New Testament.* Philadelphia: Fortress.

Hurtado, Larry H.

1985   "Jesus as Lordly Example in Philippians 2:5-11." In *From
            Jesus to Paul.* Edited by Peter Richardson and John C.
            Hurd. Waterloo: Wilfred Lauieer University Press, 113-
            126.

Jewett, Robert

1970   "Conflicting Movements in the Early Church as Reflected
            in Philippians." *NovT* 12: 362-389.

1971   "The Agitators and the Galatian Congregation." *NTS* 17:
            198-212.

Johnson, Luke T.

1978   "II Timothy and the Polemic Against False Teachers: A
            Reexamination." *JRelS* 6: 1-24.

Käsemann, Ernst
1968   "A Critical Analysis of Philippians 2:5-11." In *God and Christ: Existence and Province.* Edited by Robert Funk. New York: Harper & Row, 45-88.
1971   *Perspectives on Paul.* Philadelphia: Fortress.
Keck, Leander E.
1979   *Paul and His Letters.* Philadelphia: Fortress.
Kennedy, George A.
1984   *New Testament Interpretation through Rhetorical Criticism.* Chapel Hill: University of North Carolia Press.
Kilpatrick, G. D.
1959   "Galatians 1:18. *HISTORESAI KEPHAN.*" In *New Testament Essays: Studies in Memory of T. W. Manson.* Manchester: University of Manchester Press, 144-148.
1968   "*Blepete*, Philippians 3:2." In *In Memoriam Paul Kahle.* Edited by Matthew Black and G. Fohrer. Berlin: Töpelmann, 146-148.
Koester, Helmut
1961–1962 "The Purpose of a Polemic of a Pauline Fragment." *NTS* 8: 317-332.
1979   "1 Thessalonians: Experiment in Christian Writing." In *Continuity and Discontinuity in Church History: Essays Presented to George H. Williams.* Edited by F. F. Church and Timothy George. Leiden: Brill, 33-44.
Konstan, David
1997   *Friendship in the Classical World.* Cambridge: Cambridge University Press.
Kurz, William S.
1985   "Kenotic Imitation of Paul and of Christ in Philippians 2 & 3." In *Discipleship in the New Testament.* Edited by F. Segovia. Philadelphia: Fortress, 103-126.
Lategan, Bernard
1988   "Is Paul Defending His Apostleship in Galatians?" *NTS* 34: 411-430.
Lightfoot, J. B.
1913   *St. Paul's Epistle to the Philippians.* London: Macmillan.
Lincoln, Andrew T.
1981   *Paradise Now and Not Yet: Studies in the Role of the Heavenly Dimension in Paul's Thought with Special Reference to his Eschatology.* Cambridge: Cambridge University Press.

Longenecker, Richard N.
  1990   *Galatians.* WBC. Dallas: Word.
Loymeyer, Ernst
  1953   *Die Briefe an die Philipper, an die Kolosser und an Philemon.*
             KEKNT. Göttingen: Vanderhoeck und Ruprecht.
Lyons, George
  1985   *Pauline Autobiography: Toward a New Understanding.*
             Atlanta: Scholars.
Malherbe, Abraham J.
  1970   " 'Gentle as a Nurse': The Cynic Background to 1 Thess 2."
             NovT 12: 203-217.
  1983   *Social Aspects of Early Christianity.* Philadelphia: Fortress.
  1983   "Exhortation in First Thessalonians. *NovT* 25: 238-256.
  1987   *Paul and the Thessalonians.* Philadelphia: Fortress.
  1988   *Ancient Epistolary Theorists.* Atlanta: Scholars.
  1992   "Hellenistic Moralists and the New Testament." In *Aufstieg
             und Niedergang der römischen Welt.* Edited by W. Haase and
             H. Temporini. Berlin: Walter de Gruyter, 27: 287-293.
Marshall, I. Howard
  1983   *1 & 2 Thessalonians.* NCBC. Grand Rapids: Eerdmans.
Marshall, Peter
  1987   *Enmity in Corinth: Social Conventions in Paul's Relations
             with the Corinthians.* WUNT. Tübingen: Mohr Siebeck.
Martin, Dale B.
  1990   *Slavery as Salvation: The Metaphor of Slavery in Pauline
             Christianity.* New Haven: Yale University Press.
Martin, Ralph P.
  1976   *Philippians.* NCBC. Grand Rapids: Eerdamns.
  1983   *Carmen Christi: Philippians 2:5-11 in Recent Interpretation
             and in the Setting of Early Christian Worship.* Grand Rapids:
             Eerdmans, 1983.
Martyn, J. Louis
  1983   "A Law-Observant Mission to Gentiles: The Background of
             Galatians." *MQR* 22: 221-236.
  1985   "Apocalyptic Antinomies in Paul's Letter to the Galatians."
             NTS 31: 410-424.
  1986   "The Crucial Event in the History of the Law." In *Theology
             and Ethics in Paul and His Modern Interpreters: Essays in
             Honor of Victor Paul Furnish.* Edited by E. H. Lovering Jr.
             and J. L. Sumney. Nashville: Abingdon, 48-61.

1990   "The Covenants of Hagar and Sarah." In *Faith and History:*
            Essays in Honor of Paul Meyer. Edited by J. T. Carroll, C. H.
            Cosgrove, and E. E. Johnson. Atlanta: Scholars, 160-192.

1993   "Covenant, Christ, and Church in Galatians." In *The*
            Future of Christology: Essays in Honor of Leander Keck.
            Edited by A. J. Malherbe and W. A. Meeks. Minneapolis:
            Fortress, 137-151.

1995   "Christ, the Elements of the Cosmos, and the Law in
            Galatians." In *The Social World of the First Christians: Essays*
            in Honor of Wayne A.Meeks. Edited by L. M. White and O.
            L. Yarbrough. Minneapolis: Fortress, 16-39.

1997   *Theological Issues in the Letters of Paul*. Abingdon: Nashville.

Matera, Frank J.
1992   *Galatians*. Sacra Pagina. Collegeville MN: Liturgical Press.

Meeks, Wayne A.
1981   "Review of *Galatians*." *JBL* 100: 304-307.

1991   "The Man from Heaven in Paul's Letter to the
            Philippians." In *The Future of Early Christianity*. Edited by
            Birger A. Pearson. Minneapolis: Fortress, 329-336.

Minear, Paul
1979   "The Crucified World: The Enigma of Galatians 6:14." In
            Theologia Crucis—Signum Crucis. Edited by Carl Andresen
            und Gunther Klein. Tübingen: J. C. B. Mohr, 395-407.

Mullins, T. Y.
1964   "Disclosure: A Literary Form in the New Testament." *NovT* 7:
            44-50.

Mussner, Franz
1974   *Der Galaterbrief*. HThK. Freiburg: Herder.

O'Brien, Peter T.
1991   *Commentary on Philippians*. NIGTC. Grand Rapids:
            Eerdmans.

Olbricht, Thomas H.
1990   "An Aristototelian Analysis of 1 Thessalonians." In *Greek,*
            Romans, and Christians: Essays in Honor of Abraham J.
            Malherbe. Edited by D. L. Balch, Everett Ferguson, and W.
            A. Meeks. Minneapolis: Fortress, 216-236.

Orchard, B.
1944   "A New Solution to the Galatians Problem." *BJRL* 28: 165-
            167.

Pearson, B. A.
1971   "1   Thessalonians   2:14-16:   A   Deutero-Pauline
            Interpolation." *HTR* 64: 79-94.
Rahtjen, B. D.
1959–1960 "The Three Letters of Paul to the Philippians." *NTS* 6:
            167-173
Reumann, John
1984   "Philippians 3:20-21—a Hymnic Fragment?" *NTS* 30:
            593-609.
Richard, Earl J.
1995   *First and Second Thessalonians.* Sacra Pagina. Collegeville
            MN: The Liturgical Press.
Saller, Robert P.
1982   *Personal Patronage under the Early Empire.* Cambridge:
            Cambridge University Press.
Sampley, J. Paul
1991   *Walking Between the Times: Paul's Moral Reasoning.*
            Minneapolis: Fortress.
Schlier, Heinrich
1965   *Der Brief an die Galater.* KEK. Göttingen: Vanderhoeck
            und Ruprecht.
Schmithals, Walter
1972   *Paul and the Gnostics.* Nashville: Abingdon.
Schubert, Paul
1939   *Form and Function of the Pauline Thanksgiving.* Berlin:
            Töpelmann.
Schütz, John Howard
1975   *Paul and the Anatomy of Apostolic Authority.* SNTSMS.
            Cambridge: Cambridge University Press.
Smith, Christopher C.
1996   "*Ekkleisai* in Gal 4:17: The Motif of the Excluded Lover as
            a Metaphor of Manipulation." *CBQ* 58.
Stowers, Stanley K.
1986   *Letter Writing in Greco-Roman Antiquity.* Philadelphia:
            Westminster.
1991   "Friends and Enemies in the Politics of Heaven." In *Pauline
            Theology, Vol. I: Thessalonians, Philippians, Galatians,
            Philemon.* Edited by Jouette M. Bassler. Minneapolis:
            Fortress.

Talbert, Charles H.
1967   "The Problem of Preexistence in Philippians 2:6-11." *JBL* 6:
            141-153.
Torjesen, Karen J.
1993   *When Women Were Priests: Women's Leadership in the Early
            Church and the Scandal of their Subordination in the Rise of
            Christianity.* San Francisco: Harper's.
Verseput, D. J.
1993   "Paul's Gentile Mission and the Jewish Christian
            Community: A Study of the Narrative in Galatians 1 and
            2." *NTS* 39: 36-58.
Weima, J. A. D.
1994   *Neglected Endings: The Significance of the Pauline Letter
            Closings.* JSNTSup. Sheffield: JSOT Press.
Wengst, Klaus
1988   *Humility: Solidarity with the Humiliated.* Philadelphia:
            Fortress.
White, John L.
1971   "Introductory Formulae in the Body of the Pauline Letter."
            JBL 90: 91-97.
1986   *Light from Ancient Letters.* Philadelphia: Fortress.
Wilckens, Ulrich
1972   "*hypokrinomai,* etc." In *TDNT,* 8: 559-571.
Williams, Sam K.
1987   "Again *Pistis Christou.*" *CBQ* 48: 431-447.
1989   "The Hearing of Faith: *akoē pisteōs* in Galatians 3." *NTS*
            35: 82-93.
1997   *Galatians.* ANTC. Nashville: Abingdon.
Wright, N. T.
1992   *The Climax of the Covenant.* Minneapolis: Fortress
Young, Norman H.
1987   "*Paidagōgos:* The Social Setting of a Pauline Metaphor."
            NovT 29: 150-176.

Galatians

Introduction

The Letter

Paul communicated with the churches he had established or that he intended to visit by writing letters. The more closely the letters are studied, the more obvious it becomes that they are not hastily scribbled directives or top-of-the-head reflections. Rather, they are carefully composed communications, intended to persuade readers to think or act in a particular way. Even a group of Paul's opponents, who charged him with a weak sense of presence and poor speaking skills, acknowledged that "his letters are weighty and strong" (2 Cor 10:10).

The relatively recent examination of a host of ancient letters found a century ago by archaeologists in Egypt (see White 1986) and research into Greco-Roman theorists, who either produced handbooks on letter writing or included in their rhetorical instructions directions about the composition of letters (Aristotle, Demetrius, Cicero, Quintilian, and others; see Malherbe 1988), have enriched our understanding of Paul's practice. For the most part, he follows the literary conventions found in other Greco-Roman letters or advocated by the theorists (e.g., the openings and closings of most of his letters), though on occasion his purpose in writing dictates innovation, as is evident in the opening and closing of Galatians.

Research into an ancient epistolary practice has taught modern readers not to think of Galatians as "a fiery letter of self-defense," dictated by sacred indignation, dashed off in the hustle and bustle of a busy ministry by an apostle on the go (so Deissmann 1912, 20), but as a deliberately crafted argument, attentive not only to epistolary practices, but also employing a variety of rhetorical strategies designed to convince his Gentile readers not to accept circumcision. Galatians may represent Paul's most passionate epistle, but it is a disciplined passion and for that reason more persuasive in its effect. The biting invectives, such as "you foolish Galatians!" (Gal 3:1) or "I wish those who unsettle you would castrate themselves!" (5:12), are not to be written off as impulsive outbursts. They function as part and parcel of a carefully constructed and forceful argument made with the implied readers.

The commentary on Galatians by Hans Dieter Betz (1979) was the first to examine the letter carefully in terms of its rhetorical strategies. Betz labels Galatians as an example of the "apologetic letter," a form of juridical rhetoric. Paul is the defendant, under attack by accusers (the opponents), and in the letter he makes his case before a jury (the Galatian readers). The context makes the letter a self-apology, delivered not in person but in written form (14-25). Betz contends that Paul chooses to defend himself and the gospel he preaches by presenting a defense of the Spirit. Since his readers have received the Spirit, he can make his case by appealing to their experience and by calling on them as firsthand witnesses. While he uses other appeals, such as scriptural proofs and reminders of past friendship with the readers, the argument from experience becomes the center of his defense (28-33).

While Betz's analysis has blazed a new and important trail into the form and structure of the Pauline letters, and a trail others have followed, his decision to label Galatians as judicial rhetoric has been widely criticized. First, Betz is not able to offer a single example of an actual apologetic letter in antiquity with which to compare Galatians. His case for Galatians' being such a letter rests exclusively on the writings of rhetorical theorists and not on concrete models, and that "does not inspire confidence in his thesis" (Meeks 1981, 306). Second, a tacit assumption of Betz's work is that once a generic model for a literary composition is recognized, then it can serve as the essential key for unlocking the mysteries of the text. In many instances this proves to be the case, but it ignores the fact that literary innovation was an important feature of the period and that often ancient letters did not reflect a single model but a blending of various literary forms and patterns. Identifying the literary genre may be used heuristically to expose characteristics of the communication, but applied rigidly, it can become a straightjacket into which the contents of the letter are forced (Aune 1981, 324).

Third, the judgment that it is an apologetic letter and a specimen of juridical rhetoric hardly fits the contents of Galatians. Rather than projecting a forensic setting and being a defense of Paul's apostleship, of justification by faith, or of the Spirit, the letter is best read primarily (though not exclusively) as an example of deliberative rhetoric. In deliberative rhetoric the fictive setting is that of a political assembly where the speaker/writer is seeking to convince the audience that it is in its best interest to take a particular action in the future. Paul writes to the Galatians not so much to answer charges against himself or the gospel as to urge the Gentile readers to resist the pressure to be circumcised and to live free and faithful lives.

In connection with this, two particular points of rhetorical form militate against Betz's judgment that Galatians represents juridical rhetoric. First, in juridical rhetoric the narrative section is central because it relates the facts of the case under dispute. But the narrative section of this letter (1:11–2:14) does not mention the circumstances of the dispute in Galatia. It deals with the story of Paul's call/conversion, his meeting with the Jerusalem apostles, and his conflict with Peter at Antioch. However, as Quintilian notes, in deliberative rhetoric the *narratio* appropriately includes external matters, matters that have to do more with the speaker than with the dispute itself (*Institutio Oratoria* 4.2. 11-12). Second, as George Kennedy points out, Betz has a difficult time finding a place in the argument of the letter for the extensive section of exhortations in Galatians (5:13–6:10) because, as he recognizes, exhortation is not normally a part of judicial rhetoric. On the other hand, exhortation is a prominent form of deliberative rhetoric (Kennedy 1984, 144-152; Hall 1987, 277-287).

For many reasons, Galatians, at least in general, is more aptly described as an example of deliberative rhetoric than of judicial rhetoric. The aim of the letter is more to persuade the Galatians of the invalidity of circumcision than to defend Paul and his apostleship. This is said without an effort to squeeze all the parts of the letter into any one rhetorical category.

Despite the criticism of Betz's proposals, his work has made interpreters sensitive to the interplay between epistolary form and rhetorical strategies. Paul is writing a communication that reflects his awareness of the literary conventions of Greco-Roman letters and at the same time demonstrates considerable skill in making convincing arguments. The attention to both letter form and rhetoric become critical in reading Galatians.

Authorship

Only rarely in the history of New Testament scholarship has the Pauline authorship of Galatians been questioned. Even F. C. Baur, the leading figure in the Tübingen school in the mid-nineteenth century, included Galatians as one of only four letters that came directly from the apostle. Galatians is so "Pauline" that it normally functions as a benchmark against which to measure the authenticity of other letters in the Pauline corpus.

The letter bears Paul's name as sender (1:1) and reports much about the background and whereabouts of the apostle. In attesting to the power of the gospel to transform people, Paul reflects on his own past as an active and engaged Jew, who harassed the church, apparently for religious reasons, since he speaks of his progress in and zeal for the traditions of Judaism (1:13-14). His "conversion" and commission to be a missionary to the Gentiles (1:15-16) is followed by an undefined period in Arabia, a stay in Damascus, and three years later a visit to Peter and James at Jerusalem (1:17-20). The immediate scenario (1:21) leaves Paul in the districts of Syria (the area around Antioch) and Cilicia (the area around Tarsus).

The autobiographical section also reports two other incidents prior to the time of writing the letter. One is the visit "after fourteen years" to Jerusalem, with Barnabas and Titus, where Paul resists the pressure of interlopers to have Titus circumcised (2:1-5) and where he and Barnabas receive an endorsement from the Jerusalem leaders (Peter, James, and John) to continue to preach the gospel among the Gentiles (2:6-10).

The other incident is the confrontation at Antioch, where Paul challenges Peter for withdrawing from table fellowship with non-Jews (2:11-14). The reports of both incidents have to be treated with caution in any attempt either to reconstruct the historical whereabouts of Paul or to define his relationships with the Jerusalem apostles. The Jerusalem meeting has to be compared with visits to Jerusalem mentioned in Acts (e.g., 9:26-29; 11:30; 12:25; 15:1-29), none of which exactly parallels Gal 2:1-10. Furthermore, both incidents in Galatians 2 are told in such a way as to serve Paul's rhetorical intention, to make the case why Gentiles in Galatia should not submit to circumcision. Modern historical interests are ill served by an uncritical employment of the reports.

Despite the historical questions, however, the autobiographical material in Galatians serves to confirm that the apostle himself wrote the letter and not a later follower or imitator of Paul.

The "Story" of the Letter

While letters are not in the strict sense narratives (as the Gospels are), they nevertheless relate stories. Often deeply embedded in the message can be detected an ongoing saga between writer and implied readers, of which the letter itself is an important event. Particularly since the reconstruction of the historical circumstances surrounding this letter (i.e., who the Galatians were, when and from where the letter was written, who the persons were whom Paul attacks in the letter) is so inconclusive, it is important first to ferret out the story that the letter tells. It is clearly Paul's own version of how things have turned out. The others parties, such as the original readers or the troublemakers in Galatia or even Peter, might have told the story differently, but Paul's account is the place to begin.

It starts with a visit Paul made to the area of Galatia, where he became sick and had to remain for some time. The Galatian people, to whom he later wrote this letter, showed him gracious hospitality. Though his illness apparently allowed them reason to scorn Paul, they extended him a notably warm welcome (Gal 4:13-14). The incident gave Paul the chance to preach the gospel in the area (1:8-9; 4:13), for the people to experience an extraordinary outpouring of the Spirit accompanied by miracles (3:5), and for Christian communities to be formed, made up primarily of Gentile converts (4:8). The relationship was such that Paul could speak of these people as "my little children" (4:19).

Whether Paul visited the Galatian area a second time or not (it can be inferred from the Greek words *to proteron* in 4:13) is uncertain. But shortly after the first (or second) visit there, a group of itinerant evangelists, apparently Jewish Christian missionaries like Paul, came into the Galatian communities advocating a message different from the one Paul had preached. They, too, called for faith in Jesus as the Messiah, but they also believed that God was reaching out to non-Jews through the Torah and that Gentiles must receive circumcision as a sign of their inclusion into the people of God. The logic of their case, no doubt largely resting on their interpretation of several Old Testament texts, seemed persuasive to some among the Christian communities in Galatia. At least Paul took their preaching with utmost seriousness (1:6-7; 5:2-4, 7-8; 6:12-13).

How word reached Paul of the activity of these teachers in Galatia is not said, but he penned this powerful letter to counter their message and to reaffirm the singularity of the gospel of Christ. Paul went on the offensive in attacking both the motives and the theology of these itinerant missionaries, who in distorting the Christian message had actually perverted it (1:6-7; 5:2). Forcing circumcision on Gentile believers meant that non-Jews would have to become Jews in order to be a part of God's family. If the agitators are successful, they will have thoroughly subverted the gospel and have achieved a total unraveling of Paul's own ministry in Galatia (4:11).

There are no hints in the letter to indicate how the story went following the reception of the letter. Though he expresses a desire to be present with them in person (4:20), nothing is said about specific plans Paul has to visit the area in the near future to follow up on the letter. In the final analysis, how successful the letter was in Galatia is not known. The story of the letter has to end without closure.

Historical Circumstances

The historian, of course, has to push beyond the letter's story to evaluate the data, to compare them with information from other appropriate sources, and to propose a reconstruction of the circumstances. In doing so, the picture becomes cloudy, particularly because the chronology of Paul's activity in Acts and the chronology of Paul's activity in Galatians do not easily correlate.

Recipients

Who were the intended recipients of the letter ("the churches of Galatia," 1:1) and where did they live? The Gauls (Celts) migrated from central Europe in various directions, some as far west as Britain, others as far southeast as Asia Minor. The latter group settled in the third century BCE in a relatively small area in northern Asia Minor, just north of Cappadocia and Phrygia. Their primary cities were Ancyra, Pessinus, and Tavium. From the beginning of the second century the area increasingly came under Roman control, until 25 BCE when Galatia was reorganized by Augustus as a Roman province. A couple of decades later the province was expanded northward to include portions of Paphlagonia and southward to encompass parts of Lycaonia, Pisidia, and Phrygia. Thus when Paul wrote in the middle of the first century CE, Galatia was a Roman province covering the major portion of central Asia Minor.

How did Paul use the term "Galatia" (Gal 1:2)? Were the churches to which he wrote primarily in the north where the Gauls originally settled (ethnic Galatia), or were they in the south, in the extended Roman territory (provincial Galatia)? Since the middle of the nineteenth century, the question has sparked considerable division among commentators, some choosing ethnic Galatia and arguing for a north Galatia hypothesis (e.g., Lightfoot, Moffatt, Kümmel), others choosing provincial Galatia and arguing for a south Galatia hypothesis (e.g., Ramsay, Burton, Bruce).

The north Galatia hypothesis rests largely on the comment in Acts 16:6 and 18:23 that Paul traveled "through the region of Phyrgia and Galatia." Since the two territories are distinguished from one another, it would seem that the author of Acts is using "Galatia" to designate the more limited northern area, where the Gauls originally settled (ethnic Galatia). If Paul is using the term the same way that Luke (in Acts) does, then the destination of the letter would have been the towns in ethnic Galatia, possibly Ancyra, Tavium, and Pessinus.

The south Galatia hypothesis leans more heavily on the material in Acts 13:4–14:28, where an extensive account is given of Paul's visits to the towns of Pisidian Antioch, Iconium, Lystra, and Derbe, which were included in the extended Roman province. Though Luke does not actually use the term "Galatia" for these towns, the argument is that in the first century CE they would have naturally been identified as Galatian.

Both hypotheses are fragile at best. There is no assurance that Paul employs the term "Galatia" in the same way that Luke does, nor is there any convincing proof that the towns in the southern portion of Asia Minor mentioned in Acts 13–14 are the ones Paul addressed in the letter. Nothing in the rather extensive Acts account of the visits at Pisidian Antioch, Iconium, Lystra, and Derbe correlates with Paul's own statement that the preaching of the gospel in Galatia was occasioned by his becoming ill and by the warm welcome he received from the citizens of the area (Gal 4:13-14).

The north or ethnic Galatian hypothesis has the fewer problems associated with it and therefore seems the more likely choice. But it needs to said that beyond the dating of the letter and issues of Pauline chronology, nothing theologically significant hangs on the decision whether Paul in Gal 1:1 intends ethnic or provincial Galatia. No exegetical or theological decision rests on the determination of whether he writes to a northern or southern audience.

Date

The inability to determine where the readers of the letter lived simply adds to the tenuousness in assigning it a date. In light of Acts, if Paul wrote to the northern area where the Gauls originally settled, then he visited there for the first time on his so-called second missionary journey (Acts 16:6) and a second time on his third journey (Acts 18:23). The letter most likely would have been written during an Ephesian ministry subsequent to these visits and would be dated in the middle 50s CE. In the sequence of Paul's other letters, Galatians would come most likely after the Corinthian correspondence and before Romans. If, however, the letter is addressed to the churches in the south, which were visited twice on the first missionary journey, Galatians could come early, perhaps even the first of the Pauline letters in the canon.

But there are other factors to be taken into account in arriving at a date. Gal 2:1-10 records Paul's second visit to Jerusalem to meet with the leaders of the church. Acts, on the other hand, records five visits of Paul to Jerusalem, the second of which is the so-called famine visit of Acts 11:29-30. Paul and Barnabas carried the "relief" gathered by the church at Antioch for their stricken sisters and brothers at Jerusalem. No indication is given at that time of a discussion between Paul, Barnabas, and the Jerusalem leaders over the issue of circumcision. The third visit in Acts, the so-called Jerusalem council, is described in some detail in Acts 15:1-35. The initial issue of the meeting is whether circumcision should be required of Gentiles entering the church (15:5), but the meeting concludes with a different agenda—a set of agreements that regulate table fellowship between Jews and Gentiles (15:19-20).

Though there are multiple variations on each position, commentators are inclined to take one of two sides. Some argue that the visit of Gal 2:1-10 is paralleled by Acts 11:29-30. Since Gal 2:2 seems to indicate that the meeting was a private one, the writer of Acts did not need to provide a detailed accounting of it. Further, they point to the many discrepancies between the Gal 2:1-10 visit and Acts 15:1-35 meeting—that Paul and Barnabas were commissioned by the Antioch church (rather than going "by revelation"); that the meeting in Acts 15 is a public one and not a private one; that a set of agreements for table fellowship (often referred to as "the apostolic decrees") was reached that included abstinence for Gentiles from "things polluted by idols and from fornication and from whatever has been strangled and from blood" (Acts 15:19-20); and that subsequently a letter was sent to the Antioch church detailing the agreements. How could Paul's account in Gal 2:1-10 and the Acts 15 account differ so much in reporting the same meeting? It makes more sense, they contend, that Paul and Barnabas on the famine visit privately consulted with the Jerusalem authorities about their projected mission to the Gentiles, that they went on their so-called first missionary journey, after which they returned for the Jerusalem council meeting, dealing with a dispute that had arisen over table fellowship. Why isn't the Jerusalem council of Acts 15 not mentioned in Galatians? The most logical answer is because it had not yet taken place. Thus the date of Galatians is early, at the end of the first journey and before the Acts 15 meeting, around 49, making Galatians likely the first of Paul's letters. (For a full statement of this position, see Longenecker, lxxii-lxxxiii.)

Other commentators, however, argue for identifying the visits of Gal 2:1-10 and Acts 15:1-35. They point to the immense commonalties of the accounts: the same geographical structure (Antioch and Jerusalem), the same participants (in one group Paul, Barnabas, and Titus, or as Acts reads, "some of the others"; in another group James and Peter; in a third group those advocating circumcision); the same topic of dispute (the circumcision of Gentiles); and the same result (the exemption of Gentiles from circumcision). The Galatians account could be taken to report both a public and a private meeting (Gal 2:2). As for the discrepancies between the two accounts, commentators are inclined to acknowledge that Acts is not always historically accurate—that the famine visit of Acts 11:29-30 was probably inserted in the narrative to stress the faithful service of Paul and Barnabas to Jerusalem on behalf of the Antioch church and that the set of agreements (the "apostolic decrees") was a compromise arrived at later (without Paul's concurrence) and added to the text. (For a statement of this position, see Becker 1993, 85-99.)

Identifying the visits of Gal 2:1-10 and Acts 15 allows for a later date for the letter, not only after the Jerusalem council, but also after a subsequent conflict with Peter reported in Gal 2:11-14. Galatians would come just before or just after the Corinthian correspondence.

Suffice it here to say that a great deal of uncertainty surrounds the geographical location of the original readers and the correlation of the visits to Jerusalem in Acts and Galatians, and this in turn creates uncertainty about dating the letter. A judicious estimate places the letter somewhere between 50 and 56 CE.

The Missionaries

Another debated feature of the historical circumstances of the letter is the precise identity of the itinerant missionaries who came into the Galatian congregations and became the cause for Paul's writing the letter. (We shall alternately refer to them as "agitators" and "advocates of circumcision.") They are carefully distinguished from the Galatian readers, who are always addressed with the second person pronoun, and they apparently come from outside the community since Paul speaks of a sudden and unanticipated change that came over the Galatians (1:6). Since they are linked with circumcision and festival observance, they are of Jewish background, and the letter clearly implies that they thought of themselves as Christians.

The agitators are specifically mentioned in five passages in Galatians: 1:6-7; 3:1; 4:17; 5:7-12; 6:12-13. They taught a message called "gospel," which Paul thoroughly discounted. For him, it represented a perversion of the one true gospel and served only to disturb and intimidate (*tarassō*, 1:7; 5:10) the Galatians. The agitators made a big issue of the necessity of circumcision, which in turn evoked Paul's humorous parody in 5:12 ("I wish those who bother you would simply castrate themselves!").

Apparently the advocates of circumcision had at least a measure of success in Galatia. Paul speaks of the readers having been "bewitched" (3:1), having deserted the God who called them (1:6), and no longer running well, as they once had (5:7). In fact, Paul accuses the agitators of being success-driven, of wanting to "put on a good show in the flesh" (6:12).

Three questions need to be raised with the text in order to gain a better understanding of the identity of this group. First, did these circumcision-advocates attack Paul? Was a part of their presentation a deliberate effort to undermine the authority of the apostle, to discredit his message by discrediting his apostleship? Many commentators answer yes to both of these questions, primarily on the grounds of Galatians 1–2, and many study Bibles label some portion of this section "Paul's Vindication of his Apostleship." They mirror-read these two chapters—i.e., read beyond and between the lines—and conclude that the autobiographical material is basically a defense against allegations that Paul is a second class apostle. Behind each of Paul's affirmations, denials, and reports of meetings in Galatians 1–2 lie charges he was answering to clear his name and thus his message. Basically the accusation was that he received his credentials initially from the Jerusalem leaders to preach, but when he went into Syria and Cilicia, he accommodated the gospel to make it more palatable to Gentiles by no longer requiring circumcision. His independence made him something of a renegade and brought about the disapproval of the Jerusalem apostles. (See Bruce 1982, 19-32.)

This writer contends that the traditional position reads too much beyond and between the lines of Galatians 1–2. The autobiographical material makes much better rhetorical sense when taken as a paradigm for the power of the gospel to transform human life than when taken as an apology. Rather than being defensive, Paul goes on the offensive to argue the singularity of the message of faith in Christ and to accuse the itinerant missionaries of completely misunderstanding what that message is. (Details of this position won't be argued here since they can be found in the commentary on Galatians 1–2.) Martyn even objects to the use of the term "opponents" to describe these advocates of a law-observant gospel because it assumes that they derive their identity from their opposition to Paul. "In the main it is not they who are reacting to Paul's theology, but rather he who is reacting to theirs" (Martyn 1983, 235; somewhat differently expressed in the reprinted essay in *Issues*, 8-9).

Second, what did this group advocate that evoked from Paul such a passionate response? Three times in the letter the expression "compel to be circumcised" is used (2:3, 14; 6:12), indicating that one of the essential tenets of their teaching was the necessity for non-Jews to be circumcised in order to be fully members of the family of God.

In Gal 3:6-29, in a complex argument involving Old Testament texts, Paul responds to the demand for circumcision. He sets out to answer the question, which the agitators themselves may have initially raised, "Who are Abraham's descendants?" No doubt the agitators answered that those who are circumcised are the true offspring of Abraham (cf. Gen 17:9-14). Using Gen 15:6 and 12:3 as his key texts, Paul argues instead that people of faith, those who belong to Christ, are Abraham's descendants and that baptism has removed any significant distinction between Jew and non-Jew, i.e., between circumcision and uncircumcision.

In addition to circumcision, the agitators may have urged the observance of the Jewish festivals (4:10-11) and possibly the keeping of kosher food laws (2:11-14), though these issues do not figure as prominently in Paul's response as does circumcision.

What the agitators did *not* propose is a form of legalism that demands that people must keep the law in order to be saved. It is Paul who says that if circumcision is the gateway into the people of God, then the law must be kept in its entirety (5:3), and it is Paul who declares that the agitators have not themselves observed the whole law (6:13). It is inaccurate to suggest that Paul is fighting against people who contend for a salvation by works and who think that humans must earn God's favor by keeping the law. Individual salvation is not so much the theme of Galatians as the question of who belongs to the people of God. (For a full discussion of the agitators, their message, and the attractiveness of their proposals, see Barclay 1988, 36-74.)

Third, what motivated this group to come into the Galatian communities and teach Christ and circumcision? Two proposed answers are particularly worth consideration.

Robert Jewett has noted that there was a strong nationalistic mood in Palestine during the middle of the first century that finally erupted in the Jewish revolt against the Romans in 66 CE. The more zealous Jews demanded complete separation from Gentiles and directed considerable attention and energy against any who were Gentile sympathizers. The pressure, Jewett argues, stimulated Jewish Christians in Judea into a campaign to avert the suspicion that they were associated with Gentiles. They were under the impression, perhaps incorrectly, that the circumcision of Gentile Christians would prevent Zealot reprisals. They thought that if they could succeed in circumcising Gentile members of various Christian communities, the Zealots would leave them alone. Galatians 6:12 is particularly appropriate for Jewett's proposal: "It is those who want to put on a good show in the flesh that try to compel you to be circumcised—only that they may avoid persecution for the cross of Christ." Though the agitators' overt appeal may have stressed matters such as the importance of Gen 17:9-14 or circumcision as the sign of perfection, what motivated their missionary activity in Galatia was not so much theology as the desire to protect themselves against their nationalistic countrymen (Jewett 1971, 204-206).

Second, Martyn discovers in two second-century sources from Jewish Christianity indication of law-observant missions to Gentiles, one source even claiming that such a mission predated Paul's mission to the Gentiles. (The sources are *The Ascents of James* and *The Preachings of Peter.*) In the light of these sources, Martyn describes the itinerant teachers in Galatia as Jewish Christians who have an ecumenical vision and recognize that in the Messiah God is reaching out to the Gentiles. The difference between their position and Paul's is that they understand this outreach to happen through the law and not apart from it. They were no doubt trained interpreters of scripture and made their case by interpreting texts, all of which explains the heavily exegetical nature of Paul's response. They were motivated not by an effort to avoid Zealot pressure or by a desire to undermine Pauline authority, but "by a passion to share with the entire world the only gift they believed to have the power to liberate humankind from the grip of evil, the Law of God's Messiah" (Martyn 1983, 235).

Jewett's proposal leans heavily on an analysis of the political climate in Judea and assumes that it has generated a mission of circumcision-advocacy into areas as far away as Asia Minor. One has to wonder how a mission in such a distant place as Galatia would have had much effect on the treatment of Jewish Christians by the Zealots in and around Jerusalem. While Martyn has been criticized for relying on Jewish Christian sources of doubtful value in positing law-observant missions to Gentiles, the scenario he draws of the engagement between Paul and other Jewish Christian missionaries makes good sense of the argument of the letter.

Structure of the Letter

Analyses of the structure of Galatians are usually based on one of three premises. First, there are commentators who begin with the conventions that have emerged in Greco-Roman letter writing, either from the ancient theorists who have written about epistolary form or from actual letters themselves. It is assumed that Paul follows the patterns of his contemporaries and employs the basic structures appropriate to the type of letter he is writing. For example, Betz understands Galatians to be an apologetic letter, and though he has to make modifications at points, his analysis of the structure derives from what the ancient theorists have taught about apologetic letters. His outline of Galatians is as follows (Betz 1979, 14-25):

I. Epistolary Prescript (1:1-5)
   (Opening, greeting)
II. Exordium (1:6-11)
   (Occasion for writing)
III. Narratio (1:12–2:14)
   (Statement of the facts of the case)
IV. Propositio (2:15-21)
   (What is agreed upon and what remains contested)
V. Probatio (3:1–4:31)
   (System of arguments or proofs)
VI. Exhortio (5:1–6:10)
   (Exhortations)
VII. Epistolary Postscript (6:11-18)
   (Closing)

Second, there are a few commentators who discern a literary pattern in the letter and propose an outline that is the expression of that literary design. For example, John Bligh contends that Galatians is symmetrically constructed, along chiastic lines (a, b, b, a). The titles for each section of Bligh's outline, though based on content rather than literary or formal patterns, are chosen to highlight the parallels in the chiastic structure (Bligh 1969, 39):

A   Prologue (1:1-12)
B   Autobiographical section (1:13–2:10)
C   Justification by faith (2:11–3:4)
D   Arguments from scripture (3:5-29)
E   Central chiasm (4:1-10)
D' Argument from scripture (4:11-31)
C' Justification by faith (5:1-10)
B' Moral section (5:11–6:11)
A' Epilogue (6:12-18)

A third type of structural analysis evolves directly from the theological argument of the letter. Apart from the opening and closing of the letter, no particular attention is given to traditional epistolary patterns or to a discernible literary design. Bruce proposes such an outline, determined almost exclusively by the theological contents of the letter (Bruce 1982, 57):

I. Salutation (1:1-5)
II. No other gospel (1:6-10)
III. Autobiographical sketch: Paul's independent gospel (1:11–2:14)
IV. Faith receives the promise (2:15–5:1)
V. Christian freedom (5:2-12)
VI. Flesh and Spirit (5:13-26)
VII. Mutual help and service (6:1-10)
VIII. Concluding comments and final greeting (6:11-18)

None of these proposals is presented as the actual strategy Paul used in writing the letter. That would be to claim too much. Each has a heuristic function—to enable readers to discern features in the letter that otherwise might be obscured.

The analysis offered here assumes that Paul follows (with modifications) the traditional letter form (opening, body, including paraenesis, and closing) and within the body of the letter develops the theological case being presented to his implied readers. In comparison with his other letters, the two modifications of note in Galatians are the substitution of an astonishment-rebuke formula for the prayer of thanksgiving (1:6-10) and the closing, which summarizes the issue of the letter more extensively than the closings of other letters and omits conventional features such as greetings to or from friends and the holy kiss (6:11-18).

I. Opening (1:1-10)
    A. Salutation (1:1-5)
    B. Astonishment-rebuke formula (1:6-10)
II. Body (1:11–6:10)
    A. The authority of the gospel (1:11–2:21)
        1. The origin and power of the gospel (1:11-24)
        2. The truth of the gospel at Jerusalem (2:1-10)
        3. The truth of the gospel at Antioch (2:11-14)
        4. Justification by the faithfulness of Christ (2:15-21)
    B. Appeals to the readers (3:1–5:12)
        1. An argument from experience: reception of the Spirit (3:1-5)
        2. An initial argument from scripture (3:6–4:7)
            a. People of faith are Abraham's descendants (3:6-14)
            b. The promise and the law (3:15-25)
            c. Those in Christ are Abraham's descendants (3:26-29)
            d. God's liberating action in Christ (4:1-7)
            e. A warning not to revert to slavery (4:8-11)

Message of the Letter

Three theological categories immediately surface when one asks about the enduring message of Galatians: its christocentrism, its attention to the Holy Spirit, and its concern for the nature and composition of the people of God. We shall look at each of these categories, with special attention to the first.

Jesus Christ

While Galatians is written to deal with a specific situation in the congregations of the area and is particularly responsive to the teaching being propagated by the agitators, the message of the letter (or more technically put, its theology) is not to be equated with a mere rehearsal of Paul's response. Paul does not lift up the agitators' arguments and analyze them point by point. Instead, he takes the discussion to a different level by insisting on the singularity of the gospel and the coming of Jesus Christ as the gospel's exclusive content. From first to last, the letter is about the significance of Christ (1:1, 3-4; 6:12-18), and what is said in reply to the agitators only makes sense in light this christocentrism. (See Gaventa 1991,147-159.) Four dimensions are particularly evident in the letter.

The Actions of God. Because the Son is "sent" by God to redeem those under the law (4:4-5), the actions of Christ are the actions of God. Even the event of Christ's self-giving for human sins happens "according to the will of our God and Father" (1:4). These texts underscore what is prominent also in the other letters of Paul, namely that God is the initiator of the gospel, that even in the death of Jesus, God turns out to be the protagonist. There is no notion of Jesus as a lonely and courageous hero, taking up the cause of humanity in its brokenness and forcing God's hand to change the course of history. Nor does God, following the extraordinary self-sacrifice on the cross, step in to reprieve an otherwise martyred Jesus by raising him from the dead. Instead, Paul's christology makes it possible to see Christ's actions as God's actions. Put another way, Christ's actions—his self-giving love (2:20), his taking on himself the curse deserved by humans (3:10-13), his redeeming those under the law (4:4-5)—constitute the self-revelation of God.

An Apocalyptic Event. The term "apocalyptic" has a variety of definitions, but in Galatians (with no mention of the return of Christ) it is a way of declaring Christ's advent to be a decisive, world-changing event that inaugurates a history shaped by the gospel. It wields a death-blow to the old world and at the same time establishes a brand new world. It is not merely the possibility or offer of something different, to which humans are invited to turn; it is the declaration that God in Christ has created something new.

Nowhere does this become clearer than in the closing of the letter when the case for the gospel is sharply put in terms of parallel alternatives (6:12-17). On the one side are the agitators who compel Gentiles to be circumcised, who avoid persecution for the cross, and who boast in the circumcisions they have brought about. On the other side is Paul, for whom circumcision and uncircumcision are no longer significant categories, who bears in his body the marks of Jesus, and who boasts only in the cross of Christ. These contrasts, however, are but subsets of the fundamental apocalyptic opposition, "the world" and the "new creation." The coming of Christ has brought the fatal crippling of one and the inauguration of the other. (See Cousar 1990, 137-148.)

This means, as Martyn has clearly shown, that the present is the time of the war of liberation commenced by the invasion of Christ. "The New Creation has dawned; but in true apocalyptic fashion its Jerusalem is, as yet, still above." The letter is written in the hopes that the Galatians, in hearing it read, will be seized once again by the apocalyptic nature of Christ's coming, will learn again how and where the battle lines are drawn, and will be summoned to take their places in the struggle (Martyn 1985, 410-424; quote from 420; reprinted in *Issues* 1997, 111-123).

The Cross. The resurrection is explicitly mentioned only in the first verse, while Jesus' crucifixion and the connection of believers to it appear time and again. Are not readers always to infer the resurrection when the crucifixion is explicit? Yes and no. On the one hand, Paul has no interest in a pre-resurrected Christ (nor in a risen Christ who has not been crucified). The Christ of Galatians is clearly alive and not dead. On the other hand, often in Paul's letters the crucifixion carries a particular theological cutting edge that is blunted if resurrection is too easily assumed (see 1 Cor 2:2). This is the case with Galatians.

In addition to its apocalyptic significance, the cross functions theologically in two ways in Galatians. First, Jesus' death is the remedy for human sin. Paul begins with this in the salutation by identifying Jesus as the one "who gave himself up for our sins to set us free from the present evil age" (1:4; 2:20). Then in 3:10-13, employing two texts from Deuteronomy (27:26; 21:23), he details how Christ in his death takes away the curse of the law by becoming accursed himself. He does this so that the blessing of Abraham might come to Gentiles as well as to Jews. Christ crucified is God's answer to human sin.

Second, Jesus' death becomes the pattern for life within communities of faith. An example is Gal 2:19-20. In arguing that he had died to the law but was alive to God, Paul explains, "I have been crucified with Christ; it is no longer I who live, but Christ who lives in me. And the life I now live in the flesh I live by the faith of the Son of God, who loved me and gave himself for me." The perfect tense ("I have been crucified") points to a past action that has continuing effects for the present and highlights the cruciform nature of Christian experience. Being crucified with Christ is not a temporary stage on a journey toward a blissful resurrection, without pain, anguish, and struggle. It remains the daily experience of the community justified and ordered by the power of God. As such, faithfulness to the crucified Jesus puts believers at risk and makes them subject to the world's hostility and violence (see 5:11; 6:11, 17).

Christ and the Law. From time to time, commentators have detected an ambivalence, if not a contradiction, in the way in which the law is presented in Galatians. On the one hand, the law brings a curse to those who rely on it (3:10). It is a "Johnny-come-lately" on the scene, arriving 430 years after the promise given to Abraham (3:17). It exercises a temporary function as a power to imprison and as a disciplinarian for children (3:23-24), but "now that faith has come," we are no longer subject to its controlling power (3:25). On the other hand, the law is declared fulfilled in the love-commandment (5:14) and is spoken of now as "the law of Christ" (6:2). Is Paul speaking out of both sides of his mouth when he writes of the law first in negative and then in positive terms?

Paul talks this way because something has happened in the history of the law to change its status. Christ has taken the curse of the law on himself in order to redeem those under its curse (3:13). As God's Son, he entered the human situation as one "born under law" to set free those enslaved by law (4:4-6). Having its curse removed, the law is now restored to its original place. Paul appeals to its authority (4:21 and sees its relevance for the daily life of the churches—all because Christ silences the cursing voice of the law and brings it to completion. Thus it becomes "the law of Christ." (See Martyn 1996, 48-61; reprinted in *Issues* 1997, 235-249.)

Holy Spirit

Closely connected to the christology of Galatians is *the presentation of the Spirit.* In 4:4-6 Paul parallels the expression "God sent forth his Son" with "God sent forth the Spirit of his Son," indicating the interrelated character of both missions. Christ's work brings the adoption of persons as God's children, and the Spirit makes the experience real in human lives as people are enabled to call God "Abba."

The most striking feature of the Spirit in Galatians is its warfare with the flesh and the ethical implications of the conflict (5:16–6:10). As God's power of the new age, the Spirit is opposed by the another orb of power, the flesh, that seeks to vandalize the new creation and to wreak havoc with its blessings. In light of this struggle, the readers of the letter are exhorted not only to look to the Spirit as the source of their Christian experience, but also as the guide for their moral lives. Having crucified the flesh, they are to "live by the Spirit" (5:16), "walk by the Spirit" (5:25), and "sow to the Spirit" (6:8)—all expressions of their commitment to join in the cosmic struggle initiated by the coming of Christ.

The People of God

Finally, Galatians is concerned with the nature and composition of *the people of God.* Over against the insistence on circumcision as one of the essential marks of membership, Paul vigorously contends that belonging to Christ (and nothing else) characterizes the descendants of Abraham (3:29). But Paul goes on to draw specific implications about the unity and parity of the people of God.

> For in Christ Jesus you are all children of God through faith. As many as are baptized into Christ have clothed yourselves with Christ. There is no longer Jew or Greek, there is no longer slave or free, there is no longer male and female; for all of you are one in Christ Jesus. (3:26-28)

Whether or not Paul understood the full importance of his words, they nevertheless appropriately function to describe the church as a community in which ethnic, social, and gender distinctions are to carry no nuance of higher/lower, superior/inferior, or privileged/disenfranchised.

A Striking Beginning

(Galatians 1:1-10)

In one sense, Galatians has a normal beginning, in the conventional form of the Greco-Roman letters: from senders to recipients, followed by a greeting. To readers who know Paul's communications, the language is also familiar— "Paul an apostle," "the brother and sisters with me," "to the churches," "grace to you and peace," "to whom be the glory forever and ever. Amen." And yet from even an initial reading one discovers that the opening departs in significant ways from the usual pattern of other Pauline letters and sets the tone for what follows. Among these are:

- two sharp denials regarding Paul's apostleship (1:1)
- the statement of Paul's co-authors (1:2)
- the terse depiction of the recipients (1:2b)
- the extensive greeting, confessional in character (1:4)
- the omission of the usual prayer of thanksgiving in favor of a statement of astonishment and rebuke (1:6-9)
- two enigmatic questions and an affirmation, which conclude the opening (1:10)

Denial of Paul's Apostleship

(1:1)

Rather than Paul's usual self-identification "Paul an apostle of Christ Jesus" (2 Cor 1:1) or "called to be an apostle" (Rom 1:1), the reader is met with denials, "not from humans or through a human" and with a full statement of the source of his apostleship, "but through Jesus Christ and God the Father who raised him from the dead" (1:1). One way to interpret this unusual beginning is to make the assumption that Paul's status as apostle is under siege in Galatia from the agitators and that from the outset he is making a defense. The charge against him would be that his apostleship was not of so great a consequence as he claimed, that he had received his commission either from the Jerusalem leaders or from the Antioch church and was accountable to them (e.g., Bruce 1982, 72; Dunn 1993, 25-26).

We cannot rule out the probability that the agitators tried to discredit Paul's apostleship. Since the charges are never specified in the letter (as they are, e.g., in 2 Cor 10:10-12) and can only be read between the lines, caution is in order. Paul may simply be laying a foundation for what is a major theme of the first chapter—namely a contrast between God and humankind. In 1:10 he poses the sharp alternatives of seeking approval from humans or from God and follows with a declaration that the gospel he preaches does not function in a human way and cannot be judged according to human criteria. He bases this on the fact that he received it not from a human source but "through a revelation of Jesus Christ" (1:11-12). In light of these later references, it is just possible that 1:1, with its sharp contrast between a human and a divine origin for his apostleship, is not to be taken as a piece of a self-apology, a spontaneous defense against allegations of the agitators, but the beginning of an argument about the exclusive character of the gospel.

The term "apostle" (*apostolos*) can be used in the New Testament in a general sense to designate anyone who is sent with the delegated authority of the sender (e.g., John 13:16; 2 Cor 8:23; Phil 2:25). But in 1:1 it is clearly used in the more limited sense of a group of disciples who had a specific commission from Christ and who served in a significant leadership capacity in the early church. "Apostle" and its derivatives occur only four times in the letter (1:1, 17, 19; 2:8).

Co-Authors
(1:2)

The inclusion of co-authors in the opening of the letter is not unusual with Paul. He does so in five other letters also. In some cases, the co-author may have been the amanuensis, who took Paul's dictation. But in 1:2a the co-authors are "all the brothers and sisters with me." The expression may carry the subtle suggestion that his argument comes with the endorsement and support of others, who share his view about the nature of the gospel. The familial language is appropriate in light of the designation of God as Father in 1:1.

Recipients
(1:2b)

The addressees are stated without a word of elaboration in 1:2b, no conventional expressions to affirm their status as members of God's people (such as "beloved," "saints," or "those sanctified in Christ"). The concise address likely reflects the tense atmosphere surrounding Paul's relations with the Galatians. (On the uncertainty of the precise location of Galatia, see the Introduction.)

Confessional Greeting
(1:4)

If the address is terse, the greeting is expansive. Rather than the simple "grace and peace," one finds an elaborate acknowledgment of Christ's saving work, followed by an ascription that usually appears in the body of letters (1:3-5). For a number of reasons, verse 4 reads like a confessional formula from the early church (the opening substantive participle; the verb "set free, deliver" [*exelētai*], found nowhere else in Paul; "sins" in the plural, uncommon in Paul; and "the present evil age," an expression not found elsewhere in the New Testament). Since the prayer of thanksgiving in other Pauline letters usually sets the agenda for the matters that follow and since there is no prayer of thanksgiving in Galatians, the greeting serves such a function. It provides a strong theological foundation for the argument of the letter. Moreover, if perchance the confessional formula were already known and in use in the Galatian congregations, then its rhetorical effect would have been even more forceful.

The confession has three distinct features. First is the declaration of Jesus' self-giving "for our sins," reminiscent of the same expression in the traditional formula in 1 Cor 15:3 ("Christ died for our sins in accordance with the scriptures"). In fact, the Greek preposition "for" (*hyper*) becomes the clue for detecting a varied application of the formula throughout the Pauline letters (e.g., Gal 2:20; 3:13; Rom 5:6, 8; 1 Thess 5:10; 2 Cor 5:14). When used in connection with Christ's death, it seems to carry the notion of "in behalf of" or "in place of." As Hultgren observes, it functions as an unambiguous, declarative statement. There are no conditions set alongside the formula, no reduction of its scope to a subjective apprehension. "It is not said that it [Christ's death] happened for the sake of the elect or even for those who would come to believe in the death as atoning. Instead the 'objective' and 'universal' character of the atoning death of Christ is what constitutes the gospel as being truly good news" (Hultgren 1987, 50-51).

Second is the use of Jewish apocalyptic categories to describe what Christ's death frees people from—"this present evil age." This age is "narrow, sorrowful, toilsome, full of dangers, and involved in great hardships" (2 Esd 7:12) and in God's time is to be displaced by a new age of peace and justice.

Paul announces in Galatians that God has acted, that Christ's death has delivered people from the clutches of the old age, that a "new creation" has been established (6:15). The Galatians by their fascination with circumcision and what it represents are reverting to "this present evil age" (4:8-9).

Third, the death of Christ happens "according to the will of our God and Father." Tragic and horrific as the crucifixion was (and Paul recognizes it as such), it did not occur outside the divine will. Paul shows no interest whatsoever in tracking down the perpetrators of the crime or in assigning blame for the murder of Jesus. Instead, he portrays the event on a broader canvas in terms of God's purposes for human life and history. God turns out to be the protagonist in Christ's death (Rom 5:8). The confession appropriately concludes with an ascription of glory to the God, whose character is seen in the self-giving Christ.

Statement of Astonishment
(1:6-9)

The lack of an expression of thanksgiving and the presence of a statement of astonishment and rebuke are not surprising in Greco-Roman letter writing. In fact, the verb "I am astonished" (*thaumazō*) is used regularly to introduce the writer's dissatisfaction or irritation with an action or proposal of the recipient. But for readers familiar with other Pauline letters, the replacement of the prayer of thanksgiving or blessing with a statement of astonishment and rebuke is noteworthy since it only happens in Galatians. It indicates Paul's determination immediately to get to the business of the letter. The issue is urgent.

The structure of the section 1:6-9 includes an astonishment-rebuke statement, that argues for the singularity of the gospel (1:6-7), followed by a double curse, that reinforces the same point (1:8-9). Those who are confusing the Galatians may call their message "gospel," but Paul vigorously disavows it.

Who the agitators were is a matter of great discussion (see the Introduction). Most likely, they were Jewish Christians, who came into the Galatian congregations with an ecumenical vision similar to Paul's. Whether or not they were sponsored by the Jerusalem church is uncertain. They claimed Jesus as Messiah, but, unlike Paul, they affirmed that God reaches out to non-Jews through the law. Specifically in Galatia this means that circumcision, prescribed in passages such as Gen 17:9-14, is the gateway through which Gentiles enter the people of God. They likely pushed the observance of important religious festivals (4:10) and perhaps (though by no means certain) kosher food regulations (2:11-14), which, with circumcision, would have functioned for them as boundary markers distinguishing the people of God from other people. From Paul's perspective the insistence on these legal stipulations disturbs (the Greek verb *tarassō* can connote even intimidation) the congregations and thoroughly distorts the gospel.

While issues such as circumcision may not seem so momentous to modern readers, they obviously were to Paul. What is his complaint? Later in the letter he will write about the gospel and the people of God, but at the outset Paul's concern is with the uniqueness of the gospel, its unparalleled character. The grace of God expressed in the death of Christ is all that the community of faith needs for its present and future salvation. To argue the necessity of additional religious practices, such as circumcision, is to imply that divine grace is inadequate and to rob the gospel of its character as good news. Paul is amazed that the Galatians are attracted to the message of the agitators since they are "so quickly [or so easily] deserting the one who called you in the grace of Christ" (1:6). The Galatians are not forsaking Paul; they are forsaking the gospel of Christ. The uniqueness and sufficiency of the gospel are called into question by the requirement of circumcision.

The noun and verb for "gospel" appear five times in 1:6-9. With the potential curses declared in 1:8-9, "gospel" takes on supreme authority. It becomes the exclusive norm by which religious expressions are measured. Not only do the agitators not have the right to impose other restrictions, but neither do Paul nor his missionary cohorts ("we") nor even an angelic messenger. The use of the parallel curses (i.e., offering the guilty to the judgment of God) makes this doubly forceful. In line with 1:6-9, the "gospel" functions as a norm in two other scenarios in Galatians: It exposes the false believers who want to force the circumcision of Titus (2:3-5), and it judges the inconsistency of Peter at Antioch, who withdraws from eating with the Gentiles (2:14).

Questions and an Affirmation
(1:10)

On the surface 1:10 seems enigmatic—two rhetorical questions, followed by a statement that makes pleasing people and being a servant of Christ mutually exclusive. How the verse is connected to what precedes or follows is unclear. Some commentators seek to solve the complications of the verse by mirror-reading, by saying that Paul is responding to allegations by the agitators that he is a people-pleaser, currying the favor of Gentiles by not insisting on their circumcision (Longenecker 1990, 18; Dunn 1993, 49-50). Others see the verse as an example of rhetorical irony. The "man pleaser" was a notorious figure in ancient political rhetoric, who tried to persuade people by pleasing them. Paul is emphatically denying that he should be confused with such a character (Betz 1979, 55-56).

A more plausible solution is to recognize the broader context of the chapter. In 1:1 humans are set in sharp contrast to Christ and God ("neither from humans nor through a human, but through Jesus Christ and God the Father"). In 1:11 the same pair of opposites is established—"the gospel that was preached by me is not according to a human [i.e., measured by human norms]; for I did not receive it from a human nor was I taught it, but it came through a revelation of Jesus Christ." In verse 1 Paul claims that his apostleship had not a human but a divine source, and in verse 11 he claims the same for the gospel he preached. Why should he not in verse 10 pose the same alternative for the nature of his ministry? The two questions do exactly that, and Paul places himself on the divine rather than the human side.

This may seem like a daring move to make, except that in 1:10c he clarifies his status on the divine side of the contrast. He is "a *slave* of Christ," implying absolute allegiance and loyalty, but probably more. The verb "please" (*areskō*) often occurs in contexts of slavery; the slave's purpose is to please the master. Furthermore, the only one who legitimately judges a slave and to whom the slave is alone answerable is the slave's master. By labeling himself "a slave of Christ," Paul declares that not only his allegiance but also his accountability is solely to Christ (see Martin 1990, 51, 59-60).

In relation to other Pauline letters, the opening of Galatians is both distinctive and informative. The denials connected with Paul's apostleship (1:1) and the omission of a prayer of thanksgiving get the reader's attention immediately. The unusual statement of coauthorship and the laconic address (1:2), combined with the statement of astonishment and rebuke (1:6-9), indicate that Paul is deeply concerned about the recipients and about the welfare of the gospel in their midst.

Furthermore, the opening establishes at least two theological matters. First, the event of Christ's giving himself for sins is apocalyptic. It delivers humans "from the present evil age." To think apocalyptically is to think in dualistic categories, and the apostle does this with his opposition between God and humans. Second, two fundamental features of the gospel are its established authority and its uniqueness. The gospel judges those who proclaimed it, and the gospel resists the imposition of other requirements.

The Origin and Power
of the Gospel

(Galatians 1:11-24)

Though the first person pronoun has been already used in the opening of the letter, it is at 1:11 that the long autobiographical section begins that continues through the end of the second chapter. Since the letters do not contain much firsthand information about the apostle and his whereabouts, the material found here is of special interest to historians seeking to reconstruct the chronology of Paul's life and the life of the early church. The interest of this commentary, however, is primarily literary and theological rather than historical, and attention will be focused on the structure of the section, its rhetorical impact and message.

A big issue involved in the reading of chapters 1 and 2, to which allusion has already been made, has to do with whether or not the chapters are an apology in which the apostle is defending himself and clarifying his relation to the Jerusalem leaders. In this case, the assumption would be that part of the agitators' strategy in Galatia was to undermine Paul's authority, to say that his status as an apostle was questionable. One charge they brought against him, so the assumption goes, was that his commission came from the Jerusalem authorities to preach a law-observant gospel, but along the way, to please Gentiles who found circumcision distasteful or painful, he adjusted his message to make it a law-free gospel. Removing the requirement of circumcision would have made the message more appealing to non-Jews. Thus Paul is portrayed as something of a renegade, and his gospel with no warrant but his own. Evidence for this reconstructed scenario is drawn from 1:10, where Paul responds to the charge of being a "man-pleaser" and from the report of the Jerusalem meeting in 2:1-10 where Paul declares that he and Barnabas received an endorsement for their mission from the leaders there (see Bruce 1982, 19-32).

Other interpreters have understood the charges against Paul somewhat differently. They have suggested that the allegation was that he was too dependent on the Jerusalem figures for his credentials, to which Paul responds in the letter by insisting that his gospel is from God and not from humans and by reporting in 2:11-14 his conflict with Peter at Antioch (see Schmithals 1972, 13-32). The two incidents show Paul's assertion of independence from the Jerusalem authorities.

Both re-creations of the possible charges brought against Paul by the agitators—one that he is too independent of the Jerusalem authorities, the other that he is too dependent on them—are derived from the letter itself, but they come from mirror-reading the letter. Simply put, mirror-reading means using the text as a mirror to reflect issues and actions that are not directly (but presumably are indirectly) stated. For example, strong denials such as those found in 1:1 regarding Paul's apostleship are inferred to be responses to accusations made by opponents. While it cannot be totally avoided, however, mirror-reading must be used with great caution. (On mirror-reading, see Lyons 1985, 75-121; Barclay 1987, 73-93.)

Reading Galatians this way is complicated by two factors. First, the modern reader is hearing only one part of a conversation (Paul's part) and can only guess at what is happening in Galatia. Because Paul's rhetoric becomes heated and biting at times, it is doubly difficult to use it as an accurate reflector for the true situation in the communities. Second, Paul is not writing to the agitators who might be making allegations against him. He is addressing the Galatian Christians about the agitators, As John Barclay has observed, points are often made in the letter to pry the Galatians away from their attachment to the agitators, points that need not be read as directed at or descriptive of the agitators themselves. (Barclay 1987, 75).

Less than honorable comments could certainly have been made about Paul by the agitators. Charges may even have been leveled at him, but the stance taken in this commentary is that Gal 1–2 is, initially at least, not to be read as a defense against allegations. These chapters make too much sense when read without the supposition of a self-apology. The strong case made for the singularity of the gospel, its origin and power, sufficiently accounts for the material in the section without the necessity of reading between or beyond the lines. The section may be outlined as follows:

A. Thesis: The gospel—not a human matter, but an apocalypse of Jesus
     Christ, (1:11-12)
B. The origin and power of the gospel: personal testimony (1:13-24)
     1. Paul's earlier life in Judaism (1:13-14)
     2. God's call (1:15-16)
     3. Paul's subsequent whereabouts (1:17-21)
     4. The response of the Judean churches (1:22-24)

Thesis
(1:11-12)

The body of Paul's letters always begins with an introductory formula and with the direct address "brothers and sisters." In five of the letters the formula is one of disclosure ("I want you to know . . ." or "We do not want you to be ignorant of . . ."), in two letters a formula of request ("Now I appeal to you . . ."). Parallels can be drawn to other letters of the Greco-Roman period, suggesting that recalling information already shared or conveying new information served at the outset to create a basis of mutuality on which the argument could proceed. Not so with Galatians. The opening has already identified the polemical nature of the letter, and the astonishment-statement has expressed Paul's dismay at the vulnerability of the Galatians to the "different gospel" of the agitators. Verses 11-12 begin the body of the letter in a conventional fashion, but instead of serving as a bridge-builder to the readers, they make the basic assertion that the next two chapters seek to validate.

The structure and translation of 1:11-12 is critical.

For I want you to know, brothers and sisters, that the gospel that was preached by me
    is not *a human matter;*
            for neither from a human did I receive it, nor was I taught it,
    but by *an apocalypse of Jesus Christ.*

The basic contrast is between the gospel as a human matter (*kata anthropon*) and the gospel as received through a revelation (*apokalupsis*) of Jesus Christ. The NRSV translates a critical preposition in 1:11 (*kata*) to read "*of* human origin," making 1:11 parallel to 1:12. The preposition, however, denotes quality rather than source. Verse 11 is saying is that the gospel is not measured by or subject to the normal canons people use to determine what is true or false. It has its own logic and works in its own way. As Lategan notes, "The gospel does not conform to human criteria, does not take human considerations into account. It does not function in a human way, does not honor human preferences. This is what distinguishes it from the 'other gospel' " (Lategan 1988, 420). This nonhuman factor then is further elaborated in 1:12a by saying that the gospel does not have a human origin nor was Paul taught it by other humans.

What does Paul mean when he writes that the gospel came as a "revelation of Jesus Christ"? When used in the undisputed letters of Paul, the Greek noun *apokalupsis* denotes a revelation of someone or something, but carries with it more significance than simply a drawing back of the curtain to display an object previously hidden. It often designates an eschatological disclosure from heaven, the unveiling of the divine future (Rom 2:5; 8:19; 1 Cor 1:7). Paul writes here of his own experience of receiving the gospel, but in labeling it an "apocalypse" he stresses its divine origin and its eschatological character. It is a divine breakthrough, God's invasion into his life, that Paul does not arrive at on his own or with the help of others. It comes unsolicited. As he later writes, "God was pleased to reveal (*apokalupsai*) his Son to me" (1:15-16). As eschatological, it is more than a mere dream or vision about Paul and his destiny; it has to do with the course of history, with God's cosmic purposes, or as 6:15 puts it, with a "new creation."

A further word about "gospel." The noun, together with its cognate verb, has dominated the section 1:6-12. It is called "the gospel of Christ;" it exposes its shadow figure ("a different gospel"); it judges the proclaimers of the message (1:8-9); it cannot be measured by human criteria; and it came to Paul not from a human source but via a particular disclosure, called "an apocalypse of Jesus Christ." What is this "gospel"? The truth is that Paul does not argue his case for the "gospel" in these first two chapters of the letter by stating and then analyzing its *contents* (as he does in 1 Cor 15), but by asserting its character as *power*.

In receiving the gospel initially, the Galatians were rescued out of "this present evil age" (1:4) and set "in the grace of Christ" (1:6). In responding positively to the agitators, they are deserting not only a doctrine but also "the one who called you" (1:6). Their transfer from the dominion of one to the dominion of another happened in the preaching and receiving of the gospel, and in the mission of the agitators this transfer is being threatened. The gospel is foremost an active power, especially since it comes immediately from a divine source. To use the words from Romans, "It is the power of God for salvation" (Rom 1:16).

In light of this, when Paul declares that he was not "taught" the gospel, he is not denigrating statements of the gospel as tradition (such as 1 Cor 15:3-8) nor is he ignoring the importance of the instruction of others. It might be put this way: Paul's secondary concern in Galatians is *how* the gospel was received (by tradition or immediate revelation); his primary concern is *from whom* it came (from humans or God). That it comes from God confirms its power.

Personal Testimony
(1:13-24)

To further the case for the gospel as divine power, a personal testimony follows. His own "biography of reversal" serves as a paradigm of the gospel's effect. The section 1:13-24 is divided into four subsections:

Paul's earlier life in Judaism	(1:13-14)
God's call	(1:15-16)
Paul's subsequent whereabouts	(1:17-21)
Response of the Judean churches	(1:22-24)

Paul's Earlier Life in Judaism
(1:13-14)

The Galatians no doubt knew of Paul's past; it was no secret (1:13). Two aspects of his previous life in Judaism are highlighted here: his harassment of the church and his advancement in and zeal for the traditions of his ancestors. The details are not so specific as they are in Phil 3:5-6, where Paul lists his credentials, both inherited and achieved.

The text poses a connection between Paul's harassment of the church and his advancement in the Jewish religion. The key word is "zealous" (1:14; "as to zeal, one who persecutes the church," Phil 3:6; cf. 1 Cor 15:9). In the Pauline letters it does not carry overtones that would suggest an association with the anti-Roman revolutionaries known as the Zealots. It was simply Paul's "zealous" pursuit of the ancestral traditions, particularly traditions of the Maccabean period, that led to his pursuit of the church. "He saw himself as following in the traditions of those who had acted forcefully to defend that which was proper to Judaism" (Gaventa 1985, 26).

God's Call
(1:15-16)

"But when God, the one who had set me apart from my mother's womb and had called me through his grace was pleased to reveal his Son to me, so that I might proclaim him among the Gentiles . . ." Now comes the change, the dramatic reversal accomplished in and through the gospel.

Here we make three observations about verses 15 and 16. First, the shift in subjects is striking. The narrative begins with "I" as the subject ("I was persecuting," "I advanced," "I was more zealous"), but at 1:15 changes so that God becomes the initiator of the action. (Some Greek manuscripts

actually omit the word "God," making the subject "the one who set me apart
from my mother's womb . . .") Paul expresses no unhappiness with his early
life in Judaism, no frustration with the law, nothing to suggest that he was
anxiously searching for something new and different. God's action at his
birth ("set me apart before I was born") is paralleled by God's action in calling and revealing. At a particular moment of God's own pleasure God took
the initiative and abruptly intervened to transform his life and future.

Second, the substance of the transforming experience is the apocalypse
of Jesus Christ. The infinitive used in 1:16 (*apokalupsai*) is cognate with the
noun of 1:12 (*apokalupsis*), underscoring again the eschatological significance of the experience. God's revealing of the Son to Paul not only involved
a radical assault on his previous life, but also that assault was part of God's
world-changing activity, the bringing of a new creation.

Third, the apocalypse of Christ has a purpose—"that I might proclaim
him among the Gentiles" (1:16). The one Greek sentence that runs from
1:15 to 1:17 is long and complex, but it serves to depict both the transformation and commissioning of Paul as a single event. He is not first called
and then after a sufficient period of maturation and growth given the task of
being an apostle to the Gentiles. The two belong together.

This emphasis on mission is further supported by the use in 1:15-16 of
language derived from the call-stories of two prophets of the Old Testament
(Jeremiah and the Servant). Interestingly, both prophetic stories include the
phrase "to the nations" (Jer 1:5; Isa 49:1-6), which parallels "among the
Gentiles" (1:16). God's mission beyond the boundaries of Judaism is not a
new idea God concocted recently; it lies at the heart of God's plans from the
time of the prophets. No doubt the Galatian readers (or hearers) would discern in the association of Paul's call with the prophetic calls a message for
their situation as recipients of the expansion of God's mission to the
Gentiles.

A comparison of this story of Paul's call/conversion with the accounts in
Acts is instructive. On three occasions Acts records Paul's experience on the
Damascus Road (Acts 9:1-19; 22:3-16; 26:1-20). The accounts are fairly
elaborate, including details such as the reason why Paul was going to
Damascus, the sudden light from heaven, the mysterious voice of Jesus, the
help of his traveling companions, and the subsequent visit to Ananias, a
disciple in Damascus, who interpreted the experience for him. The reports of
the incident play a critical role in the narrative structure of Acts.

In sharp contrast, mention of the call/conversion in Paul's letters is relatively rare (only Gal 1:13-24 and Phil 3:4-11), and the accounts are barren
of the details found in Acts. When Paul tells his own story, he divulges

nothing of his feelings during or after the incident, no historical circumstances, no light, no voice, no Damascus Road. He does not engage in any introspective probing of the event, nor does he show any interest in the circumstantial information. The reports are thoroughly theological in character. For instance, the incident in Gal 1:11-24 primarily functions as a witness to the power of the gospel (as will be more evident in 1:22-24) and to its divine source. The details of the event, which would be of great interest to the historian or to the modern reader, are not present.

The statement in 1:16 that Paul did not immediately consult with others and did not initially go to Jerusalem seems a bit abrupt, until we remember that the major concern of the section is with the uniqueness of the gospel, including its divine origin. No one else, including the leaders of the Jerusalem church, contributed to the interpretation of the message, even those who were apostles before him. Paul's gospel does not originate with other church officials.

Paul's Subsequent Whereabouts
(1:17-21)

Paul goes to Arabia and then returns to Damascus. "Arabia" is a loosely defined area. While it included the immense desert east of the Gulf of Aqaba, the term could be used for the more proximate Nabataean kingdom that prospered during the first century. Though one of Nabatea's main centers was Petra in the south, the territory stretched north almost to Damascus. What Paul did and how long he stayed in Arabia apparently is not of importance to the case he is making with the Galatians. The popular notion that he went on a spiritual retreat to prepare for his new calling is speculation.

Paul's first visit to Jerusalem, mentioned in Galatians, comes in 1:18, "after three years." The most debated part of the narrative is the statement of the trip's purpose. The Greek infinitive used here (*historēsai*) could be translated "to get information from" Cephas (Kilpatrick 1959, 144-149), or the more noncommittal "to visit" Cephas (Betz 1979, 76). From uses elsewhere in Greek literature of the period, it is hard to exclude from the verb the notion of "getting information." But Paul's narrative is bare; the topics of conversation between the two apostles are not indicated. In any case, a visit to Peter "after three years" to inquire about Jesus in no way jeopardizes the contention that Paul received the gospel through a divine apocalypse and not from human sources.

Response of the Judean Churches
(1:22-24)

The conclusion to Paul's personal testimony is critical in that it includes the response of the churches in Judea. Since Paul was active in Syria and Cilicia, the Christian communities in Judea were not personally acquainted with him and would not have recognized him had they seen him. And yet the word had come to them that the notorious persecutor of the church was now proclaiming the same gospel he had once so vigorously opposed. The news of the transformative power of the gospel was out. Rather than being suspicious or resentful as they had reason to be, these predominantly Jewish Christians "glorified God."

The positive response of the Judean churches confirms Paul's personal story. The change in his life and directions was not merely internal or superficial, a shift here and an adjustment there. The text emphasizes that the transformation was behavioral—from persecuting the church to proclaiming the faith. Others have observed and declared what happened to Paul, and the end result among the Judean churches was the worship of God.

At this stage in the letter the unique character of the gospel Paul preaches has been clearly established. It does not adhere to human standards, nor did it originate with human beings. Rather, it functions as God's transformative power. Paul's own story is primary evidence. The personalizing of the effects of the gospel in terms of his autobiography helps to set it apart from "the other gospel" being advocated in Galatia. Given the fact that circumcision seems to be the critical issue, the mention of the positive response of the Judean churches (1:22-24), with their predominantly Jewish constituencies, is a concluding tour de force in the argument.

The Truth of the Gospel

(Galatians 2:1-21)

The second chapter of Galatians is comprised of three sections, clearly connected. The autobiographical section begun at 1:13 is continued through the first two of the sections as Paul relates incidents that occurred at Jerusalem and at Antioch. The third section (2:15-21), while serving as a theological reflection on the Antioch experience, abandons the narrative mode and presents the proposition that will be vigorously argued in chapters 3 and 4 of the letter. The structure of the chapter is simple:

The truth of the gospel at Jerusalem	(2:1-10)
The truth of the gospel at Antioch	(2:11-14)
Justification by the faithfulness of Christ	(2:15-21)

The narrative portions of the chapter (2:1-14) are fraught with historical and rhetorical and theological questions. While the focus of the commentary is primarily literary and theological, the historical issues cannot be totally ignored. We shall try to keep the two somewhat separate and carefully identified. Both sets of questions are important, but they carry differing significance for the interpreter.

The Truth of the Gospel at Jerusalem
(2:1-10)

The historical questions surrounding this second visit of Paul to Jerusalem abound. The most debated matter is the relationship of this visit with the various visits of Paul to Jerusalem mentioned in Acts. Since the paralleling of the visits has been discussed earlier in connection with the date of the letter (see Introduction), there is no need to rehash the issue here. It is enough to say that the rhetorical force and the theological interpretation of Gal 2:1-10 are not materially affected by how the visits of Galatians and Acts are related. The report of the visit in 2:1-10 has three distinct phases.

Announcement of the visit and its purpose   (2:1-2)
Refusal to circumcise Titus   (2:3-5)
Results of the meeting with the Jerusalem leaders   (2:6-10)

Announcement of the Visit and Its Purpose
(2:1-2)

The time of the visit is uncertain. Does the "fourteen years" designate the time between Paul's call and the second visit, or between the return to Damascus and the second visit, or between the first and second visits? The mention of "again" may support the last of these three options, though it is hard to be certain.

Although the time of the visit is uncertain, the people who made the trip are known: Paul, Barnabas, and Titus. Barnabas is not mentioned often in the Pauline letters (only in 2:1, 9, 13; 1 Cor 9:6). Most of what is known about him comes from Acts. He was respected at Jerusalem as a Levite who had sold a piece of property and donated the proceeds to the church. Fittingly, he became Paul's sponsor on his first trip to Jerusalem following the Damascus Road experience (Acts 9:26-28). He generally functioned with Paul as a link joining Jewish and Gentile segments of the early church. His presence in both incidents in Gal 2 is interesting, siding first with Paul at Jerusalem but with Peter at Antioch. This would not have gone unnoticed by the Galatian readers.

Titus is familiar from his ambassadorial role in connection with the Corinthian community (e.g., 2 Cor 2:13; 7:6, 13-14; 8:6). What becomes critical here is that he is a Greek and thus uncircumcised. Whether Paul deliberately took him along for this reason is of course unknown, but he becomes a *cause celebre* for an important issue.

Why was the trip to Jerusalem made? Verse 2 says that Paul went to Jerusalem "in response to a revelation" (*kata apokalupsin*). This could suggest that Paul had a specific dream or vision in which God directed him to go to Jerusalem. His inclusion of it here would close off any notion that he had been summoned by the Jerusalem leaders, who might have been displeased with him, or that he had been commissioned by the Antioch church (Acts 15:1-2). But this interpretation seems unlikely. As we have previously noted, *apokalupsis* ("revelation") is primarily used in the Pauline letters for God's eschatological activity relating to the gospel—the coming of Christ (1 Cor

1:7), God's righteous judgment on the day of wrath (Rom 2:5), the divine mystery kept secret for long ages (Rom 16:25; cf. Eph 3:3). As Howard points out, even when the term is used for the reception of a revelation by another individual (1 Cor 14:6, 26), it is not an oracular command for the person to go somewhere or to do something, but involves an interpretation of the gospel that edifies the community (Howard 1990, 38).

More likely, "revelation" in 2:2 is to be connected to its earlier uses in Galatians (1:11, 16). Paul goes to Jerusalem to lay before the leaders the "apocalypse" that had happened to him—the revelation of God's Son and the commission to preach the gospel among the Gentiles. This life-changing, world-reordering event was both the motivation for his trip and the substance of his message.

How then is one to interpret the acknowledgment that Paul's visit was "lest I was not running, or had run, in vain" (2:2)? Does this imply that Paul was investing the Jerusalem leaders with the authority to decide whether or not he should preach a gospel without circumcision to the Gentiles? Hardly. Paul harbors no doubts about the truth of the gospel and his role in going to the non-Jewish world. Such an implication would countermand the whole of Gal 1 and especially the thesis stated in 1:11-12.

At stake in the trip to Jerusalem was the solidarity of the people of God. The one gospel, vigorously argued for in Gal 1–2, demanded a unified people. Paul had engaged in an extensive mission among the Gentiles, had established churches in Asia Minor, and it was time now to seek the endorsement of the Jerusalem apostles for his mission in order that the church might not be splintered into two separate, essentially Jewish and non-Jewish groups. Though a missionary to the Gentiles, Paul remained fundamentally a Jew and cherished for himself and for the congregations he established their connections with the mother church and through them continuity with Israel.

Refusal to Circumcise Titus
(2:3-5)

Separating the announcement of the Jerusalem meeting from the statement of the results of the meeting, this unusual scenario appears, telling of "false brothers" slipping in secretly to spy out "the freedom we have in Christ Jesus" and urging the circumcision of Titus. The intrusion of the incident into the natural flow of the narrative has led some commentators to speculate that the incident took place at Antioch before the Jerusalem meeting (Schlier 1965, 71); others contend that it happened at Antioch after the

Jerusalem meeting (Bruce 1982, 115-117; following Orchard, 165-167). But there is no substantial reason to locate the incident anywhere other than Jerusalem. The slipping in and spying out may in fact have occurred at the private meeting of Paul's group and the Jerusalem leaders.

The identify of the "false brothers" is uncertain. Either they or someone else thought them to be Christians since the term "brothers" is used, but then immediately the association is rejected by the label "false." They are a group that obviously denies that Gentile Christians have any place in the fellowship of believers without first becoming Jews. The failure to identify the "false brothers" precisely and the debate as to the location of the incident in no way, however, blunt the strong rhetorical effect of the report. The group demanding circumcision is pictured in the darkest light—"false brothers," who operate in secrecy, surreptitiously gaining entrance to the meeting and playing the role of undercover agents, seeking to rob believers of their freedom and seeking ultimately to enslave them. The language is highly pejorative. Galatian readers could not help but draw a connection between these advocates of circumcision and the agitators in their midst, especially when the scenario ends, "We did not yield to them even for an instant, so that the truth of the gospel might remain with *you*" (2:5). The association is clear. The activity of the agitators in Galatia is no less scandalous than the activity of the "false brothers" in Jerusalem.

The word "freedom" occurs in 2:4 for the first time and is set over against efforts to enslave. Its prominence will grow in the letter, especially with the Sarah-Hagar allegory (4:21–5:1). Here it designates the liberty of both Jewish Christians and uncircumcised Gentile Christians, who make up the Pauline group, but whose freedom could be lost if they succumb to the "false brothers." More generally, freedom depicts the situation of those whom Christ has delivered "from the present evil age" (1:4), those called by the gospel of grace (1:6).

Results of the Meeting with the Jerusalem Leaders
(2:6-10)

Paul's depiction of the Jerusalem apostles raises interesting questions. First, how is one to interpret the statement "what they *once were* makes no difference to me" (2:6)? Some commentators suggest that the verb tense reveals a change in Paul's attitude toward the Jerusalem apostles. Once he had accepted their authority, recognized that they held the power to say that his mission to the Gentiles could have been "in vain," but by the time he writes the letter he is no longer prepared to grant them such authority. The change that occurred ("once were") had to do with Paul's acknowledgment of their role and status (Dunn 1990, 118-122). But this seems to be an awkward reading of 2:6 and presumes a change in Paul's attitude that is otherwise unexplained. If Paul had undergone such an alteration in his own attitude toward the Jerusalem apostles, he does not indicate where or why such a change took place.

A simpler and more plausible reading of 2:6 understands the past tense as a reference to the fact that Peter, James, and John had been physical companions of Jesus, as disciples and as brother, and could claim a special relationship (what they "once were"). This no doubt added to their stature among the early Christians and thrust them immediately into leadership roles in the Jerusalem church. Paul's apostleship, on the other hand, originated from "a revelation of Jesus Christ," and he does not consider his status in any way secondary or inferior to those who had been eyewitnesses of Jesus' ministry. Paul's case is buttressed by reference to the recurring Old Testament theme of God's impartiality ("God does not accept the face of a person").

Also questionable is the possibility of irony in Paul's description of the Jerusalem leaders. The relationships between Paul's group and Peter, James, and John appear amiable. The mood of the meeting is harmonious, and the agreements (as reported) are arrived at without contention or serious debate. But *three* times (2:3, 6 [twice]) the Jerusalem apostles are described as "*those acknowledged to be*" (sometimes translated "those reputed to be;" literally, "those who seemed to be"). It is hard to avoid the conclusion that Paul writes of them with less than full appreciation. In a sense, the text shows him walking a tight rope. On the one hand, he accepts their endorsement of his mission and deems it important enough to include in his letter to the Galatians. They concur in his concern for a united people, undivided by the matter of circumcision. On the other hand, Paul does not want in any way to appear subservient to the Jerusalem apostles. He is accountable to the gospel (1:6), not to the authorities in the Jerusalem church, and this primary accountability must not be imperiled by seeming to make too much of their approval. Betz translates the phrase in 2:3, 6 (twice), "men of eminence" and comments that the expression "allows Paul both to acknowledge the fact that these men possess authority and power and to remain at a distance with regard to his own subservience to such authority" (Betz 1979, 92). This ambivalent stance toward the leaders becomes particularly significant in light of the challenge made to Peter's authority in Antioch reported in the next section (2:11-14).

Four results of the meeting at Jerusalem are indicated. The first is subtle, but important. The Jerusalem leaders concurred with the decision not to circumcise Titus. The language of 2:3 ("Titus was not compelled to be circumcised") can be interpreted to imply that the leaders would have preferred Titus' circumcision but did not insist on it, or the language can be interpreted to mean that from the beginning they agreed wholeheartedly with Paul's decision not to have Titus circumcised. In either situation, the test case as to the potential circumcision of a non-Jew is settled. The Jerusalem authorities not only agreed in principle, but they actually demonstrated their agreement in terms of a particular Greek individual.

The second result of the meeting was the apostles' endorsement of Paul's message. The leaders "added nothing to my message" (2:6, NIV). Paul puts the issue very delicately, because, while the support of the Jerusalem apostles strengthens his case with the Galatian readers, he does not want to hand over to them the authority to dictate what he should preach. Happily, they added nothing—such as circumcision, food regulations, or Sabbath observance—to the gospel he had been proclaiming.

The third result was a more positive one concerning mission—a mutual acknowledgment of Peter's work among the Jews and Paul's among the non-Jews (2:7-9). The Jerusalem apostles had apparently heard of Paul's exploits in Asia Minor and recognized the Spirit's activity in the churches he had established. It proved to be convincing evidence of God's work among non-Jews, which they could acknowledge and bless.

Exactly what is implied by the recognition of two missions, one among Jews and one among Gentiles, is not clear. It could hardly be a geographical division. Since many more Jews in the first century lived in the Diaspora than in Palestine, it is unlikely that the Jerusalem leaders were limiting their activity to Palestine. If an ethnic division were implied, then this would have made racially mixed churches (such as the one at Antioch) scarce. The agreement did not keep Paul away from Jewish groups (1 Cor 9:20-21), nor did it keep Peter from predominantly Gentile groups (2:11-14). Dunn is right: the agreement means simply that Paul and Barnabas were recognized as the voices for Gentiles in the church, working predominantly among them, and that Peter, James, and John are to be spokespersons for Jewish Christians, among whom they primarily labor (Dunn 1993, 111). The "right hand of fellowship" (*koinonia*) seals the agreement and commits them to a ministry of mutual recognition.

The final result of the Jerusalem meeting had to do with remembering the poor (2:10). The Jerusalem group initiates the request, and Paul immediately concurs. On the surface, "the poor" would seem to be an unambiguous term, designating people socioeconomically deprived, except that the term had come to be closely associated in Jewish writings with humility and piety and to be a term used for members of the Jerusalem church. Paul writes to the Romans about those who shared their resources "with the poor among the saints at Jerusalem" (Rom 15:26).

Rather than being a general concern for impoverished people, 2:10 seems primarily to refer to the economically or piously "poor" among the believers in Jerusalem. An offering was taken by Paul from the churches of Asia Minor and Greece for the Jerusalem church as a symbol of Gentile indebtedness to Jews (Rom 15:27; 2 Cor 8-9), and the Galatians actively participated (1 Cor 16:1-3).

Longenecker, however, rightly points out that the verb "remember" is in the present tense, implying a continuous activity, and may convey more than a single gift. The request to "remember the poor" continually would include not only the offering, but also keeping the Christians at Jerusalem regularly in their minds and affections (Longenecker 1990, 60).

The reporting of the second Jerusalem visit is a crucial component of Paul's case with his intended readers. The Jerusalem authorities confirm that the gospel of grace is decisive, sufficient, and cannot be contained in one ethnic expression, as symbolized by circumcision. As Paul reports the meeting, the Jerusalem authorities agree that Titus should not be circumcised, that Paul's message needs no supplement, that his mission to the Gentiles is valid, and that he should keep before his congregations the needs of the mother church. Underlying the specific agreements is the one gospel that has been recognized by the apostles of the church. If there are lingering doubts in the minds of the Galatians whether Paul's message is idiosyncratic or unrecognized by the Jerusalem leaders, the report of 2:1-10 should lay them to rest. In the language of the letter, "the truth of the gospel" (2:5) prevailed at Jerusalem.

The Truth of the Gospel in Antioch
(2:11-14)

Interpreters of Gal 2:11-14 often have been puzzled that two of the church's key leaders, both prominent in the foundational stories of the Christian faith, should have differed as sharply as Paul and Peter did at Antioch over the issue of table fellowship. In the early centuries of the church's life, theologians struggled to account for the embarrassing fact that one apostle (in most circles taken to be the chief apostle) was reprimanded publicly by another apostle and then the incident was recorded in a letter widely circulated among the churches. In a Jewish Christian document called "The

Preachings of Peter" (early third century CE) Peter is given a chance to rebut
Paul's charges.

> But if you [Paul, called in the document Simon] were visited by him
> [Jesus] for the space of an hour and were instructed by him and thereby
> have become an apostle, then proclaim his words, expound what he has
> taught, be a friend to his apostles, and do not contend with me, who am
> his confidant; for you have in hostility withstood me, who am a firm rock,
> the foundation stone of the church. If you were not an enemy, then you
> would not slander me and revile my preaching in order that I may not be
> believed when I proclaim what I have heard in my own person from the
> Lord, as if I were condemned and you were acknowledged. And if you call
> me condemned, then you accuse God, who revealed Christ to me, and dis-
> parage him who called me blessed on account of the revelation. But if you
> really desire to cooperate with the truth, then learn first from us what we
> have learned from him and, as a learner of the truth, become a fellow-
> worker with us (*Pseudo-Clementine Homily* XVII, 19).

The writer, taking up Peter's cause in the debate, goes on to accuse Paul of
being "lawless" and "a hostile person."

Tertullian, in his writings against the Marcionites, sought to justify
Paul's behavior at Antioch. The problem, he argued, is that Paul at the time
was only a new convert, "inexperienced in grace," very zealous because his
own apostleship was called into question. He acted immaturely in opposing
Peter, something he would not have done later, since he wrote in 1 Cor 9:20,
"To those under the law I became as one under the law. . . ." Peter had
certainly done nothing of blame (*Adversus Marcionem* I. 20). Clement of
Alexandria dealt with the embarrassment of the conflict by suggesting that
the "Cephas" mentioned in Gal 2:11, 14 was not the apostle Peter but
another person of the same name from the circle of the seventy disciples
(Eusebius, *Ecclesiastical History* I.12.2). His solution conveniently solved the
problem, but had no historical basis and never gained wide acceptance.

For a period of ten years, Jerome and Augustine engaged in a rather
heated correspondence over the nature of the conflict at Antioch. Jerome,
following an earlier interpretation by Origen, argued that Peter's decision to
withdraw from eating with the Gentile Christians could be explained by the
fact that he was being true to his calling to be a missionary to the Jews (Gal
2:7), just as Paul was faithful to his calling as a missionary to Gentiles. Peter
withdrew in order to prevent confusion from arising in the minds of Jewish
Christians about their continued obligation to the law. After all, Paul had

initiated the circumcision of Timothy (Acts 16:1-3), which proved he was really no different from Peter.

On the other hand, Augustine differed sharply with Jerome's exoneration of Peter, arguing that it made Paul in his rebuke of Peter in Gal 2:14 to be a liar. Peter's behavior was reprehensible, Augustine contended. And yet in a concluding letter to Jerome, he also lifted Peter up as a symbol of "sacred humility," one who accepted his rebuke without complaint and "gave a more precious and holy example to posterity than Paul did" (*Letters* 28, 40, 75, 82). Clearly in the early church, immense energy was invested in the effort to mitigate the opposition between the two prominent apostles and especially to picture Peter in a more positive light than the embarrassing portrait Paul provides in Gal 2:11-14. (For a brief history of the interpretation of Gal 2:11-14, see Mussner 1974, 146-167).

Modern historians have been interested in the incident at Antioch for different reasons than the theologians in the early church. They see it as a pivotal event in the early church's struggle to define itself in relation to its Jewish heritage. While the Jerusalem meeting (2:1-10) indicates agreement between the leaders of the Jewish and Gentile wings of the church, the Antioch incident indicates a disagreement. Paul's version is the only canonical account of the confrontation, and thus the details of the confrontation are critical.

The fairly terse report raises a number of intriguing questions:

• What brought Peter to Antioch in the first place?
• Did the confrontation with Paul occur before or after the meeting at Jerusalem?
• What was the nature of the table fellowship between Jewish and Gentile Christians at Antioch and at Jerusalem, and under what conditions was it practiced?
• Were the Jewish food regulations observed totally, in part, or not at all?
• Who was the group that came to Antioch "from James" (2:12)?
• What did they say to Peter to cause him to change his custom of sharing table fellowship with Gentiles?
• Why did Peter withdraw?
• Was the issue food regulations or association with Gentiles?
• Was Peter's decision to withdraw a practical, *ad hoc* matter, or did Peter have a theological reason for his actions?
• Who were "the circumcision" whom Peter feared (2:12)?
• What persuaded the other Jewish Christians, and especially Barnabas, to join Peter in the walkout?
• Who finally won the day at Antioch?

Commentators differ widely in their answers to these questions. I shall pose a historical scenario that takes account of both what is said and unsaid by Paul and in the process will deal with the significant exegetical matters.

It is not surprising that Peter should come to Antioch (2:11), since Acts records considerable coming and going between the congregations at Jerusalem and Antioch (Acts 11:19-26, 30; 15:1-4, 22, 30; 18:22). On this particular visit he apparently stayed some time since Paul indicates (by an imperfect verb tense) that Peter's custom at Antioch was to eat with the Gentiles (presumably Gentile Christians). What food did they eat? Dunn argues that the Antioch meals observed the basic food regulations prescribed by the Torah. Pork was not used, and when meat was served, particular care was taken to assure that the animal had been slaughtered in the proper manner (the Noachite laws). When the group from James arrived, however, they were shocked with what seemed to them a far too slack observance of the regulations. They demanded a more scrupulous interpretation of the Torah, to include ritual purity (such as cleansing of the hands) and tithing the food (Dunn 1990, 148-163; see the critique by Esler 1994, 52-69).

The major problem with Dunn's interpretation is that nothing is mentioned in the text with regard to food. The Galatian readers, who may or may not have understood the nuances of the Jewish regulations, are given no clues about a more or less strict observance of the laws. What seems at issue in the text is not the menu of the meals but the guest list.

A more probable explanation takes note of the fierce nationalism that prevailed throughout Palestine and Syria during the middle decades of the first century, up to the Jewish revolt against Rome in 66–70. Following the ideology of the Maccabean period, the Zealots sought to cleanse Israel by removing all impure persons. Hippolytus reports as typical of a Zealot of one persuasion that "when he hears that someone has been speaking about God and his laws, but is not circumcised, he lies in wait for him and when he finds him alone threatens him with death if does not let himself be circumcised. If he does not obey, he is not spared, but killed" (*Philosophumena*; cited by Hengel 1989, 70 and 197). It was important that the land be kept pure and that Israel's sacred privileges not be desecrated or usurped by unclean people.

The Jewish Christians in Judea surely felt this separatist pressure intensely and sent a delegation to Antioch ("certain people from James") to urge Peter to cease and desist in his associations with Gentiles at Antioch (no matter what food was served at the meals). While Peter may be relatively safe in Antioch eating with Gentiles, his fellow believers at Jerusalem are vulnerable. As word filters back to Jerusalem about his behavior at Antioch, they are put at risk. How he responds carries implications for their situation. The "circumcision" (inaccurately rendered in the NRSV as "the circumcision faction") Peter fears then are the Jews, who in their nationalistic fervor are exerting pressure on the Jewish Christians at Jerusalem (Jewett 1971, 204-206).

The decision Peter faces is both practical and theological. Does he continue participating in the congregational meals and put his colleagues in Jerusalem at risk, or does he withdraw from table fellowship, which then means abandoning the Gentiles? Critics of this scenario argue that, had this been Peter's dilemma, he could have called a "congregational meeting" and explained to the church at Antioch why he was withdrawing. This move might have lessened, if not removed, the conflict with Paul.

But this criticism ignores the critical theological issues at stake for Paul. First, Peter may well have explained the reasons for his actions to the Antioch congregation, but for Paul, taking strategies to avoid persecution for the cross of Christ is simply unacceptable (6:12). He himself had suffered greatly in the service of the gospel and never saw it as a negative but as an occasion for union with the crucified Christ (2 Cor 4:7-15; 11:23-29). Thus, Peter's "explanation" of the potential persecution that might occur in Jerusalem would hardly have carried much weight with Paul.

Second, the decision to withdraw from table fellowship with the Gentile Christians violates the singularity of the gospel because it puts fellowship in the church on some other basis than the grace of Christ alone. Gentiles, in being abandoned at the table by Peter and the others, are made second class citizens. Only if they fully take on the Jewish mantle can they be accepted into the same community with Peter, Barnabas, and the other Jewish Christians. Paul wants Peter to resist the demands of the delegation from Jerusalem just as he had resisted the "false brothers" who urged the circumcision of Titus (2:3-5). If one followed Peter's line of thinking, Christ and circumcision would become codistinguishing marks of the people of God, precisely what the agitators at Galatia were advocating. For Paul, this constitutes not walking "according to the truth of the gospel" (2:14).

The word "hypocrisy" (sometimes translated "insincerity") is twice used in 2:13, suggesting that Paul's complaint with Peter's behavior may be personal, having to do with a lack of principle. Cullmann makes much of this and argues that the psychological pattern of Peter evident in the Synoptics (impulsive claims of loyalty and then failures in the time of trial) is apparent in Galatians (Cullmann 1962, 50-53).

For two reasons, Cullmann's interpretation fails to be persuasive. First, the Greek word *hupokrisis* in Hellenistic Judaism is always used in a negative sense, but rarely to mean "hypocrisy." More often it is used broadly to denote "apostasy" or "defiance of God" (Wilckens, 565). Peter is being condemned, but not simply for a character flaw. Second, Peter must have had a theological reason for his withdrawal since Barnabas, Paul's longtime companion and advocate for the Gentiles, was persuaded to join him. It would have been highly unlikely that Barnabas would have sided with Peter had he not seen a reasonable cause for Peter's decision.

Paul puts the issue succinctly in his question to Peter. "If you, a Jew, have come to Antioch and have lived as Gentiles do, sharing table fellowship with them openly, and have lived not as Jews do who separate themselves from Gentiles, how can you now, by your walkout, force them to become Jews?" (2:14, paraphrased). Peter's inconsistent conduct betrays him. Once he was committed to an inclusive community on the grounds of the gospel alone ("live like a Gentile and not like a Jew"). But his withdrawal from the table means that circumcision is substituted for the gospel and that Gentile Christians must become Jews in order to participate in the people of God.

Who won the day at Antioch? The best guess is that in the short run Peter did. At least the Jewish Christian segment of the Antioch church sided with him. If Peter had changed his mind again and decided to rejoin the Gentiles in table fellowship, either at the moment or at any time before Paul wrote the letter, it would surely have been mentioned in the letter.

The rhetorical issue to be raised is how this confrontation with Peter functions in the letter to the Galatians. What does its reporting do for Paul's argument, particularly for the initial readers? First, the Gentiles in Galatia are bound to associate with the Gentile Christians who have been abandoned by Peter and the others at Antioch. They can empathize with their experience. Furthermore, they can recognize Paul as the defense attorney for both groups. The word "compel" is the key. Just as Paul defended Titus against a forced circumcision (2:3-5), so he defends the Gentiles at Antioch against another forced circumcision (2:14) and in the letter likewise defends the Galatians (6:12).

Second, what is most remarkable about this passage is the silence of Peter. While a later Jewish Christian document ("The Preachings of Peter") allows Peter a rebuttal, the narrator of Galatians gives him no voice at all. He does not utter a word in the report of the meeting, either directly or indirectly, not even in response to Paul's indicting question (2:14). Matera comments, "There is nothing he can say because Paul confronted him with the truth of the gospel" (Matera 1992, 90). Peter's actions speak for him and leave the readers to surmise that there is no explanation, no refutation of the message of God's grace.

Third, the conflict with Peter triggers the more theological statement of the issue of the letter, as laid out in 2:15-21. Peter's behavior is not merely inconsistent; it violates a conviction that Peter and Paul share, namely that a person is not justified by "works of the law" but by the faithfulness of Jesus Christ. The scenario provides a dramatic entre to the proposition of the letter, stated in the next paragraph.

Since the incident at Antioch concludes the narrative portion of the letter (1:11–2:14), it is important to recall the thesis with which the section began, namely, that the gospel Paul preached is not a human matter but comes as a revelation of Jesus Christ. This thesis has been substantiated by a rehearsal of the apostle's "biography of reversal" (1:13-16), by a report of an incident at Jerusalem where the "truth of the gospel" prevailed in a conflict (2:5), and by a recounting of the confrontation with Peter and his cohorts who "were not acting consistently with the truth of the gospel" (2:14).

Another feature of the rhetoric helps to reinforce the thesis. Paul is consistently pictured in this section as something of an outsider, recognized by the Judean congregations (1:22-24) and the Jerusalem apostles (2:6-10), yet dependent on neither. Notice the ways his independence is stressed:

• Following his call/conversion, he did not confer with anyone (1:16).
• Initially he did not go to Jerusalem to visit the apostles (1:17).
• The Jerusalem apostles added nothing to his message (2:6).
• The Jerusalem apostles are depicted with some indifference (2:6).
• Paul alone defends the cause of the Gentiles at Antioch (2:11-14).

Rather than being details that would enhance his own authority with the readers, these features of the narrative stress that the message Paul preaches among the Gentiles has its roots in God's apocalypse of Jesus Christ (1:12) and nowhere else, specifically not in the Jewish Christian community. There is no effort to discredit the Jerusalem authorities or to drum Peter out of the apostolic circle for his behavior at Antioch. Paul simply assures his readers that his ministry among the Gentiles and the noncircumcision gospel of grace he proclaims have a divine origin and are not subject to compromises and accommodations (Verseput 1993, 36-58).

Justification by the Faithfulness of Christ
(2:15-21)

While Betz's categorization of Galatians as an apologetic letter is inaccurate, his identification of 2:15-21 as the letter's *propositio* is on target. The ancient rhetorical manuals placed the *propositio* before the detailed arguments of the letter in order to sum up the points of agreement and to set up the issues to be discussed in the later sections (Betz 1979, 113-114). Gal 2:15-21 fits this role. Verses 15-16 express the consensus on which Paul and the Jewish Christians agree. Verse 17 raises an objection, which may or may not have been voiced by the agitators. The objection is denied and then responded to in 2:18-20 with expressions (law, faith, crucifixion with Christ, the self-giving of Christ) that receive fuller treatment in the chapters that follow. Verse 21 concludes the *propositio* with a strong statement that declares a commitment to divine grace (2:21a) and that exposes the theological logic of the letter (2:21b). The movement through the section looks like this:

The points of agreement: (2:15-16)
    justification through Christ's faithfulness
An objection raised: (2:17)
    If we are found to be sinners, does this make Christ a servant of sin?
The objection responded to: (2:18-20)
    (a) A return to the Law would make one a transgressor.
    (b) Crucifixion with Christ means dying to the Law.
A concluding affirmation: (2:21)
    The significance of Christ's death is the critical issue.

While 2:15-21 serves as the *propositio* of the letter, it must not be severed from 2:11-14. The original readers (and hearers), with no quotation marks or paragraphing or subtitles to help them, would assume in 2:15 a continuation of Paul's words to Peter at Antioch. The "we" for them would specifically include Paul and Peter and perhaps Barnabas and the other Jewish Christians. At what point the initial readers would have realized that they were no longer listening in on the conversation at Antioch is hard to tell. Thus it is important that the *propositio* be closely tied to the report of the social event that precedes it, lest it be isolated and made to address matters other than Jewish Christians and Gentile Christians bound together by a single gospel and united in table fellowship.

The Points of Agreement
(2:15-16)

While Paul, Peter, the Jewish Christians, and the Galatian readers may have agreed on the precise sense of the single Greek sentence (2:15-16), not all commentators since have been so astute. Part of the problem is that the text is loaded with "abbreviations," short phrases that stand for bigger theological issues. Four such expressions warrant special discussion. First is the phrase "Gentile sinners" (literally, "sinners of the Gentiles"). For those standing within Israel, Gentiles are by definition "sinners" because they lack the covenantal relationship with God and the Torah (see 1 Macc 2:48). On occasion the writers of the Gospels use "Gentiles" and "sinners" interchangeably (Matt 5:47=Luke 6:33). In 2:15 part of the rhetoric in Paul's siding with Peter and the other Jewish Christians is that he adopts the Jewish perspective on Gentiles.

The second critical expression is the word "justify" (*dikaioō*), used three times in 2:15-16 and once in 2:17, with the noun appearing in 2:21. The verb comes from the same root as the Greek noun for "righteousness" or "justice" (*dikaiosunē*), but we have no verb in English that can indicate the semantic connection. Furthermore, the English verb "justify" is more often than not used in a completely different sense to mean "to explain one's behavior" or "to make excuses for." The action involved in the Greek verb, however, is the notion of setting or making things right. Leander Keck suggests the translation "rectify," to put people or things that are out of kilter into a right relationship (Keck 1979, 118-123). The common understanding then that Paul and Peter share is that persons are set in a right relationship with God (are rectified) by the faith of Jesus Christ and not by works of the law. This agreement is sealed by a citation from Ps 143:2: "because no one will be justified by works of the law."

Third, what is meant by the phrase "works of the law," which appears twice in 2:16? In the context of the Antioch incident as well as the Galatian problem, it seems obvious that by "works of the law" is meant primarily circumcision and in 4:10 calendar or festival observances. They are the obligations stipulated by the Mosaic law that are particularly under question. They, along with the kosher food regulations, are the boundary markers that in the first century identified the Jewish people. Peter's withdrawal from the table had to do with disassociating with uncircumcised people (see Dunn 1990, 215-225). Certainly "works of the law" does *not* connote the indeterminate amount of good deeds one must do to earn one's salvation. The agitators would no doubt agree with Paul, Peter, and the Jewish Christians that salvation is a divine gift and not something one achieves.

But a further question has to be asked. Why then use the expression "works of the law"? Why not use "circumcision," a familiar Pauline term and more specific in the context than "works of the law"? As will become clear in the next two chapters of the letter, Paul has a serious complaint with what is apparently the agitators' understanding of the law. The "revelation of Jesus

Christ" has given him a new perspective on the Mosaic law, both negative and positive, that will be developed in chapter 3. He prepares for the later discussion by using in 2:16 "works of the law."

Fourth, the Greek expression *pistis Christou* ("faith of Christ" or "faith in Christ") has received much attention. It occurs seven times in the Pauline letters (Gal 2:16 [twice], 20; 3:22; Rom 3:22, 26; Phil 3:9). Under the influence of the Reformation readings of Paul, most translators since the time of the King James Version (Authorized Version) in 1611 have taken "of Christ" to be an objective genitive and have rendered the phrase "faith in Christ," on the assumption that the faith referred to is a human's trust in Christ. In recent years, however, more scholars have been drawn to the subjective genitive and the translation "faith (or faithfulness) of Christ" (see, e.g., Hays 1983; Matera 1992, 99-102). In 2:16 the latter rendering helps to remove the redundancy of the verse ("we have believed in Christ Jesus") and sharpens the contrast between "works of the law" (something humans do) and "the faithfulness of Christ" (something Christ does). The word *pistis* has a broad range of meanings, including not only trust, faith, and confidence, but also faithfulness, reliability, and fidelity. Since "faith" is used in 3:23, 25 for the advent of Christ and justification is "in Christ" in 2:17, it seems likely that in 2:16 the "faith" that justifies is Christ's act of obedience ("faithfulness") and not human trust in Christ. (See also the discussion at Phil 3:9.)

Having dealt with the theological abbreviations packed into 2:15-16, we can now paraphrase the points of agreement, "Peter, you and I are Jews by birth and are not 'Gentile sinners,' yet we know that a person is not set in a right relationship with God by doing what the law prescribes but only through the faithfulness of Jesus Christ. We also have come to believe in Christ Jesus, so that we might be set right with God through Christ's faithfulness and not by doing what the law prescribes, because, as Ps 143:2 says, 'No one will be set right with God by the law's prescriptions.' "

An Objection Raised
(2:17)

Beyond the common ground, a question is raised about the implications. "If in seeking to be justified in Christ, we too turn out to be 'sinners,' does that then make Christ a servant of sin?" The objection may have arisen from something the agitators have alleged about the potential moral chaos of abandoning the Mosaic law, but more likely it comes from the encounter at Antioch. Eating with Gentiles had led Peter, Paul, and the other Jewish Christians to be labeled "sinners" like the Gentiles (2:15). Does this turn

Christ into sin's promoter? The immediate response is "Rubbish" (Paul's familiar *mē genoito*).

Response to the Objection
(2:18-20)

The text offers two observations about the objection that still reflect the conflict at Antioch and yet go far beyond it. They telegraph the critique of the law that will follow in 3:10–4:11. First, the language of construction and deconstruction clarifies that a transgressor is one who rebuilds the law's perspective (2:18). To reverse the decision of faith and to regress to the time before the "revelation of Jesus Christ" turn one into a true law-breaker. (Notice that in responding to the objection, the pronoun appropriately shifts from the plural to the singular. It is not, however, a return to the autobiographical first person of 1:11–2:14, but an "I" that includes all those who share Paul's perspective.)

The second response moves the argument quite a pace. The reason why the law won't work is because "through the law I died to the law, so that I might live to God. I have been crucified with Christ" (2:19). Betz is correct here in noting that "through the law" is one of those theological "abbreviations" that is elaborated elsewhere. In 3:19-25 the law is given an active role in making its subjects prisoners and guarding them until they are finally freed from it by the coming of "faith" (Betz 1979, 122). Rather than being justified by service to the law, they discover in Christ freedom from the law's dominion.

Dying to the law and living to God then are explained in the statement "I have been crucified with Christ." The law itself is not destroyed, but union with the crucified Christ brings an entirely different relationship to the law. The perfect tense of the verb is highly significant, because it captures both the punctiliar action of dying to the law and the continuing life of service to God. What does it mean to be and remain co-crucified with Christ? Three things are specified. First, the "I" dies in the crucifixion with Christ (see 5:24). Second, what now lives is not a transformed "I" but Christ, risen as the crucified One. Third, the actual life of believers ("the life I now live in the flesh") is made possible by the faithfulness of God's Son, a faithfulness defined in terms of his love and self-giving death.

The language of 2:19b-20 is so bold that it grabs the readers' attention. It goes beyond the issue of Jews and Gentiles together at the table to hint at the radical significance of Christ's death and of the believer's participation with him. To be crucified with Christ means that one has died to the law, the very law that has given identity to the Jewish people and has mandated their way of life, including their separation from the Gentiles. Obviously more explanation is needed to indicate what these verses mean (so chapter 3), but for the moment Paul has alerted readers to the brand new world brought about by "the revelation of Jesus Christ."

A Concluding Affirmation
(2:21)

Since Paul has accused the Galatians of having deserted "the one who called you in the grace of Christ" (1:6), it is appropriate that he concludes the *propositio* with the statement that his message and ministry do not nullify God's grace. (It seems unlikely, even though it is stated in the negative, that 2:21a is a refutation of a charge against Paul. Why would he be accused of nullifying the grace of God?)

This statement then is followed by a sweeping statement that reveals the "theological logic" used throughout the letter. "If righteousness [NRSV: justification] comes through the law, then Christ died for nothing" (2:21b). The noun "righteousness" (*dikaiosunē*) recalls the various verbal uses of "justify" (*diakioō*) in 2:16-17. Being rectified (i.e., being set right with God) through the law and being rectified through Christ's death are mutually exclusive. Whereas Paul once sought righteousness through the law (Phil 3:6, 9), "the revelation of Jesus Christ" (1:12) has changed everything. Now the crucifixion of Christ (and not the law) functions as the theological norm against which all other proposals are measured. In the case of the agitators' proposal, it falls short in that it makes the death of Christ unnecessary.

The stage is set for the specific arguments to be made in the remainder of the letter that will seek to convince the readers of the proposition laid out in 2:15-21. The first two chapters are gripping in the way they narrate the critical events of Paul's story and state the letter's issue in daring and forceful prose. They have not only grabbed the readers' attention, but also have relentlessly held up before them the non-circumcision message of grace as the one and only gospel worth hearing. The task now is to argue the case for the decisive, world-changing character of Jesus' death as it correlates to the promise given to Abraham, as it impinges on an understanding of the law, and as it is shapes the moral life believers are called to live.

An Argument from Experience

(Galatians 3:1-5)

The first two chapters of Galatians have articulated the significance of the gospel, its divine origin, and how its power has been evident in the life of the Christian community. Paul has made himself a centerpiece in the argument by telling his own story of transformation and by reporting his engagements with the pillar apostles in Jerusalem and with Peter in Antioch. Whether or not some of this material also serves to answer allegations brought against him by the agitators is not at all clear. The section concludes with the statement of the letter's proposition, which is deftly intertwined with the speech made to Peter.

The statement of the proposition (2:15-21) is followed by the longest section of the letter, in which specific arguments are placed before the readers (3:1–5:12). The arguments consist of various strategic appeals, some forcing the readers to reflect on their own experiences of receiving the gospel (3:1-5; 4:12-20), others inviting their attention to particular texts of scriptures (3:6-29; 4:21-31). Their intent is to convince the Galatians of the freedom given in Jesus Christ, in the hope that they may be seized once again by the power of the gospel and reject the overtures of the agitators. The section closes with some strong, personal admonitions from the apostle that warn of the dire consequences of succumbing to the attraction of circumcision (5:1-12). Sharp distinctions are drawn between the old age, where circumcision and uncircumcision are critical matters, and the new age, where awaiting God's righteous verdict, believers are engaged in ministries of love.

An outline of the arguments-section is as follows:

A. An appeal to experiences of the readers: the reception of the Spirit (3:1-5)
B. An initial argument from scripture (3:6–4:11)
C. A personal appeal to the readers (4:12-20)
D. A further argument from scripture (4:21-31)
E. Admonitions: Do not abandon your freedom (5:1-12)

We turn now to the first of the arguments. In the body of the letter thus far (1:11-2:21), the readers have been in the background. While they have been mentioned on occasion (1:11, 13; 2:5), the focus has been elsewhere. At 3:1, however, a major change occurs, that picks up where 1:7 left off—with the Galatians' desertion of the gospel. Attention is shifted abruptly from the autobiographical narrative and its concluding proposition to the situation of the readers. The opening address of 3:1 ("You foolish Galatians!") is jarring, indicating the sharp and aggressive character of the appeal. The charge (see the word "foolish" also in 3:3) is not that the readers are stupid or uneducated, but that they lack the ability to discriminate, to separate the wheat from the chaff, to discern the gospel from the not-gospel.

The appeal takes the form of five rhetorical questions that make the readers think about their initial experiences in receiving the gospel and the gift of the Spirit and bring to focus the fundamental issue stated in the proposition (2:15-21). First, "Who has bewitched you, before whose eyes Jesus Christ was publicly portrayed as crucified?" (3:1, RSV). The question plays on the ancient notion that persons or things could be put under a spell by an evil eye. How could the Galatians, who have heard the gospel of the crucified Christ, let themselves be charmed by the agitators' magic?

They know that their conversion from not knowing God to being known by God (4:9) came from the message of the cross (1:4; 2:20; 3:13) and not from keeping the law's proscriptions. The question draws the attention of the readers away from the agenda and issues presented by the agitators and back to the gospel that transformed them.

The clause that precedes the second rhetorical question ("The only thing I want to learn from you is this," 3:2) highlights its importance. "Did you receive the Spirit by the works of the law or by the message of faith?" Several exegetical issues emerge in the simple question. First, the expression "works of the law" (in 3:2, 5) has already appeared in 2:16, and, as we noted there, it denotes in context circumcision and perhaps Sabbath and festival observances (4:10). These are the requirements of the Mosaic law that are particularly at issue in the Galatian community. There is no reason to interpret the phrase as shorthand for works-righteousness or the earning of one's salvation by doing good deeds.

Why is a more inclusive term like "works of the law" used rather than "circumcision"? The answer becomes clear later in chapter 3 when the argument moves beyond circumcision to a critique of the law. Since the agitators are correct in their argument that the Mosaic law demands circumcision (Gen 17:9-14), Paul's case against circumcision as a requirement for membership in the people of God will necessitate a reevaluation of the law and its function.

Second, the phrase in 3:2 (and also in 3:5) rendered here as "by the message of faith" ("by believing what you have heard" [NRSV]; "by hearing with faith" [RSV]) is semantically ambiguous and open to several translations. The Greek word *akoē* can mean either the act of hearing or the message that is heard; the noun *pistis* can mean the act of believing or the message that is believed.

When all the options are laid out, the basic issue, as Hays notes, has to do with the antithesis in the text. Is the contrast between two forms of human activity (doing works of the law versus hearing the faith) or between a human activity (doing works of the law) and a divine activity (the proclaimed message)? If the former contrast is implied, then the NRSV or RSV reading (or "the hearing of faith") is appropriate. If the latter contrast is implied, then "by the message of faith" (or "by the message that creates faith") is appropriate. I have chosen the latter because of the sharp antithesis between the human and divine that runs throughout chapter 1 (vv. 1, 10, 11, 12) and shapes the understanding of the entire letter. In addressing the issue facing the Galatians, Paul is not advocating one human activity to replace another, but is opposing any human activity that usurps the exclusive place of God's activity declared in the gospel. (For a full discussion of the issues, see Hays 1983, 143-149; and Williams 1989, 82-93.)

Third, the word "Spirit" appears here for the first time in the letter and will be a major topic in chapters 5 and 6. In both Hebrew and Greek, the term means both "wind" and "breath" and carries the connotations of power and liveliness. When used as a theological term, as is true most often in Galatians, it signifies God's lively activity, the divine reality at work in the human community. Paul's question presumes that the conversion of the Galatians (when the message of Christ crucified was preached) was characterized by the reception of the Spirit.

The third rhetorical question (3:3) follows on the heels of the second, but probes a bit deeper. It shifts the focus from the time of the Galatians' conversion to the present situation in the community. "Having begun with the Spirit, are you now seeking to attain perfection by the flesh?" The Greek verb can be translated either as a middle voice ("are you now ending?") or as a passive voice ("are you now seeking to attain perfection?"). The latter is a bit stronger, if the agitators, as seems likely, are making the case that circumcision is not to be chosen in lieu of faith but as the completion or fulfillment of faith.

The use of "flesh" connoting circumcision is intriguing (see 5:13, 16-21, 24 for a more complete treatment of the Greek word). On the one hand, it is obviously descriptive of the process of circumcision, the removal of a piece of flesh from the male body. On the other hand, it is a bold move particularly in light of the later argument of the letter. Readers would not miss the association of such a cherished religious practice as circumcision with "the works of the flesh," including such things as fornication, impurity, licentiousness, idolatry, drunkenness, and carousing (5:19-20).

The fourth rhetorical question (3:4) is brief. "Did you experience so many things in vain—if they really were in vain?" The initial reception of the Spirit evidently was a rich experience for the Galatians, which threatens to be for naught. The caveat at the end of the sentence expresses the hope that the experiences will not be in vain.

The final rhetorical question (3:5) repeats the second one in posing the alternatives of "works of the law" and "the message of faith," but also reminds the Galatians of the richness of their past life in Christ. God (though the word is not actually used in the Greek) is depicted as the one who is the source of both the Spirit and the mighty works done in their midst. To choose circumcision is to turn one's back on a mountain of experiential evidence.

The five questions provide a forceful introduction to the long section of arguments. The answers to the questions are obvious and, since they come from the Galatians' own experience, constitute indisputable evidence. The readers cannot deny their own rich history, replete with the extraordinary things God has done in the community. The key, of course, is that they all happened at the preaching of the gospel ("Jesus Christ publicly exhibited as crucified"; "the message of faith") and are completely independent of circumcision or law-observance.

The appeal to experience, while different in rhetorical form and style from the argument from scripture (which follows in 3:6-29), is closely joined in content. In fact, a strong case can be made for taking 3:1-14 to be a unified argument. As 3:1-5 points the Galatians to their initial reception of the Spirit, 3:6-14 explains how Gentiles apart from the law can be recipients of the Spirit. Verse 14 brings the argument to a climax by linking the Gentiles' fulfillment of the blessing to Abraham with the reception of the Spirit through faith.

An Initial Argument from Scripture

(Galatians 3:6–4:11)

Before turning to the arguments from scripture made in Galatians 3–4, it is appropriate to ask: What difference does it make that the appeal to the readers' initial experience in receiving the gospel (3:1-5) *precedes* the scriptural argument (3:6–4:7)? Two comments. First, the argument from experience recalls for both writer and initial readers the Spirit-centered nature of their community life (3:2, 3, 5) and reminds modern readers that the Old Testament texts cited in 3:6–4:11 are interpreted from the perspective of that experience (including the preaching of the crucified Christ, the gift of the Spirit, and the inclusion of the Gentiles). To put it another way, the fulfillment of the texts precedes their interpretation. As Hays comments, "Only because he sees in the Christian community the fulfillment of the promised blessing does Paul venture a retrospective interpretation of its latent sense" (Hays 1989, 109). Otherwise, Paul's handling of the Old Testament texts seems arbitrary and manipulative.

Second, the point drawn from the interpretation of the Old Testament texts, that "in Christ Jesus the blessing of Abraham might come to the Gentiles," is made parallel to the reception of the "promise of the Spirit" (3:14). The very experience of the Galatians in receiving the Spirit confirms the point being made, that Gentiles are included among the descendants of Abraham by faith. Jews and Gentiles ("we") are bound together by their common reception of the promised Spirit.

The initial passage containing the argument from scriptural texts unfolds, topically, in the following manner:

A. People of faith as Abraham's descendants (3:6-14)
B. The promise and the law (3:15-25)
C. Those in Christ as Abraham's descendants (3:26-29)
D. God's liberating action in Christ (4:1-7)
E. A warning not to revert to slavery (4:8-11)

The first three sections deal explicitly with Old Testament texts (3:6-14, 26-29) and the issue of the Mosaic law (3:15-25). The fourth section specifies how God turns slaves into worshiping children and heirs (4:1-7). The final section issues a warning to the readers not to turn back to slavery (4:8-11).

People of Faith as Abraham's Descendants
(3:6-14)

The argument of the first section unfolds in three stages. The first stage (3:6-9), drawing on two texts from the story of Abraham in Genesis, makes the point that people of faith (in 3:1-5 inclusive of the Gentile readers) are recipients of Abraham's blessing. The second stage (3:10-13), citing texts from Deuteronomy, Habbakuk, and Leviticus, establishes that the law brings a curse and that Christ has redeemed "us" from the curse. The third stage (3:14) draws the conclusion from the two previous stages of the argument that in Christ Abraham's blessing comes on the Gentiles, a blessing confirmed by the giving and receiving of the promised Spirit.

First Stage of the Argument
(3:6-9)

The figure of Abraham is prominent throughout 3:6-29. Why Abraham? It is likely that the agitators in Galatia had drawn heavily on the stories of the patriarch in making their case for the necessity of circumcision. They would have been closely in tune with Jewish writings of the period that insisted Abraham's faith and his acceptance of circumcision must be held together when speaking of his righteousness. (For references, see Longenecker 1990, 110-112.) According to Gen 17:9-14, circumcision was initiated with Abraham, including the stipulation that "any uncircumcised male who is not circumcised in the flesh of his foreskin shall be cut off from his people; he has broken my covenant" (17:14). The point that the agitators insisted on and that Paul has to counter is that circumcision is demanded by the Mosaic law and is a distinguishing mark of those who are heirs of Abraham's blessing. The fundamental question in the debate then is, "Who are the descendants of Abraham and on what basis?"

Paul's counterargument begins with the quotation of Gen 15:6 ("Abraham believed God, and it was reckoned to him as righteousness"). Then he draws the somewhat surprising conclusion that "people of (identified by) faith" (*hoi ek pisteōs*) are Abraham's children (3:7). The surprise lies in the fact that the phrase "children of Abraham" does not occur in Gen 15:6, nor is the Genesis text concerned with the issue Paul is addressing, namely who are Abraham's descendants. It is likely, as Martyn has suggested, that the expression "children of Abraham" has been part of the agitators' vocabulary in arguing the case for circumcision with the Galatians and that the surprising conclusion Paul draws can be explained by the fact that he is joining an exegetical discussion already in progress (Martyn, 1993,139; reprinted in *Issues*, 162-163).

The NRSV in its translation of 3:7 and 3:9 turns the Greek noun for "faith" (*pistis*) into a verb ("those who believe"), implying that those who believe as Abraham believed are his descendants. But such a translation ignores the heavy freight that the noun "faith" has come to carry in the argument. In 2:15-16 "faith" is associated with the faithfulness of Christ, an association reaffirmed later in the letter when "faith" serves as a metonym for "Christ" (3:23, 25). Furthermore, in 3:8 the phrase "by faith," at least in the first instance, does not designate what the Gentiles must do to receive the blessing of Abraham, but rather describes the way God functions in justifying them. As Howard notes, there are three aspects of faith that are "temporally and causally antecedent to the Christian's faith," namely, God's faithfulness to the promise, Abraham's faith, and the faith of Christ (Howard 1990, 58). Thus in the context of Galatians when the phrase "those of faith" occurs, it connotes more than simply people who believe. "People identified by faith" in 3:7, 9 is a shorthand expression for those whom God has justified on the basis of the faithfulness of Christ and in response to the promise to Abraham.

The identification of the children of Abraham as those characterized by faith is bolstered in 3:8 by a composite quotation from Gen 12:3 and 18:8 (cf. 22:18), strikingly introduced, "And the scripture, foreseeing that God by faith would justify the Gentiles, declared the gospel beforehand to Abraham, saying, 'All the Gentiles shall be blessed in you.' " The early glimpse of the gospel given to the patriarch had to do with God's intentions to bless all the Gentiles in and through Abraham and his seed ("in you"). The inclusion of the Gentiles is not, Paul argues, a recent addition to the divine intentions nor does it represent a change in God's plans. It is there from the beginning as God's promise to Abraham. In answer to the question under debate ("Who are Abraham's descendants and on what basis?"), 3:7 and 3:9 both make clear that those "of faith," including specifically Gentiles, are children of Abraham and recipients of his blessing.

Second Stage of the Argument
(3:10-13)

Having stated that the blessing of Abraham is extended to those characterized by faith, Paul now takes the offensive, contending that "as many as are
of the works of the law" (3:10, literally) are "under a curse." Deut 27:26 is
cited to identify the curse: "Cursed is everyone who does not continue in all
the things written in the book of the law to do them." Commentators have
often identified the "curse" of the law as its unfulfillability. The logic runs:
no one can possibly meet all of the law's demands, and any infraction leads
to condemnation. Therefore, instead of trying to earn one's way to God by
keeping the law, one should believe in Christ, who removes the curse of the
law. But this explanation ignores both the fact that the law itself had always
taken account of transgressions and had provided a means of forgiveness and
the fact that Paul remains fairly positive about the possibility of keeping the
law. He describes himself as "blameless" regarding righteousness under the
law (Phil 3:6).

It is more likely that the law's "curse" lies in its power to suppress. Later
verses state that "scripture has *imprisoned* all things under the power of sin"
(3:22), that "before faith came, we were *imprisoned and guarded* under the
law" (3:23), that "the law was our *guardian* until Christ came" (3:24). These
all suggest that prior to the advent of Christ, the law functioned to restrain
and suppress humanity. At the heart of this suppression was the division of
the world into law and not-law, into Jew and Gentile, into circumcision and
uncircumcision. Thus the Gentiles did not escape the law's curse. They were
not under the law in precisely the same way that Jews were; nevertheless,
they were "under the curse" in that they were kept from the promises of
God. They were excluded, isolated by the wall the law erected and victims of
the antinomies it created. They were rejected (see Howard 1990, 58-62).

The argument moves a step further in 3:11-12 in the interpretation of
two more Old Testament texts. First, Hab 2:4 is cited to prove the "obvious"
fact that no one is to be justified "by law." Hays has suggestively argued that
"the righteous one" (*ho dikaios*) in the citation does not have generic significance, denoting anyone who is righteous, but refers specifically to the
Messiah. "The righteous one" is a frequent designation for Jesus in the New
Testament (Acts 3:14; 7:52; 22:14; 1 Pet 3:18; 1 John 2:1), and it is not
implausible to think that Paul would have understood the Septuagint of Hab
2:4 messianically. If Hays is correct, then the logic of 3:11 would run like
this: The Messiah sets the pattern for justification and life. Since he lived and

died by faith, justification can be no other way than by faith—certainly not "by law" (Hays 1983, 151-157, 206-207).

Second, the quotation of Lev 18:5 in 3:12 ("The one who does these things shall live by them") is no doubt triggered by the use in Hab 2:4 of the verb "shall live." While the juxtaposition of the two Old Testament texts would have posed no contradiction for Jews, who regarded doing the law as an essential ingredient of faith, they clearly pose a contradiction for Paul. What the law promises in Lev 18:5, it cannot deliver. Only those of faith will live. Thus law and faith turn out to be mutually exclusive ways of claiming one's identity (see Dahl 1977, 170.)

The argument in 3:13 becomes more explicitly christological. Christ, by becoming a curse for us, "redeemed us from the curse of the law." The structure of the verse is that of an interchange (such as in 4:4-5; 2 Cor 5:21; Rom 8:3-4). Christ becomes what we are (cursed) in order that we might become as he is (free). The citation from Deut 21:23 links the manner of Christ's death (hanging on a tree) with the actuality of the curse. It is as if the law has done its job, performed its condemning function ("curse") at the cross, and has exhausted itself so that it ceases to be effective. In light of the previous discussion regarding the suppressive nature of the law, the "us" who are redeemed from the curse of the law include not only Jews but also Gentiles.

Third Stage of the Argument
(3:14)

The preceding argument leads to two conclusions. First, Christ's redemption of Jews and Gentiles from the curse of the law results in "the blessing of Abraham," announced in Gen 12:3, reaching its fulfillment. The Gentiles are now numbered among the recipients of the blessings—i.e., God in faithfulness to the promise to Abraham justifies the Gentiles in Christ (3:8). Second, "the gift of the Spirit is evidentiary proof of God's acceptance" (Dahl 1977, 133). Verse 14 is composed of two parallel purposive clauses:

> that to the Gentiles the blessing might come in Christ,
> that we might receive the promise of the Spirit by faith.

It is unlikely that the two clauses are to be separated or made sequential. The inclusion of the Gentiles in the blessing of Abraham *and* the reception of the Spirit, the eschatological gift *par excellence*, are together features of the radical new age that the "apocalypse of Christ" has brought and that fulfill the promise.

Both conclusions drawn in 3:14 reach back to the previous appeal to experience (3:1-5) and tie together the entire section that runs from 3:1 through 3:14. The public preaching of the crucified Christ (3:1), whose death removed the curse of the law, and the Galatians' rich endowment with the Spirit (3:2-5) are the foundation for Paul's case that the Gentiles belong in the community of God's people by faith and not by circumcision.

The Promise and the Law
(3:15-25)

Prior to 3:10 the word "law" has been used sparingly in the letter, mostly in the expression "works of the law" (2:16; 3:2, 5; cf. also 2:19, 21). We have noted that in the context of the issue in Galatia, the phrase "works of the law" denotes primarily circumcision (plus the observance of special days in 4:10), the badge of identity for the Jewish people. With 3:10 and more specifically 3:15–4:5, the subject more deliberately changes to law (and in each of its usages the Mosaic law is to be understood), what it can and cannot do with and to the people of God.

Why this attention to law? First, it is clear that the law advocates circumcision for all those who are members of God's family (cf. Gen 17:9-14). If a case is going to be made that circumcision is *not* required for Gentile believers, then a reevaluation of the law is needed. What authority does the law have? How does it stand in relation to the promise made to Abraham in Gen 12:3 (see 3:8)? Second, the agitators who have come into Galatia to advocate circumcision no doubt were skillful interpreters of the Mosaic law and put a lot weight on the law as a complement to the gospel. Their ecumenical vision differed from Paul's precisely in that they saw no tension between the law and Messiah. Paul, therefore, has some theological work to do (in 3:15–4:5) to clarify the place of the law in relationship to the good news of Jesus Christ.

Though there are several contested exegetical details along the way, the section 3:15-25 progresses fairly clearly according to the following structure:

Introduction of an analogy involving an irrevocable will	(3:15)
The promises to Abraham and his seed	(3:16)
Application of the analogy:	(3:17-18)
a late-arriving law cannot change the promise,	
What is the law's purpose?	(3:19-20)
Is the law then opposed to the promises?	(3:21)
The law's role as temporary guardian	(3:22-25)

The analogy drawn from daily life is straightforward: a person's will, once ratified, cannot be added to or annulled (3:15). How this declaration in actual fact reflected Greek, Roman, or Jewish legal practices is not at all clear (for a discussion, see Longenecker 1990, 127-130), but the use of the declaration in the argument of 3:15-18 is obvious. The Greek word translated as "will" (*diathēkē*) is, with few exceptions, used in Hellenistic times for one's "last will and testament." But critical for the argument is the awareness that the same Greek word is employed by the Septuagint translators for the term "covenant" (Hebrew: *berith*), and the NRSV appropriately renders the same Greek word as "will" in 3:15 and as "covenant" in 3:17.

Between the analogy (3:15) and its application (3:17-18) an important clarification is made about the promises given to Abraham. Repeatedly in the Genesis narrative, the phrase "and to your seed (or offspring)" is used to refer to Abraham's descendants as recipients of God's promises (Gen 12:7; 13:15-16; 17:7-8; 24:7). The singular in these texts functions as a collective noun, an implied plural. Paul, however, plays on the singular of the noun "seed" from these narratives and takes it to refer not to those who biologically have descended from Abraham and are his natural progeny (so identified by circumcision), but to Christ, in whom the promises are fulfilled. By pointedly rejecting the plural interpretation of "seed," Paul denies that the promises of God come automatically to those who can claim to be a branch of Abraham's family tree. By identifying the "seed" as Christ, he redefines the marks that characterize Abraham's family. While this discussion of the singular and plural of "seed" may seem like exegetical hair-splitting to modern readers, it is crucial to the argument, as will become evident in 3:29.

In 3:17-18 the analogy laid out in 3:15 is taken up again and aptly applied to the covenant (*diathēkē*) and the law. The fact that the law does not come into Israel's life until the time of Moses means that it cannot abrogate or modify the covenant previously established with Abraham. As the next paragraph indicates (3:19-25), the law has a function to perform, but in doing so, it does not qualify the prior promise that God has made to Abraham. This promise, unfulfilled until the coming of Christ, remains inviolable.

No doubt behind the argument of this section lies the message of the agitators in Galatia, who linked the covenant promises with the law, thus finding a warrant for circumcision and the observance of special days. For Paul, however, such a linkage would nullify the promises. His response is to drive a sharp wedge between promise and law and to contend that no matter how sacred the law is, it cannot modify God's promise to Abraham.

The topic of the law is too important, however, for Paul to leave without further clarification. He follows with two logical questions: What is the law's purpose (3:19)? And is the law opposed to the promises (3:21)?

The first question gets a threefold reply. First, the law "was added because of transgressions." Rather than being an original actor, it arrived on the stage late and had a particular role to play in response to human transgressions (to be discussed further in 3:22-25). Though it is not spelled out here as it is in Romans (5:13; 7:7-8), a factor in this role is that the law serves to define transgressions, to "make wrongdoing a legal offense" (NEB), to show certain deeds for what they really are—sins, acts against God.

Second, the law was temporary, playing its part until Christ appeared on the scene, as the one "to whom the promise has been made." Jewish readers would find here a sharp contradiction of their tradition, since the Jews consistently thought of the law as immortal and not subject to change. Numerous references refer to the "imperishable" and eternal character of the law (Wisd of Sol 18:4; Sir 24:9; 2 Esd 9:37; etc. cf. Matt 5:17-18).

Third, the law was given to the people "through angels by a mediator," making it inferior to the promise, which had been spoken to Abraham directly and needed no mediator (3:8). Two other verses in the New Testament speak of the law as having been established by angels (Acts 7:53; Heb 2:2), but only in Galatians is this terminology used to infer that the law's status is subordinate to that of the promise.

The second question flows naturally from Paul's having divorced the law and the promise. "Is the law opposed to the promises of God?" (3:21). The response is an immediate "No," followed by an oblique explanation. The law cannot be a viable rival to the promise because it does not have the capacity to give life. Had it been a lifegiving source (as much of the Jewish tradition claimed it was), it would have been an agent of righteousness and would have stood in opposition to the promise. But since it is not the source of life or righteousness, then it can play its subordinate and proper role.

What is its role? It "imprisoned all things under the power of sin" (3:22). It shut down all avenues of escape for everyone (Jews and non-Jews), leaving only one "out"—the faithful obedience of Jesus Christ. Through Christ the promise made to Abraham can finally be given to those who believe. (The word "scripture" rather than "law" is used as the subject in 3:22 apparently because some particular, but unstated, passage is implied, as in 3:8.)

The final verses of the section (3:23-25) add an additional metaphor for the law that helps to clarify further its proper function. The *paidagogos* (NRSV: "disciplinarian") was usually a domestic slave, a member of Greco-Roman (and possibly Jewish) households, who had primary responsibility for a child until the child came of age, sometime after puberty. His specific job was to protect and guard the child (for example, in going to and from school), to see that the child used good grammar and diction, and to serve as a moral guide. Libanius includes this description of the guardian role:

> For pedagogues are guards of the blossoming youth, they are keepers, they are like a fortified wall; they drive out the undesirable lovers, thrusting them away and keeping them out, not allowing them to fraternize with the boys, they beat off the lovers' assaults, becoming like barking dogs to wolves. (*Orations* 58.7)

Such protection involved twenty-four-hour surveillance and the imposition of restrictions, limitations, and confinements for the child. Since 3:23-25 links the image of the jailer guarding the prisoner with that of the *paidagogos*, what Paul highlights by the metaphor is not so much the law's teaching or disciplining function but its restrictive role, its curtailing of freedoms. This it did by dividing the world into law and not-law, by segregating circumcision from uncircumcision, by building a wall between Jews and Gentiles (see Young 1987, 150-176).

As the *paidagogos* was temporary, serving only until the child reached late adolescence, so the law's role as guardian ends with the coming of Christ. No longer is one subject to its restrictions and limitations. The antinomies it established are abolished. The way is paved for the breaking down of all sorts of barriers (3:28), but especially that between Jew and Gentile. Interestingly, the word "faith" is twice used as a metonym for Christ (3:23, 25), reflecting the cruciality of Christ's faith(fulness) in creating the new world declared in 3:26-29.   No Distinction!

Those in Christ as Abraham's Descendants
(3:26-29)

Freedom from the confinement of jail and from the restrictions of the *paidagogos* is given a strong christological underpinning in the remaining verses of the chapter (3:26-29), as Paul describes the relationships now appropriate in the new creation and then draws a final conclusion. The conjunctions and particles that link the verses provide the structure for the section. The word *gar* ("for") appears three times in the paragraph to explain the cause of the previous statements, and the final verse (3:29) is shaped as an inference from what has preceded it. The logic runs like this:

Since faith has come, we are no longer under a guardian (3:25).
[Why no longer under a guardian?]
For (*gar*) in Christ Jesus you are all children of God through faith (3:26).
[Why children of God through faith?]
For (*gar*) as many of you as were baptized into Christ have <u>clothed yourselves
with Christ</u> (3:27).   *or naked...*

Picture <   There is no longer Jew or Greek, *Has no ethnicity*
              there is no longer slave or free, *Neither slave nor free*
              there is no longer male and female. *Male clothed in a dress*
[Why these divisions no longer?]
For (*gar*) all of you are one in Christ Jesus (3:28).
And (*de*) since (*ei*) you belong to Christ, then (*ara*) you are Abraham's seed,
      heirs according to the promise (3:29).

Four exegetical issues need to be considered before drawing conclusions
from the logic of this passage. First, throughout this section the pronouns are
disconcerting. In 3:23-25 the first person plural ("we" and "our") is used; in
3:26-29 the second person plural ("you"); in 4:3-5 the first person plural
("we" and "us") ; in 4:6 both the second person plural ("you") and the first
person plural ("our"); in 4:7 the second person singular ("you"); and in 4:8-
10 the second person plural ("you"). Some commentators draw a sharp line
with the use of the pronouns contending that the "we" denotes the Jews and
"you" the Gentiles. Thus in 3:23-25 when the topic is the restrictive but
temporary role of the law, "we" is most natural for Paul, himself a Jew, to use,
and in 3:26-29 the address ("you") is directly to the Galatian readers (almost
exclusively Gentiles).

On the one hand, this seems to be a valid judgment. The shift is made
because one or the other group is most prominent in the argument and is
singled out. On the other hand, it is clear that the law has its restrictive effect
on Gentiles as well as Jews by its exclusiveness, by the split it creates between
circumcision and uncircumcision. In 4:3 and 10 both groups ("we" and
"you") are enslaved under "the elemental spirits of the world"; in 3:13 both
are redeemed from the curse of the law. None has priority over the other.
Therefore, some parts of the argument may be more directly applicable to
Jews than to Gentiles (or vice versa), but never to the exclusion of the other.
The section focuses not on the discrimination between the two groups, but
on their common plight—in bondage to the law and in redemption from
the law.

A second exegetical issue has to do with the possible presence in 3:26-28
of a pre-Pauline baptismal formula. Comparisons with 1 Cor 12:13 and Col
3:11 reveal a similar use of the word "all" and a similar set of contrasts as

found in 3:28, making it likely that all three texts represent versions of a liturgy that would have been used at baptismal celebrations in the early church (see Betz 1979, 181-185). If this is the case, then it may be that the Galatians were already familiar with the content of 3:26-28 as a part of their worshiping experience and that its significance is being recalled in the debate with the agitators. Here the liturgical formula brings the argument of chapter 3 to a critical point by denying any significance in the Christian community to the distinctions of race, social status, or gender.

Third, in connection with baptism the imagery of "clothing oneself" is used (3:27). It may have come readily to mind from the practice in the early church of disrobing before baptism and of taking a new garment after baptism. The imagery, however, is found in the Old Testament in numerous places, where Zion is urged to "put on strength" (Isa 52:1; 51:9) and the priests are to be "clothed with righteousness" and "with salvation" (Ps 132:9,16; cf. Isa 61:10). Here baptism entails being clothed "with Christ" (3:27), meaning that the one baptized takes on a Christ-formed life, a life shaped by the "one who loved me and gave himself for me" (2:20).

A fourth exegetical issue surrounds the phrase "there is no longer male and female" in 3:28. This portion of the baptismal liturgy is unique to Galatians (i.e., it is not found in 1 Cor 12:13 or Col 3:11), and the use of "and" (instead of "nor") breaks the parallelism with the other pairs in the verse. The expression no doubt reflects Gen 1:27 ("male and female he created them"), where it is immediately followed by the command, "Be fruitful and multiply, and fill the earth." The association with procreation and fertility makes it difficult to understand the statement in Galatians ("there is no longer male and female") as abolishing sexual differences, as is proposed in Gnostic writings (e.g., Gospel of Thomas 22, 114). In the new creation, men remain men, and women remain women. The categorization of the community by race, social status, and gender, leading to patriarchal hierarchies, no longer exists. The community now receives its constitutive identity from Christ.

Verse 29, with its "since" ("if") . . . "then" structure, draws a sweeping conclusion to the argument begun at 3:6. The case has been laid out that the promise was given to Abraham "and to his offspring" and that Christ is the sole "offspring" of Abraham (3:16). But now in 3:29 Christ is taken to be a corporate figure, and those who are baptized into Christ, who have "clothed yourselves with Christ," and who are "one in Christ" share with him the benefits of being Abraham's offspring and heirs according to the promise. Thus the question, posed at the beginning of the section, "Who are the descendants of Abraham?" is answered: those whose identity is found in Christ.

God's Liberating Action in Christ
(4:1-7)

The opening phrase of chapter 4 ("My point is this" NRSV) indicates that the function of the following paragraph (4:1-7) is primarily a recapitulation of 3:23-29. And yet the restatement of the argument comes with new images and an intriguing parallelism in 4:4-7. Furthermore, it sets the stage for the warning of 4:8-11, that the readers not revert to a status of slavery from which they have only recently been freed.

In 3:23-29 the coming of Christ ("faith" in 3:23, 25) creates a movement for God's people from confinement "under law" to the status of God's children, Abraham's offspring, and heirs according to the promise. With the controlling images of a jailer (3:22) and a *paidagogos* (NRSV: "disciplinarian"), the text depicts the confinement and restraint under the law, that only come to an end with the advent of Christ. The same movement can be traced in 4:1-7. The sending of God's Son and the Spirit of God's Son radically alters the situation of God's people. From being minors, with no more rights than slaves, confined "under guardians and trustees," they move to being children and heirs.

The structure of the paragraph is clear. It begins with the analogy of minors in the situation of confinement (4:1-2) and then appropriates the image for the people of God (4:3-6), drawing a final conclusion in 4:7.

Three exegetical issues warrant particular comment. First, it is difficult to reconstruct precisely the historical sources of the inheritance practices that have shaped this passage, whether Jewish law, Roman law, or Hellenistic law that continued in the first century to be observed in certain locales in the eastern provinces. The text may simply reflect the proprietary structure of Roman households, where the heads exercised such authority that members under their care could not own property and thus were no better than slaves. Has the time of inheritance been set by a now deceased father or by a father who is away from home for an extended period? Details are uncertain, but the focus of the passage is clearly on the plight of minors, who until they reach a certain age determined by the father are under the control of guardians and trustees.

The "guardian" (*epitropos*) was a person appointed by the father, who had legal responsibilities for the child. The figure appears in one of Jesus' parables as the paymaster (Matt 20:8). The "trustee" (*oikonomos*) normally came from the slave class, but functioned as the administrator of the family estate. He, too, is depicted in the parables: as "a manager whom the master will put in charge of his slaves" (Luke 12:42) and a steward with enough access to the family possessions to be able to squander them (Luke 16:1-9). Whatever their precise function in the structure of the Greco-Roman family, in 4:2, they parallel the *paidagogos* of 3:24-25: both have control over the child until a time set by the father, and both represent the Mosaic law.

Second, in appropriating the analogy of the minor, the Greek expression *ta stoicheia tou kosmou* (NRSV: "the elemental spirits of the world") is used (4:3), which poses a broad range of possible renderings. For *stoicheion*, the Greek lexicon (BAGD) lists the following:

- "elements (of learning), fundamental principles," such as the letters of the alphabet (cf. Heb 5:12)
- "elemental substances the basic elements from which everything in the natural world is made and of which it is composed," traditionally thought of as earth, air, fire, and water
- "elemental spirits, which the syncretistic religious tendencies of later antiquity associated with the physical elements"
- "heavenly bodies," such as the signs of the zodiac

The differences in the various printed versions of the New Testament (and their marginal readings) indicate the high degree of uncertainty about the phrase.

"Elemental substances" is more widely attested in ancient literature than the others and would normally be the preferred option. For the understanding of 4:3, 9, however, the distinction debated among commentators between "elemental substances" and "elemental spirits" may not be all that helpful. The Greek word *stoicheion* is not used in association with "spirits' until the third century, but Jews of the intertestamental period traditionally accused Gentiles of worshipping the "elemental substances" as gods.

> For all men who were ignorant of God were foolish by nature; and they were unable from the good things that are seen to know him who exists, nor did they recognize the craftsman while paying heed to his works; but they supposed that either fire or wind or swift air, or the circle of the stars, or turbulent water, or the luminaries of heaven were the gods that rule the world. (Wisd of Sol 13:1-2; Philo, *De Vit Cont* 3; *De Decal* 52-53)

Moreover, the context of Gal 4:3 and 9 attributes to the substances of a quasipersonal existence. They are agents of enslavement (4:3) and are compared to "beings that by nature are not gods" (4:9). In 4:3 Paul then is doing no less than depicting life under the law as the unconditional subservience to alien masters.

The third exegetical issue surrounds the perplexing use of the personal pronouns in 4:3-6. In 4:3 and 4:5 the first person plural is used ("we" and "us"), while in 4:6 the second person plural ("you") appears alongside another first person plural ("our"). As noted earlier (in connection with 3:23-27), some commentators conclude that when the first person is used, Jews are intended (Paul's identification of himself as a Jew, so 2:15) and when the second person is used the Gentile readers are addressed. The abrupt shifting back and forth in the section 3:23–4:7, however, calls into question such a neat distinction. Though one group may be more in the forefront of the argument by the use of the pronoun, it is unlikely that either group (Jews or Gentiles) is excluded from either pronoun. As Martyn states it, "Paul's careful alternation of pronouns and verb subjects . . . is surely a psychologically effective means of insisting on the undifferentiated monolith of humanity before Christ" (Martyn 1995, 17). The comparison between 4:3 and 4:9 confirms Martyn's observation.

The beginning of the paragraph (4:1-3) thus paints a picture of humanity as dispossessed minors, resembling slaves in their servitude to the law's fundamental demands. The law creates a bondage that leaves its clients in a servile state, until such time as God determines.

The text turns then to the word of liberation (4:4-7). The structure of these verses is significant.

> *But* when the fullness of time had come,
>> God sent his Son,
>>> born of woman,
>>> born under the law,
>> in order that he might redeem those under the law,
>> in order that we might receive adoption.
> *And* because you are children,
>> God sent the Spirit of his Son
>>> into our hearts,
>>> crying, "Abba! Father!"
> *So* you are no longer a slave but a child,
>> and since a child also an heir through God.

The parallelism is striking: between the two "sendings" of God (4:4, 6); between the two conditions of the Son's advent ("born of woman," "born under the law"); and between the two "in order that" clauses (4:5). Furthermore, the three conjunctions ("but" in 4:4, "and" in 4:6, and "so" in

4:7) direct the precise movement within the section from an initial contrast with what precedes it, through the two initiatives of God, to a final conclusion. Whether or not these verses contain a pre-Pauline creedal statement (as some commentators argue) or reflect a common Christian "sending" formula that emerged from the Jewish wisdom tradition (as other commentators argue), their final form reflects a careful and deliberate structure.

The emphasis in 4:4-7 on the divine initiative is strong. God is the subject of both the sending of the Son and the sending of the Spirit. The expression "the fullness of time" (4:4) is equivalent to "the date set by the father" in 4:2. In an awkward expression in 4:7 that scribes copying the manuscripts tried in various ways to make less strange, God is even made the agent of inheritance ("an heir *through God*"). The breaking out of bondage to the law comes only at the instigation of God. While the language here is not specifically apocalyptic, the thought resonates with the earlier apocalyptic emphasis of the letter.

The verb "redeem" (*exagorazō*) in 4:5 recalls the use of the same verb in 3:13 and flags the parallelism between the passages. In 3:13, Christ became a curse for us, to redeem us from the curse of the law; in 4:5, Christ is born under the law, to redeem those who were under the law. The image in both passages is that of an interchange between two parties: Christ becomes what we are ("under the law") in order that we might be redeemed and become what he is (God's child). (See Hooker *Adam* 1990, 33, 59-60.)

God's sending of the Spirit in human hearts confirms the new status as adopted children and makes possible the cry of "Abba! Father!" (4:6). It is unusual to find here in a letter written to a Gentile audience the phrase "Abba!", which continues the untranslated Aramaic term alongside its Greek equivalent (see also Rom 8:15). The early church obviously found something special in this intimate expression for God and preserved it in its original form. Jesus had used it in his time of anguish (Mark 14:36), and it may possibly lie behind the opening words to the Lord's Prayer (Luke 11:2; Matt 6:9). The Spirit now leads adopted children to address God in this unprecedented way.

The paragraph reaches a conclusion in 4:7. The result of God's sending of the Son and of the Spirit is that "you" (singular) no longer remain a slave, but a child and an heir. The use of the singular, when the plural has been employed throughout, personalizes the affirmation for listeners in the Galatian audiences who hear the letter read. Being an heir refers to the inheritance of the promise made to Abraham that in his seed all the nations (read "Gentiles") would be blessed (3:29).

A Warning Not to Revert to Slavery
(4:8-11)

Following an appeal to the experience of the readers (3:1-5) and a long and detailed appeal to scripture (3:6–4:7), Paul concludes this section with a warning (4:8-11). The tone of the warning is more that of concern than rebuke, leading as it does to the personal appeal of 4:12-20. Yet clearly hidden in the concern is Paul's frustration over the Galatians' interest in the message of the agitators. The concluding statement of the section (4:11) is a sigh expressing not so much resignation as perplexity, that the readers could give up so much so quickly.

The section contains a statement of the readers' move from a pagan past to knowing God (4:8-9a), a question posing the consequences of their attraction to the law (4:9b), an acknowledgment of their fascination with (if not actual observance of) the Jewish calendar (4:10), and an expression of the apostle's anxiety over the situation of the readers (4:11).

The structure of 4:8-9a sets up the question of 4:9b. First, the readers are reminded of their pagan past ("Formerly") when they did not know God and "were enslaved to beings that by nature are not gods." The apostle could treat the polytheism of the Greco-Roman world either as the worship of deities that have no real existence (1 Cor 8:4-7; 12:2), a judgment rooted in his Jewish heritage (2 Chron 13:8-9; Isa 37:18-19; Jer 2:11), or as the worship of demons (1 Cor 10:20-21). Here the point is that the life of the Galatians prior to the coming of Christ was a bondage to appearances, to entities that masked as gods but in truth were not gods.

The Galatians' past is sharply contrasted with their present ("Now, however")— knowing the true God. But their knowledge of God is immediately defined as God's knowledge of them. The aorist passive participle (literally, "having been known by God") describes the election that has drawn the readers into the family that knows the one God and that has made them objects of divine concern and acknowledgment (Rom 8:29; 1 Cor 8:3; 13:12; Gen 18:19; Exod 33:12; Amos 3:2; Hos 13:5; Jer 1:5).

Then comes the question: In light of being chosen by God and being rescued from the worship of appearances, how can the Galatians return to their old status, enslaved to "the weak and beggarly elemental spirits" (*stoicheia,* cf. 4:3)? What makes the question so shocking is the way it equates the pagan past of the Gentiles with life under the Mosaic law. The readers, who were attracted to the message of the agitators, would no doubt have differed with the way Paul put the question. For them, circumcision and the observance of the Jewish calendar were not reversions to paganism, to enslavement to impotent and impoverished forces; they were expressions of obedience to the Torah and assurance of their inclusion among God's people. If, however, they have followed the line of the letter to this point and have nodded in approval of Paul's argument, they are faced with a real decision.

The question underscores Paul's conviction that the law, as it was interpreted by the agitators in Galatia, was equivalent to the *stoicheia*. It enslaved but had no power to give life. How could those who had heard the message of the crucified Christ, had experienced the gift of the Spirit, and had enjoyed the freedom of the gospel turn again to such bondage?

A Personal Argument

(Galatians 4:12-20)

In this section of the letter in which arguments or proofs are offered to persuade the readers (3:1–4:31), a certain shifting back and forth occurs between those rooted in the past experience of the readers (3:1-5) and Paul's relationship to them (4:12-20) and those rooted in scripture (3:6-29; 4:21-31). The alternation produces an interesting effect when approached from the point of the readers.

The first argument (3:1-5) begins with a jolting address ("You foolish Galatians!") followed by a series of questions, forcing the Galatians to recall their initial response to the gospel. Attention is aroused, and radical alternatives are posed. The second argument (3:6-29) contains a careful consideration of Old Testament texts, making hard demands on the readers to follow the sometimes hair-splitting exegesis of the apostle. Texts are pitted against each other, and critical distinctions are drawn on the basis of a noun's being singular rather than plural. The third proof (4:12-20) calls on the language of relationships—the Galatians' past relationship to Paul, the agitators' relationship to the Galatians, and Paul's current relationship with the Galatians —and employs rich metaphors. While the third appeal is much more emotional and personal in tone than the second (or the fourth), it would be inaccurate to think of it as *merely* emotional or *purely* addressed to the heart. The metaphor of labor pains, as we shall see, has an important theological connotation (4:19). The fourth argument (4:21-31) returns to the scriptures, drawing on two women and their offspring as symbols for slavery and freedom. For a group of believers in one of the Galatian communities listening to Paul's letter read (no doubt repeatedly), the interspersing of personal appeals amid the more logical arguments serves to relieve the tedium of prolonged rational debate and to maintain the interest of listeners (and readers).

The third argument, though seen by some commentators as diffuse and erratic, has a definite movement from its initial exhortation to imitate Paul

(4:12) to the final expression of frustration (4:20). It can be outlined in the following manner:

A. An exhortation to imitate Paul (4:12a)
B. A reminder of the Galatians' previous welcome of Paul (4:12b-16)
C. An alert to the agitators' strategy (4:17-18)
D. An expression of Paul's concern and his frustration (4:19-20)

An Exhortation to Imitate Paul
(4:12a)

Paul does not actually use the word "imitator" in 4:12 as he does in 1 Cor 4:16 and 11:1, but the force of the exhortation is the same nevertheless. It raises two questions. What has Paul "become" that the readers should imitate, and what does such an imitation mean for them? In answering the former question, one recalls the autobiographical sections of the letter where the "changes" in Paul are depicted. From being a zealous advocate for the traditions of his ancestors and a persecutor of the church, he became a preacher to the very people he had persecuted (1:13-16, 22-23). It was the grace of God that led him not only to preach, but also to contend for the place in the community for non-Jews without their having to undergo the rite of circumcision (2:11-14). Though with all the proper credentials as a Jew, he has "become" like his believing Gentile readers, identified not by law but by the gospel.

Paul asks his readers, whom he appropriately addresses as "brothers and sisters," to remain as they are and not forsake the grace that drew them into the believing community for a life under the law. This means rejecting the message of the agitators, who argue that circumcision, along with faith, is an essential mark of God's people and accepting a membership among Abraham's offspring that has nothing to do with legal observances.

A Reminder of the Galatians' Previous Welcome
(4:12b-16)

In 4:13b-16 Paul invites the readers to reflect on his initial visit to Galatia ("you know") and on the warmth with which they received him. Two features of the welcome are highlighted in the text. First, in connection with his visit he contracted an illness that left him at their mercy for care and support. The illness apparently caused him to linger in Galatia and became the occasion for his extended preaching of the gospel in their midst.

Though the text invites speculation, there is no hard evidence to identify the nature of the sickness or even conclusively to connect it with Paul's "thorn in the flesh" mentioned in 2 Cor 12:7. Whatever the illness, Paul acknowledges that the Galatians had every opportunity to reject and scorn him. Verse 14 literally reads, "You did not despise me nor *did you spit me out.*" The latter verb describes the action of fending off a demon, no doubt associated with the sickness. Instead of succumbing to the temptation to disdain Paul, however, they showed him great hospitality and welcomed him as a divine angel, as Christ himself.

The second feature of the welcome was the Galatians' willingness to go far beyond the call of duty. Using a literary figure (and therefore weak evidence for determining the exact nature of the illness), Paul says that they "would have torn out" their eyes and given them to him (4:15). The proverbial expression highlights the immense sacrifice they made in his behalf, and he himself can testify to their genuine and lavish generosity.

Each of these two recollections is followed, however, by a pointed question: "What has become of the goodwill you felt?" (4:15). "Have I now become your enemy by telling you the truth?" (4:16). The contrast is sharp. The recollections do not lead to nostalgia or praise, but to amazement that the Galatians could change so rapidly. From such extravagant hospitality and such warm receptivity to the gospel preached among them, how could the Galatians lose their "good will" (literally their "state of blessing") and turn Paul into an enemy when he tells the truth (that is, when he preaches a gospel of grace)? The language of personal relationship, once strong but now threatened, makes for a powerful appeal.

An Alert to the Agitators' Strategy
(4:17-18)

In 4:17-18 the focus turns away from Paul's relationship to the Galatians to the agitators' relationship to the Galatians. The agitators are pictured as suitors courting the Galatians, which in itself is not a bad thing. "It is always good to be made much of for a good purpose." The problem lies in the intentions of the agitators' courting. "They want to exclude you, so that you may court them."

In describing the situation of the Galatians, Paul draws here on a common and pervasive motif in classical and Hellenistic literature—the "excluded lover." Deceived and manipulated by the attentions of an insincere suitor, the excluded lover finds herself or himself jilted, outside the bolted door, lamenting the deception and pleading with the lover within to open the door (e.g., Aristophanes, *Ecclesiazusae*, 938-975; see Smith 1996, 484-492 for other examples). So with the Galatians. Courted now, they will soon find themselves shrewdly tricked by the agitators into becoming the lover on the outside doing the soliciting. The "excluded lover" image calls attention both to the manipulative intentions behind the agitators' appeals (see also 6:12) and to the vulnerability of the Galatians currently being courted.

An Expression of Paul's Concern and Frustration
(4:19-20)

In the concluding portion of the personal appeal to the readers, Paul steps forward and expresses his deep concern and frustration over the situation of the Galatians (4:19-20). In doing so, he employs a complicated and somewhat strained metaphor. "My little children, for whom I am again in the pain of childbirth until Christ is formed in you." The NRSV rightly stresses that the Greek verb (*ōdinō*) refers not simply to a painful experience but specifically to the labor pains of an expectant mother. It seems a rather strange metaphor for Paul, who regularly employs paternal imagery (e.g., 1 Thess 2:11). In both the Septuagint and various places in the New Testament, however, the image is used in connection with the situation of God's people collectively and particularly with the coming day of the Lord (Mic 4:10; Isa 13:6, 8; Jer 6:24; Mark 13:8; Rev 12:2). In the other two locations where Paul uses the image, both the corporate and apocalyptic contexts are clearly in the forefront (1 Thess 5:3; Rom 8:22). Thus in Gal 4:19 Paul's birth pangs are not merely an expression of his personal concern for the Galatians; his identification is with the groanings of creation, as it awaits the completion of God's purposes.

The second portion of the metaphor seems strained since Paul cannot say "until I bring forth Christ in you" because only God does that. Thus he writes "until Christ is formed in you," referring to the formation of Christ crucified among the Galatians (Gal 2:20; 6:15). On the one hand, this crucifixion with Christ is a gift, not an accomplishment, and yet a gift the Galatians in their fascination with the message of the agitators seem prone to dismiss. On the other hand, the apocalyptic connotations of the first portion of the verse affirm that the formation of Christ is in progress until God's final triumph. Paul then is in labor as one who knows that God has decisively acted in Christ to usher in a new day, but at the same time one who must await the completion of the formation of Christ in the Galatians and in all believers. (For a detailed treatment of the image of labor pangs, see Gaventa 1990, 189-201.) Not surprisingly, Paul concludes by wishing that things were different in the Galatian communities and by honestly acknowledging that he is at his wit's end (4:20).

Three vivid metaphors then dominate this section and give force to the appeal Paul makes with the readers. The Galatians' initial welcome of the apostle was extravagant ("Had it been possible, you would have torn out your eyes and given them to me"). The agitators that have come into the communities, however, are devious. They want to manipulate the Galatians into being "excluded lovers" who end up doing the courting. Meanwhile, Paul is the anguished mother whose labor pains seem to go on and on, awaiting the formation of the crucified Christ in the communities of Galatia. The metaphors are intended to stimulate the initial readers to reflect on their situation and to provoke them to reaffirm the gospel they had heard from the apostle.

A Further Argument
from Scripture

(Galatians 4:21-31)

In the fourth of Paul's major arguments, he turns again to a scriptural proof, rooted in the reading of Old Testament texts. Leaving behind the personal appeal where he stirs the heartstrings in recalling the Galatians' warm reception of him and their ready acceptance of the gospel (4:12-20), he examines the stories of the births of Ishmael and Isaac. In doing so, Paul underscores in a fresh manner exactly who his Gentile readers are and should reckon themselves to be and what they must do in the face of the agitators who insist on the necessity of circumcision.

Though the passage represents a change in tone from the previous appeal, it nevertheless maintains an important thread of continuity. In 4:19 the readers are addressed as "my children," and in 4:21-31 the same Greek word "child/children" repeatedly occurs. The "children" affectionately addressed in the previous appeal are now being scrutinized more carefully, whether they are in fact children of slavery or children of freedom.

The passage (4:21-31) is often overlooked. Frankly, it is difficult, and the difficulty lies in the fact that, though it is based on an Old Testament story, it hardly represents a typical Pauline argument from the Old Testament. It uses expressions that seem strange ("two covenants") and makes connections that are hard to trace (Hagar and Mt. Sinai).

The position taken here is that many (though certainly not all) of the difficulties of the text arise because Paul is responding to an interpretation of the Hagar-Sarah story proposed by the agitators and already under discussion in the Galatian communities. As modern readers, we are permitted to hear a conversation that that has already moved apace. Much is assumed on the part of the initial readers, for example, the fact that neither Sarah nor Ishmael is identified by name. Moreover, it is not hard to see how the Hagar-Sarah story at a surface level could have been used by the agitators in line with their mission to the Gentiles. They believed in Christ, but saw God reaching out to non-Jews through the Torah and thus demanded that male converts be circumcised. For them, Sarah as the free woman symbolizes the family that adheres to the Torah, and Hagar represents the Gentiles.

Some interpreters downplay the significance of 4:21-31, saying that as an allegory it serves as window-dressing to what has been argued more forcefully earlier in the letter. Rather than being merely decorative, however, the passage brings the arguments of 3:1–4:31 to a climax. In response to the agitators, Paul offers a radically different reading of the Hagar-Sarah story that serves, as we shall see, two purposes: to reaffirm the identity of those in Galatia who have responded to the good news of God's grace (4:28, 31) and to urge that the message of the agitators be thoroughly rejected (4:30).

The passage is critical precisely because it has been regularly misinterpreted. It has been and continues to be read as a polemic against Judaism. The synagogue is pitted against the church, the one a religion of slavery identified with Hagar, the other producing children for freedom identified with Sarah. But this operates under the false assumption that in the sixth decade of the first century CE, Christianity was a religious entity distinct from Judaism. Admittedly, the passage is highly polemical, but it is aimed not at Judaism but at the Jewish Christian agitators who had come into Galatia on a mission preaching circumcision and law-observance as well as Christ. Paul had no reason to launch an attack on Judaism. There were few, if any, Jews among his audience. His expressed differences were with the agitators, not with Judaism.

The literary structure of 4:21-31 is clear.

A. A direct word to the readers (4:21)
B. The Hagar-Sarah story and its interpretation (4:22-27)
C. The implications of the story and its appeal to readers (4:28-31)

Before examining the various components of the passage, we need to note its genre. Paul declares that "this is an allegory" (literally, "these things speak allegorically," 4:24). The verb develops fairly late in Greek literature (first found in Philo *De Cherib.* 25) and has not by Paul's day developed a strict literary definition. Nothing more should be read into its use here than simply the notation that the persons and events carry a second significance beyond their primary or literal meaning. It may be Paul's way of concurring with the agitators that the Hagar-Sarah stories have contemporary meaning, but then of offering a very different understanding of that meaning.

One can appreciate the restraint of Paul's "allegory" when it is compared with Philo's extensive allegory of the same story in Genesis. In Philo, Abram's wife Sarah represents virtue (or philosophy). She gives to Abram (the mind) as concubine her handmaid Hagar, who symbolizes the accepted school courses (the study of grammar, music, geometry, and rhetoric). These inferior courses are but stepping stones to the higher study of philosophy. "Sarah, virtue, bears, we shall find, the same relation to Hagar, education, as the mistress to the servant-maid, or the lawful wife to the concubine, and so naturally the mind which aspires to study and to gain knowledge, the mind we call Abraham, will have Sarah, virtue, for his wife, and Hagar, the whole range of the school culture, for his concubine" (*De Cong. Quaer. Erud. Gratia*, 23).

A Direct Word to the Readers
(4:21)

The introduction to the section (4:21) is direct and pointed. The addressees are pictured as "you who want to be subject to the law." Such a group would include those in the Galatian communities who were fascinated by the message of the agitators. They had heard the exegetical arguments in favor of a law-observant Christianity, that inclusion in Abraham's true descendancy, via the line of Isaac, means embracing the covenant of circumcision. Apparently, from the way the address is worded (literally, "the ones who are wishing to be under law"), many of the Gentile readers had not yet taken the step to receive circumcision, but their interest was more than casual.

The Hagar-Sarah Story and Its Interpretation
(4:22-27)

In relating and interpreting the Hagar-Sarah story (4:22-27), drawn primarily from Gen 16 and 21, Paul sets up two contrasting parallels (though not always complete) of Abraham's descendants, based on the mothers.

slave woman: Hagar	free woman: [Sarah]
son born according to the flesh	son born through promise
Mt. Sinai	_____
bearing children into slavery	_____
the present Jerusalem	the Jerusalem above
slave children	free children

Several features of this comparison warrant comment. First, two different experiences of birth underlie the whole section (4:23). Ishmael's birth happened according to natural circumstances, nothing special or unusual about it. Hagar was younger than Sarah, and the birth is depicted in Genesis 16 as happening in the normal course of events. The birth of Isaac, on the other hand, was extraordinary due to the age of Sarah. Paul notes the differing circumstances of the births with the contrasting prepositional phrases "according to the flesh" (*kata sarka*) and "through the promise" (*di' epaggelias*). At one level the phrases are merely descriptive of the Old Testament stories of the two births. At another level, however, the words "flesh" and "promise" are words laden with meaning and critical to Paul's argument throughout the letter. "Flesh" signifies circumcision in 3:3 and the reality that opposes the Spirit, producing all sorts of destructive "works" in 5:16-21. Ishmael's birth then is associated with the very religious rite being urged by the agitators. On the other hand, the "promise," as Paul argues in chapter 3, comes to fulfillment only in Christ, enabling those who belong to Christ to be Abraham and Sarah's true heirs (3:22, 29). Isaac's extraordinary birth "through the promise" then signifies the inclusion of Gentiles, who also become Isaac's true descendants.

Second, Martyn has noted a significant change in Paul's use of the verb for begetting or giving birth. In the Septuagint accounts in Genesis 16 and 21 of the births of Ishmael and Isaac, the Greek verb *tiktō* ("bear, give birth to") is exclusively used. Paul, however, studiously avoids *tiktō* in Galatians (except in citing Isa 54:1) and instead employs in 4:23-24, 29 another verb for birthing, *gennaō*. The substitution takes on added significance when one discovers that *gennaō* is regularly used in the Pauline letters to denote the genesis of Christians and of Christian communities through the power of the gospel (e.g., Phlm 10; 1 Cor 4:14-15). In 4:29 the contrasting births are "according to the flesh" and "according to the Spirit." How churches are evangelized is the issue that occupies Paul in 4:21-31. "He uses the verb to speak of two different ways in which churches are being born at the present time, and thus of two different missions" (Martyn 1990, 179; reprinted in *Issues* 1997, 199). The mission of the agitators is identified with Hagar and Sinai and thus with slavery; the mission of Paul to the Gentiles is associated with Sarah, the free woman, whose children come via promise. Thus the allusions relate to two different ways in which the gospel is understood and Gentiles are evangelized, rather than two different religions, Judaism and Christianity.

Third, the expression "two covenants" (4:24) is highly unusual, especially since Paul does not use the term "covenant" often. One covenant corresponds to Hagar, the other to Sarah. Many commentators identify the two as the old and the new covenants, the one established at Sinai and based in the law, the other Christ-centered and expressing divine grace (cf. 1 Cor 11:25; 2 Cor 3:6). But such a reading seems out of place in this context. Paul has mentioned only one covenant thus far in Galatians, the one made with Abraham (3:15-18). It seems more likely that by using the expression "two covenants," he designates two ways of understanding the one covenant established with Abraham. One of the ways is expressed by the agitators, now aligned with Hagar, who forge a tight link between covenant and law. The other way to understand the covenant is represented by the apostle's mission to the Gentiles, in which a wedge is driven between covenant and law (see the discussion on 3:15-25). The latter is associated with the "free woman," whose child is born "through the promise."

Fourth, a somewhat mysterious, but critical, connection is drawn in 4:25 between "Hagar" (introduced with the neuter article) and Mt. Sinai. Some commentators associate "Hagar" with the Arabic word for "rock" or "cliff," providing a connection to the mountain. A simpler and more plausible explanation finds the connecting link in the mention of Arabia, which is both the location of Mt. Sinai and the land where Hagar's offspring were thought to have lived. This would illumine the first part of 4:25. But in the second half of the verse another geographical connection is drawn, based on nongeographical reasons. Mt. Sinai, though "in Arabia," is made to correspond to "the present Jerusalem," because it produces children of slavery. Though subtle and contrived, the geographical associations made in 4:25 facilitate the connection of Hagar with Mt. Sinai (and thus with the law, slavery, and the agitators), leaving Sarah as the mother of the children freed by grace.

Fifth, one of the contrasts drawn in 4:25 and 26 is between "the present Jerusalem" and "the Jerusalem above" (or "the heavenly Jerusalem"). The former phrase denotes the spiritual, if not the literal, home of the agitators, from where the law-observant mission to the Gentiles was launched. It is not unusual for Paul to use "Jerusalem" to designate the church in that city (1:17-18, 21; 1 Cor 16:3). The expression "Jerusalem above," which occurs frequently in Jewish apocalyptic writings (4 Ezra 7:26; 8:52; 13:36; 1 Enoch 53:6; 90:28-29; 2 Bar 4:2-6), appears other places in the New Testament as an expression of eschatological hope (Heb 11:10; 12:22; 13:14; Rev 3:12; 21:2, 10). Here, however, the eschatological stress falls much more on the present than on the future (note the present tense verbs in 4:26), leading Lincoln to comment rightly that "the heavenly city represents an order which is now being realized and the benefits of which can now be experienced by the believer" (Lincoln 1981, 22).

Finally, the Hagar-Sarah contrast is concluded with the somewhat surprising quotation (in 4:27) of Isa 54:1, surprising in that it does not come
from Genesis, where the Hagar-Sarah story originates. The setting of Isa 54
was the exile, where the prophet spoke to a people longing for restoration to
their homeland. Like a barren woman, forsaken by her husband, Israel lan-
guished in exile. The Isaiah text promises the return of the Lord as husband
(54:5-8), the expansion of the family tent (54:2-3), and numerous children
resulting from the union ("your descendants will possess the nations and will
settle the desolate towns," 54:3). Two things likely triggered the citation of
Isa 54:1 in Galatians: Sarah as the barren woman and the expansive growth
of the progeny that stretched "the curtains of your habitation" (54:2). It
serves as an authorizing word for Paul's aligning himself and his mission with
Sarah and Isaac.

Gal 4:21-27 represents a radical re-reading of the Hagar-Sarah story. The
agitators no doubt argued in line with Gen 21:10 that the son of the slave
woman would not be included in the inheritance alongside the son of Sarah.
The circumcised Isaac alone was the legitimate heir, and thus non-Jewish
Christians would need to be circumcised to be included in the legacy. Paul's
contrary interpretation does not focus on who is circumcised and who is not,
but on the birthing experience of each woman. Hagar, the slave woman,
gives birth "according to the flesh," linking her line with circumcision,
whereas the free woman gives birth "through the promise." Instead of associ-
ating Hagar and Ishmael with the Gentiles, as the agitators certainly would
have done, Paul associates them with those in the law-observant mission to
the Gentiles who urge circumcision.

Implications and Appeal of the Hagar-Sarah Story
(4:28-31)

In the final verses of the section (4:28-31) the implications of Paul's rendering of the Hagar-Sarah story are pointedly drawn for the readers. Two things
become clear. First, the readers are to identify themselves with the Sarah-
Isaac-free line. In case they had not followed the details of reinterpretation,
they could not miss the direct address ("brothers and sisters") of 4:28,
repeated in 4:31, and the specific conclusions: "Now *you* (emphatic "you")
are children of the promise like Isaac" and "So then we are children, not of
the slave but of the free woman." The tone is affirmative and clear. As
Gentile believers, they need not feel or act like inferior members of the
family or second-class citizens, who must receive circumcision to be fully
accepted. Even the law, as Paul has read it, confirms this (4:21).

Second, the readers are to reject the message of the agitators. Quoting Sarah's words to Abraham in Gen 21:10, Paul speaks emphatically to the readers, "Drive out the slave and her child; for the child of the slave will not share the inheritance with the child of the free woman." Having followed Paul's re-reading of the Hagar-Sarah story, the conclusion seems obvious. Rather than being "the excluded lover" left jilted and pleading for entrance (see on 4:17), the Galatians are to expel the false suitor. They are to take action to see that the pernicious influence of the agitators spreads no further in the community. Their self-awareness as children of the free woman requires this.

In 4:29 Paul speaks of two persecutions: one by Ishmael against Isaac and a contemporary persecution, carried out by those "born according to the flesh" against those "born according to the Spirit." What persecutions does Paul have in mind? At the time of Ishmael and Isaac, the reference is to Gen 21:9, where the verb translated in the NRSV as "playing" connotes mocking and jeering. Sarah demands that Hagar and Ishmael be expelled from the family because Ishmael has scorned Isaac. As for the persecution contemporaneous with the letter, the reference is evidently to the aggressive efforts of the agitators, pressuring male readers to be circumcised. Since there is no other evidence that the churches in Galatia were under violent assault from any group, the Greek verb translated "persecuted" in 4:29 (NRSV) need imply no more than annoyance or verbal harassment.

Gal 5:1 functions as a transition, both ending the argument of 4:21-31 and introducing the next section (5:1-12). Christ's act of liberation is for the purpose of freedom for all God's people. Accepting the message of the agitators represents a reversion to the life of slavery, a return to the very jail from which one has been freed. Thus the mission to the Gentiles that requires observance of the law is to be rejected.

A Warning Not to Abandon Freedom

(Galatians 5:1-12)

Chapters 3 and 4 of Galatians contain the major section of Paul's arguments. Using both personal appeals (3:1-5; 4:12-20) and scriptural proofs (3:6–4:7, 21-31), he contends that God acted decisively in the crucified Christ, with the result that the Gentile readers are children of God through the gospel and not through the law. "If you belong to Christ, then you are Abraham's seed, heirs according to the promise" (3:29); "We are children, not of the slave woman but of the free woman" (4:32).

In following the various arguments presented in chapters 3 and 4, we have noticed that Paul's case is often made in the language and style of the so-called agitators, who have preached and taught in Galatia since his departure from the area. Paul's interpretations of various scriptural texts make sense as responses to and critiques of their use of the same texts. Their arguments, however, have hung in the background of 3:1–4:31; as a matter of fact, the agitators themselves are only mentioned obliquely in this section of the letter ("they" in 4:17), and the word "circumcision" does not even appear in Galatians 3–4. It is therefore appropriate for the apostle to turn more directly to the agitators and to the issue of circumcision in the conclusion to the section of the arguments (5:1-12).

In thinking structurally about the development of the letter, commentators debate the place of 5:1-12. Two issues are critical. First, does 5:1 conclude the interpretation of the Hagar-Sarah story (and thus go with chapter 4), or does it introduce a new section? Second, however one decides the role of 5:1, what is the function of 5:2-11? Is it the conclusion to the section of arguments (3:1–4:21), or does it begin the paraenetic section of ethical injunctions, with which the body of the letter closes (at 6:10)?

Regarding the first question, 5:1 seems to stand Janus-like pointing in two directions. On the one hand, by repeating the word "freedom," the verse draws from the designation of Sarah as "the free woman" in the previous section (4:22, 23, 29), and verse 2 appears to begin in such a way as to introduce a new section ("Now I, Paul, am telling you . . ."). On the other hand, 5:1 has no conjunction connecting it to the end of chapter four, and with its concluding exhortation ("do not submit again to a yoke of slavery") it clearly points to the line of the following paragraph. Thus it is best to see 5:1 as a transitional verse that concludes the Hagar-Sarah story and at the same time leads to the warnings and rebukes of 5:2-12. The RSV acknowledges the transitional role of 5:1 by placing it in a paragraph by itself.

Regarding the second question, the issue is a bit more complex. Some commentators have taken 5:1-12 to be the beginning of the exhortation or ethical section of the letter. The shift from the mode of arguments in 3:1–4:31 to an imperative ("Stand firm, therefore") and a strong prohibition ("do not submit again to a yoke of slavery") in 5:1 seems to signal a transition to a new section. Betz divides the section here and makes 5:1 a headline to the paraenetic emphasis. This leads him to conclude that the primary function of Paul's ethics is to protect and preserve freedom. "It follows that the ethical task is the *prevention* of the loss of salvation" (Betz 1979, 257). By making a major break at 5:1, the paragraph 5:1-12 introduces and, in a sense, sets the tone for understanding the remaining ethical injunctions.

At least four factors, however, militate against beginning the ethical section at 5:1 and the depiction of Paul's ethic as merely a way of protecting one's freedom. First, the section 5:1-12 is not at all ethical in character. While 5:1 introduces the paragraph, 5:2-6 is a passionate plea to the Galatians not to be circumcised, and 5:7-12 indicts the agitators for raising the issue of circumcision for Gentiles. No particular ethical injunctions are included.

Second, the section 5:1-12 functions as a fitting ending to 3:1-4:31. It brings the personal and exegetical arguments to a pointed conclusion by laying out the serious consequences of receiving circumcision and, in turn, the response the readers are to make: reject circumcision and let the agitators be damned.

Third, Longenecker (1990, 221-222) has noted the numerous parallels between 5:1-12 and 1:6-10. Both paragraphs are harsh in tone and content. Both contain similar expressions: "the one who called you" (1:6; 5:8), "grace" (1:6; 5:4), "again" (1:9; 5:1, 3), "some who are confusing you" (1:7; 5:10). Both threaten divine judgment (1:8-9; 5:10). The first paragraph (1:6-10), which structurally replaces the omitted prayer of thanksgiving, introduces the issue of the letter. The latter paragraph (5:1-12) concludes the section of arguments. They function like brackets around the arguments.

Fourth, v. 13, repeating from 5:1 the word "freedom," serves as a more likely beginning to the paraenetic section (5:13–6:10), because it includes the positive exhortation to love. By making the major break at 5:13 rather than 5:1, the section 5:1-12 has to do with preserving freedom and preventing the loss of salvation, but is not to be confused with the ethical material, which follows in 5:13–6:10. The ethical material is more positive and particular than Betz depicts it.

The section divides into three parts.

A. An introduction (5:1)
B. A passionate plea to reject circumcision (5:2-6)
C. An indictment of the agitators (5:7-12)

Introduction

(5:1)

The repetition of the expression of freedom in the introductory verse (5:1) brings to the forefront the theme that underlies the first four chapters of the letter. The "false brothers" at Jerusalem were out to undermine the freedom in Christ that Paul and his colleagues represented, and they were resisted (2:4). The Hagar-Sarah story is told in such a way as to pit freedom against slavery (4:22, 23, 26, 30, 31). Now appropriately the theme stands at the close of the section of arguments, with an eye to stating what believers are free *from* (5:1-12). It will be repeated at the beginning of the ethical exhortations, with an eye to what believers are free *for* (5:13).

Two observations about the wording of the initial statement in 5:1: First, the Greek verb in the expression "Christ *has freed* us" is in the aorist tense, suggesting a particular point in past time, no doubt the crucifixion (cf. 3:13-14). Thus any discussion of Paul's understanding of freedom has to take account of its origin in the Christ-event. To some extent the language of freedom may reflect the practice of manumitting slaves in the first century, but more likely it recalls for the initial readers the story of Israel's deliverance from Egypt at the time of the exodus, a story regularly confessed in Jewish worship (Deut 6:20-25; 26:5-11). In both cases (the exodus and the crucifixion) freedom is rooted in a particular historical act of divine deliverance. Second, the word order in the Greek text stresses the purpose for which "Christ has set us free"—"for freedom" (a dative of advantage). The goal of freedom is the exercise of freedom, the living out of the gift given.

"Stand firm" is a favorite Pauline verb and in several cases carries the image of soldiers who are urged to close ranks and not to yield in the face of strong opposition. For example, Paul expresses confidence in the Philippian believers, facing persecution, that they are "standing firm in one spirit, striving side by side with one mind . . . in no way frightened" by their adversaries (Phil 1:27-28). Here the Galatian readers are called to close ranks with a staunch determination to counter the message of the agitators.

The imperative to stand firm then is paralleled by a prohibition: "Do not submit again to a yoke of slavery." In the Septuagint the "yoke" regularly symbolizes a relationship of total dependency, whether to human masters (2 Chron 10:4) or alien powers (Isa 47:6; Lam 5:5). Breaking the yoke means deliverance for Israel, liberation from dominion (Lev 26:13; Isa 9:4; 10:27). The Galatians themselves have known such spiritual bondage "to beings that by nature are not gods" (4:8), and they are warned here not to return to a similar enslavement by choosing to be identified by the law. The law brings its own form of bondage (3:23; 4:9). Submitting to the agitators' demand to circumcise Gentile believers is like walking back through the gate to such bondage and dependency (5:2-6).

A Passionate Plea to Reject Circumcision
(5:2-6)

In 5:2-6 four consequences are laid out for the readers if they choose circumcision, followed by two supporting reasons why they should reject it. Paul marshals his personal authority behind the appeal ("Now I, Paul, am telling you that . . ."). The tone of the paragraph is severe and uncompromising.

The first consequence of choosing circumcision is that Christ will be of no benefit (5:2). The argument throughout the letter has underscored that justification through the law and justification through Christ are mutually exclusive. "If justification comes through the law, then Christ died for nothing" (2:21). To focus on circumcision as a distinguishing feature of the believing community alongside Christ, as the agitators advocated, is to negate the significance of the death of Christ.

The second consequence is the need to attend to the entire law and not just portions of it (5:3). It is difficult from the letter to reconstruct exactly what the agitators were teaching about the particular observance of the law, beyond the matter of circumcision and attention to special days of the calendar (4:10). Paul accuses them of not keeping the law themselves (6:13), and yet the exegetical arguments in chapters 3 and 4 suggest that both parties (Paul and the agitators) treat the law as a whole. It may be that this third consequence provides no new information for the readers, but a reminder of what they already have heard, namely, that they cannot choose part of the law. A single feature, such as circumcision, makes no sense apart from the whole package.

The third consequence is a reiteration of the first but with a slight change in the imagery. The Greek verb used in 5:4 (*katargeō*) appears also in Rom 7:2 (and 7:6) to describe the release from the law experienced by the woman whose husband has died and is no longer bound by the marital code. In like manner, those seeking to be justified by law find themselves "released" from Christ, no longer benefited by or under obligation to him.

The fourth consequence is the loss of grace. Throughout the letter Paul poses sets of opposites: human approval or God's approval (1:10), slavery or freedom (4:21-31; 5:1), flesh or Spirit (3:3; 5:16-26; 6:8-9), circumcision/uncircumcision or new creation (6:15). Underlying 5:4 is the antinomy of circumcision of Gentile believers or divine grace. To choose one is to lose the other.

Verses 5 and 6 use the introductory particle "for" (*gar*), thus providing reasons why circumcision for Gentiles should be rejected. The first reason ("Through the Spirit, on the basis of faith, we eagerly wait for the hope of righteousness") is one of the few expressions of a future hope in the letter (cf. "the Jerusalem above" in 4:26 and "eternal life" in 6:8). But its importance in this context lies not its in eschatological orientation, which presumably the agitators would share, but that the hope of righteousness is to be anticipated "through the Spirit, on the basis of faith." As we have noted in earlier sections of the commentary (on 2:15-16 and 3:6-14), the noun "faith" becomes in Galatians a shorthand term, inclusive of much more than simply human trust in Christ. Behind it lies God's own faithfulness to the promises made and particularly Christ's faithfulness shown in the crucifixion. It is this faith that distinguishes the gospel Paul preaches from the gospel the agitators preach and that the Spirit makes available to the readers (cf. 3:3, 14).

The second reason why circumcision for the Gentiles should be rejected is that designations of circumcision and uncircumcision are simply rendered irrelevant by the presence of God's new creation in Christ (5:6). They are now an anachronism. Whereas they once carried immense weight as the dividing line separating Jews from non-Jews, "in Christ" they no longer do so. It is significant to note that the statement does not denigrate circumcision for Jewish people. It is not an attack on the rites sacred to Israel. Uncircumcision is no better than circumcision. Instead, it is a declaration that *in the Christian community* ("in Christ") the isolation of Jews from Gentiles is gone.

Instead of debating circumcision and uncircumcision, what matters is "faith working through love." Since throughout the previous chapters Paul has argued that God's righteousness comes through the death of Christ and is a totally unmerited gift, it may be something of surprise to hear that "faith" is active and that it effectively operates through love. And yet Paul has actually paved the way for such an expression if we take the "faith" (*pistis Christou*) spoken of twice in 2:16 as the "faith(fulness) of Christ" and not human "faith in Christ" (see the discussion at 2:15-16). The implications of the "faith(fulness) of Christ" are that when human faith is spoken of (as it is in 5:6) it is a faith shaped by the cruciformed life and death of Christ, by the "faith" of the one "who loved me and gave himself for me" (2:20). Believing then as a human experience is much more than either an intellectual acceptance of an historic fact or a passive trust. It actually "works" through love.

An Indictment of the Agitators
(5:7-12)

The final paragraph of this section (5:7-12) focuses the readers' attention squarely on the agitators and utilizes three vivid metaphors to highlight the pernicious influence they and their message have had in Galatia. First is the scenario of a race in which the Galatians are running well, only to have someone swerve into their lane, cutting them off (*egkoptō*) and preventing them from reaching their goal. The one who blocks the lane is not specifically named. Presumably the agitators (as a collective) are intended, though in another context, when the same verb is used, Satan is identified as the one who blocks the way (1 Thess 2:18). Paul no doubt knew who the culprits were in Galatia, but by asking a question ("Who prevented you . . .?) he forces the readers to provide the answer.

Second, the image of yeast that infects the whole batch of dough is used (5:9). No explicit parallels are drawn, but since yeast, a familiar symbol in the New Testament, normally appears as a negative influence (e.g., Matt 16:6, 11-12; 1 Cor 5:6-8), it makes good sense to assume that the agitators are the "yeast" with potential to spread a harmful influence through the various Galatian congregations. While their message may seem only slightly different from Paul's message, it has the capacity to undermine the nature of grace and to produce a community divided along ethnic grounds rather than united in the gospel.

The third image represents a crude, but effective, bit of humor. "I wish those who unsettle you would castrate themselves!" (5:12). The play is on the insistence of circumcision for Gentiles. If the agitators are so determined to circumcise, then let the knife slip and let them make eunuchs of themselves. Behind the verse may lie the word in the law that castration is a reason for excommunication (Deut 23:1). Instead of ensuring inclusion in the people of God, the advocates of circumcision would find themselves excluded.

One verse in this paragraph requires special comment. "If I am still preaching, why am I still being persecuted? In that case, the scandal at the cross has been removed" (5:11). Two questions arise immediately: How could the idea have arisen that Paul was "still preaching circumcision"? What is the connection between "preaching circumcision" and being persecuted? Frankly, it is difficult to arrive at answers to either question. Paul and the initial readers understand the allusions, but from a later vantage point modern readers can only make educated guesses. Regarding the first question, Paul's preaching of circumcision may be a reference to his days in Judaism, something the agitators could have cited in support of their own case. There is no indication that Paul actually engaged in proselytizing during this period of his life, but in his harassment of the church he could have been thought of as an advocate of circumcision. Another explanation is to assume that some occurrence in his ministry, such as the circumcision of Timothy (Acts 16:3), or his apparent acceptance of (or at least silence about) circumcision for male Jewish babies could have been the occasion for charges against him, that he was still preaching circumcision.

Regarding the second question, the "persecution" Paul still experiences most likely refers to the disruption the agitators caused him by their presence in Galatia. The Greek verb (*diōkō*) need not imply violence, only harassment and persistent hounding. Since the Jews would have had no reason to persecute him for preaching the gospel to Gentiles, the agitators are likely his persecutors. Paul later notes that they themselves avoid persecution for the cross of Christ (6:12).

Paul adds that advocating circumcision for Gentiles means robbing the cross of its offense, its character as a stumbling block (*skandalon*). The theme is developed more thoroughly in 1 Cor 1:17-25, where the crucified Christ, contrary to all rational explanations and external proofs, is identified as divine power and the occasion for saving God's people. But preaching "eloquent wisdom" can empty the cross of its power (1 Cor 1:17). Requiring circumcision of Gentiles has the same effect, the dilution of the gospel to the point that it is harmless.

This brings us to the end of the long section of arguments made to persuade the Galatians to hold fast to the gospel of grace initially preached to them by Paul, the message that God had invaded the world in Christ, thereby making old distinctions such as circumcision and uncircumcision no longer critical. The rhythm of arguments between intimate appeals (3:1-5; 4:12-20) and lengthy exegetical discussions (3:6–4:7, 21-31) aim at both experience and reason, at the heart and the head. The apostle is not done yet. In the conclusion of the letter (6:12-17) he restates the issue one more time. Meanwhile, there is the question of the moral implications for the readers of God's invasion of the world. To that we turn in 5:13–6:10.

Love and Law

Anyone familiar with Paul's writings is not surprised to find toward the close of the body of the letter a shift to the ethical, to exhortations about the living out of the grace-filled life given in Christ. It is not a shock to discover paraenetic sections winding up the major thrust of the letter. But a pertinent question arises about this shift. In what way is 5:13-6:10 related to the sections that precede it? Having laid out a careful argument that the gospel does not have a human origin and cannot be wedded to the Mosaic law as the agitators were advocating in Galatia, why does Paul include these exhortations at the conclusion of the body of the letter? What is their relationship to what has preceded?

In the history of scholarship a breadth of proposals has been offered as explanation, ranging from denying any connection to the previous material to postulating a second group of opponents (libertines) whom Paul has to counter in addition to the agitators. (For a survey of the more recent proposals, see Barclay 1988, 9-23.) The connections between 3:1–5:12 and 5:13–6:10, however, seem fairly obvious. The dominant themes of the latter section—freedom, love, law, Spirit, and flesh—have appeared earlier in the letter and provide a strong line of continuity between the two parts. There is no indication that Paul is responding to two different sets of opposition in Galatia. Instead, the readers, composed of the single audience being addressed, are reassured that their congregational life can be guided by the same Spirit that brought them to faith (5:25) and that they do not need to look to the law for identity and guidance. Verses 15 and 26 suggest that the Galatian community is experiencing internal dissension, no doubt over the very issues the letter addresses. Paul's argument is that the law is no balm to heal the divisions in their midst. It only aggravates the problems. But the Spirit brings the qualities that make for peace.

Another way to put this is to say that one must be cautious in reading Galatians not to drive too deep a wedge between what is theological and what is ethical. Paul does not abandon his theological "hat" for an ethical "hat" at a certain point in the letter, as if to say "Since God has done all this, now we should do the following." What ensues in 5:13–6:10 is more a description of the life of the new creation that God has effected and is effecting in Christ than a list of specific do's and don'ts for the community. The people formed by the gracious call of God are continuing to have Christ "formed" in the midst of their daily lives (4:19). The indicative mood verbs in chapters 5 and 6 are as important as the imperatives.

The section thematically divides itself into two major parts.

A. Freedom, love, and law (5:13-15)
B. Living by the Spirit (5:16–6:10)

We turn now to the first major section, and immediately discover in 5:13 an affirmation about the readers that closely parallels 5:1. One important difference between the two verses is that whereas the word order of 5:1 places the phrase "for freedom" in the prominent spot, in 5:13 "you" is emphatic (strengthened even further by the direct address "brothers and sisters"). The attention shifts from the agitators (5:7-12) to the readers.

The initial exhortation (5:13) has a double side: negatively, "see that your freedom does not become an occasion for the flesh to establish a beachhead for its activities"; and positively, "in love serve each other." The two together highlight the sharp contrast between Paul's understanding of freedom and the Stoic notion that was prevalent in the first century. Epictetus wrote, "He is free who lives as he wills, who is subject neither to compulsion, nor hinderance, nor force, whose choices are unhampered, whose desires attain their end, whose aversions do not fall into what they would avoid" (*Discourses.* 4. 1. 1). For the Stoics, people demonstrate that they are free by curbing their passions and fears, by managing well their own souls, and by cultivating a disinterestedness toward the world. Rather than being at the mercy of the ups and downs of life, they are enabled to accept whatever comes with composure and equanimity. Paul's presentation of freedom as engagement and service of one another rather than as independence and self-determination must have seemed jolting to readers with a Stoic bent.

While 5:13 is a particularly apt word for the Galatian communities disrupted to some extent by dissension, it has significance beyond its historical context. Martin Luther stated this most poignantly in his paradoxical affirmations:

A Christian is a perfectly free lord of all, subject to none.
A Christian is a perfectly dutiful servant of all, subject to all.

(Luther's Works, 31:344)

The statements belong together. The essence of Christian freedom is the loving service rendered to the neighbor.

Who is this enemy called "flesh" (*sarx*) of which the Galatians are directed in 5:13 to be wary? The word has a broad semantic meaning and is used, even in this one letter, with a variety of nuances. Without any pejorative connotations, it can designate a person's physical character (literally, "flesh and blood," 1:16) or humanity as a whole (literally, "all flesh," 2:16) or the sphere of that which is human or natural ("in the flesh," 2:20). Unlike Hellenistic dualism, Paul does not imply that "flesh" as material substance is inherently evil. It becomes for him an apt word to associate with circumcision, the removal of a piece of flesh from the human body (3:3; 6:12, 13). Its frequent contrast with "Spirit," however, casts the word in a different light (3:3; 4:29; 5:16-24; 6:8). Since "Spirit" in Galatians is not an anthropological term but designates God's powerful presence, betokening the inbreaking of the new age, "flesh" becomes associated with the world, with the old age that is passing away. It functions as a quasi-personal force, a hostile warrior in fierce combat with the Spirit (5:17).

The apocalyptic overtones of "flesh" in 5:13 as an antagonistic power are connected with the use of the word *aphormē*, translated in the NRSV as "opportunity." The term literally designates the starting point or base of operations for an expedition, and the injunction is that the "flesh" not be allowed to gain a beachhead for its wily activities. Unfortunately, the NRSV rendering of "flesh" in 5:13 as "self-indulgence" obscures the imagery.

Verse 14 then supplies a reason (*gar*) why the readers should shun the "flesh" and should serve one another in love: the law has been fulfilled (has been brought to completion) in the one word, "Love your neighbor as yourself." The more natural rendering of the Greek verb *peplerotai* (like a promise realized or a prayer answered) is probably to be preferred over "is summed up" (NRSV), a translation largely dependent on the parallelism to Rom 13:9 (where a different Greek verb is used). Paul, however, seems to be doing more than reducing the law to its essence, love. The perfect tense and passive voice of the verb indicate that something has happened to the law, with the result that love of neighbor (a citation from the law; Lev. 19:18) can now be the single divine imperative for the people of God. The verb "has been fulfilled" echoes the action of Christ in removing of the law's curse (3:13), in embodying the original promise given to Abraham (3:18), and thereby in restoring the law to its rightful identity. Martyn sums up this treatment of the verb by saying,

> In Gal 5:14, that is to say, the guiding imperative of the Law (Lev 19:18) is not the result of an insightful deed of *Paul*, his act of reducing the Law to its essence (his achievement of the *reductio in unum*). On the contrary, that guiding imperative is the result of the powerful deed of *Christ*, his act of *loosing* God's Law from the Law of Sinai, thereby addressing God's Law to the church. The Law taken in hand by Christ (Gal 6:2) is the Law that Christ has restored to its original identity and power (Gal 5:14). (Martyn 1997, 247-248)

Martyn's interpretation helps to explain the sharp tension between the negative and positive words written about the law in Galatians. In chapters 3 and 4, Paul distinguishes between two voices of the law (see the positive and negatives uses in 4:21). On the one hand, the law "curses" (3:10) and enslaves (3:23-24; 4:3-5) by dividing humanity into circumcision and uncircumcision (3:10; 5:6). On the other hand, the law (*graphē*) "preached the gospel ahead of time to Abraham" (3:8) in the covenant promise about his future "seed" (3:16-17). By taking the curse of the law upon himself (3:13) and by being the embodiment of the promise (3:16-17), Christ enables the original, promising voice of the law to be heard again, now as the primary word for the guidance of the Galatian churches.

The commonplace warning given in 5:15, that if the readers continue to fight like cats and dogs they will end up devouring one another, is a reminder that this paraenetic section is addressed first and foremost to the community and only in a secondary sense to individuals within the community. Those sitting in the Galatian congregations, listening to the letter read, would hear Paul's words spoken about their common life, which may have been in some disarray. If the conflicts sparked by the agitators were to continue, the results could be disastrous.

Living by the Spirit

(Galatians 5:16–6:10)

The command to love one's neighbor (5:14) is not immediately followed by a list of specific examples of what loving entails or of who qualifies as neighbor. Rather, the second and longest section of the paraenesis, while not abandoning the notions of law (5:18, 23; 6:2) and love (5:22), changes the dominant categories to Spirit and flesh. The contrast of Spirit and flesh marks both the beginning and the end of the section (5:16-24; 6:8). Since it is not the first time that such a contrast has appeared in the letter (see 3:3; 4:29), it provides a point of continuity in the overall argument of the letter as well as an additional framework for depicting the character of the Christian community. As we shall see, the thrust of the section is not so much to confront the readers with a choice: either serve the Spirit or serve the flesh. Instead, the use throughout of the indicative moods of various verbs indicates that the readers are being reminded that since they *have already received* the Spirit, they should live by and trust the Spirit's guidance for their common life. The Spirit produces the love that has been commanded (5:22), so that in reality God makes possible the very life required.

The section itself divides into two further subsections.

A. The Spirit at war with the flesh (5:16-26)
B. Bearing one another's burdens (6:1-10)

The Spirit at War with the Flesh
(5:16-26)

The conversation that has taken place in the Galatian congregations between the members and the agitators, prior to the writing of this letter, can only be guessed at. It is not unlikely, however, that the agitators had argued that direction for the moral life of Christians is to be derived from the Mosaic law. It provides guidance as well as identity for the people of God as they

seek to cope with life in a pagan environment and thus is posed as the antidote to the power of the "flesh." In response, Paul contends that the Spirit,
God's presence and activity in human life, is the only match for the "flesh."

The argument unfolds as follows:

The Spirit and the flesh wage war against each other.   (5:16-18)
The works of the flesh bar the way to the kingdom of God. (5:19-21)
The Spirit produces fruit that fulfills the law.   (5:22-24)
Since the Spirit has given life,   (5:25-26)
    the Spirit should guide the daily conduct of the community.

The Spirit versus the Flesh
(5:16-18)

The conflict between Spirit and flesh makes sense only when it is recognized
that Paul as an apocalyptic theologian writes of two spheres of power that
stand in fierce opposition to one another. On the one hand, the Spirit has
been sent by God in conjunction with the Son to create the new family relationships, with the result that people are no longer known as slaves but as
children (4:4-7). Throughout the New Testament the Spirit is the symbol
par excellence of the powerful inbreaking of the new age (e.g., Matt 12:28;
Luke 1:35; John 4:21-24; Acts 1:8; 2:16-21; Heb 6:4-6). In Galatians (with
the exception of 6:18), "Spirit" (*pneuma*) consistently denotes the divine
Spirit.

On the other hand, "flesh," precisely because of its polarity to the Spirit,
becomes associated with the old age, the field of force invaded by the Spirit
(see the discussion of "flesh" at 5:13). It is misleading in this context to translate *sarx* ("flesh") as "lower nature" (NEB), "sinful nature" (NIV), or "human
nature" (TEV), as if it were an anthropological term, implying that the individual is divided into two parts, a spiritual nature and a fleshly nature.
Instead, the Spirit and the flesh are two powers engaged in an apocalyptic
combat, with the battlefield being the Galatian congregations.

The Greek imperative in 5:16 rendered by the NRSV as "Live by the
Spirit" reflects the characteristically Pauline verb *peripateō* ("walk"), meaning
something like "conduct your daily life by the Spirit" (e.g., 1 Thess 2:12;
4:1,12; Rom 13:13; Phil 3:17, 18). The assumption is not that the Spirit is a
reality the readers still have to appropriate; rather, the Spirit they have
already received must be allowed to guide and direct their congregational
life.

One pesky exegetical problem occurs in the final clause of 5:17. The flesh and the Spirit are so vigorously opposed to one another that they end up frustrating each other, with the result that "you do not do the things that you want to do." Out of context, the verse could be understood as implying a permanent standoff between the Spirit and the flesh, leaving the community and the individual helpless and paralyzed.

Two points need to be made about the syntax of 5:17-18. First, verse 17 begins with a conflict between the flesh and the Spirit. They oppose one another "*in order that* you not do these things that you want to do." The clause expresses purpose (and not result) and declares the intent of each power, namely, to thwart the work of the other. As Williams comments, "The flesh and the Spirit oppose each other in order to keep Christians from doing what they might otherwise do if the other adversary were not on the field" (Williams 1997, 149). Nothing is implied about the status of the readers until 5:18. This leads to the second comment about the syntax. The opening clause of 5:18 is a first class conditional, implying that it assumes the reality of the condition. It could be translated, "But since (*ei*) you are led by the Spirit, you are not under law." The readers are not victimized by a standoff between the flesh and the Spirit because their identity and allegiance are with the Spirit.

Works of the Flesh
(5:19-21)

Fifteen specific items are listed among the obvious effects that the flesh produces (5:19-21), and at least eight are peculiarly disruptive of communal life ("enmities, strife, jealousy, anger, quarrels, dissensions, factions, envy"). The list resembles in many ways the traditional catalogues of vices and virtues that go back to Plato (*Republic 7. 536A*) and Aristotle (*Nicomachean Ethics 2. 6. 15-3. 7. 15*) and are particularly prominent in the Stoic moralists such as Epictetus (*Discourses 2. 8. 23, 24. 89-90*), Dio Chrysostom (*Orations 4. 91-96*), and the later Diogenes Laertius (*Lives,* "Zeno," 7). Both vice and virtue lists (see 5:22-23) played an important part in moral instruction throughout the Greco-Roman world. Paul, however, uses the lists not to indicate what conduct persons should avoid (or what conduct they should nurture, in the case of 5:22-23), but what the opposing powers—flesh and Spirit—produce in the life of the community. If the community is guided by the flesh, then it can expect such behavior as 5:19-21 indicates. If it walks by the Spirit, then it can anticipate "the fruit of the Spirit" (5:22-23).

Works of the Spirit
(5:22-24)

The effect of labeling the outcomes of the flesh "works" and the outcomes of the Spirit "fruit" is significant. The particular choice of "fruit" stresses even more pointedly than "works" that the characteristics included in the list are the products of the Spirit's presence and not the result of human initiative and activity. The language throughout the section is consistent—"*led by* the Spirit" (5:18), "the *fruit* of the Spirit" (5:22)," from the Spirit *will reap* eternal life" (6:8). Furthermore, the singular of the noun "fruit" suggests that the Spirit's benefits are cohesive and unified. In distinction from the "gifts" of the Spirit, which are varied and multiple (1 Cor 12:4-11), the "fruit" is indivisible.

Not surprisingly, "love" heads the list. For Paul, the choice is hardly arbitrary or accidental in light of what is stated about "love" in 1 Corinthians 13. "Love" is not one virtue to be numbered among several others, but the quintessence of the Christian life (5:6, 13-14). The remainder of the list gives further substance to the word "love" and depicts the qualities characteristic of the community in which the Spirit is active.

Verse 24 provides a somewhat surprising conclusion to the two lists found in 5:19-23 in that "Spirit" is not mentioned: "Those who belong to Christ Jesus have crucified the flesh with its passions and desires." First, particularly since the name "Christ" has not been used since 5:6, its presence here is a reminder that "belonging to Christ" and "being led by the Spirit" may be two different ways of speaking but are not two separate experiences. The Spirit for Paul is not a second gift, additional to the gift of Christ. Second, the aorist tense of the verb ("have been crucified") likely points to baptism, where believers are identified with Christ in his death (Rom 6:36) and where Christ is "put on" as a new robe (3:27). Baptism signifies death to the realm of the flesh, making its enticements no longer an option (cf. 6:14).

Guidance of the Spirit
(5:25-26)

Verse 25 reiterates 5:16a, and the two verses provide cohesiveness for the section. The verb translated in the NRSV as "guided" carries the nuance of "being in line with" as a soldier marching in rank. The verse can be paraphrased, "Since the Spirit gives us life, let us continually follow in the Spirit's steps." The Galatian communities, prior to Paul's writing, have obviously experienced disruption over the agitators' demands that Gentiles be circumcised (see also 5:15), warranting the injunctions of 5:26: "Let us not boast, provoking and being jealous of one another."

Bearing One Another's Burdens
(6:1-10)

The division between the end of chapter 5 and the beginning of chapter 6 is difficult to determine precisely. In a sense, 5:25-26 are transitional verses, which conclude the section 5:16-24 and also look forward to 6:1-10. The Greek word for "Spirit," which has been the major theme of 5:16-24, appears twice in 6:1 (in different forms) and again twice in 6:8. The exhortation "Let us not boast" could easily be the title for 6:1-10, with the emphasis on self-awareness and proper self-evaluation (in 6:1, 3-5). The NEB chooses this alternative, making the paragraph break after 5:25, whereas the RSV sets 5:25-26 as a separate paragraph. The NRSV begins a new section and paragraph with 6:1 because of the direct address ("brothers and sisters"; NRSV, "my friends"), which seems to signal a fresh start.

At first glance, the section 6:1-10 does not appear to exhibit the cohesiveness of 5:16-26. Verse 1 begins with a specific example of the kind of activity that a community that receives the Spirit should demonstrate (the restoration of one caught in a trespass), with the reminder that each person engaged in the restorative action beware of his or her own situation. The example is then interrupted by an imperative that puts the action in the form of a command (6:2). Verses 3-5, addressed to the individual, return to the matter of self-awareness. Then 6:6 seems an isolated word to the readers to encourage the support of teachers. Verses 7-8, beginning with the sharp warning ("Do not be deceived; God is not mocked") and using an agricultural proverb, return to the contrast between the Spirit and the flesh to underscore yet again that the Spirit leads to one eschatological result and the flesh to another. The final two verses (6:9-10) urge the readers to continue to do good in light of the eschatological moment.

Cohesiveness is found in 6:1-10 in the rotating pattern emerging between an address directed to the corporate congregations in Galatia followed by a word to individuals. (Barclay labels this pattern responsibility and accountability. See 1998, 149-150.)

Corporate: restore a fallen brother or sister (6:1a)
Individual: beware of yourself (singular, 6:1b)
Corporate: bear one another's burdens (6:2)
Individual: you (singular) must bear your own burden (6:3-5)

Corporate: support those among you who teach (6:6)
Individual: whatever one sows, he/she reaps (6:8)
Corporate: do good to all, especially to those in the church (6:9-10)

Four exegetical observations about this section: First, the scenario sketched in 6:1 is forceful, even though the Greek is not entirely clear. The verb translated as "detected" (NRSV) or "overtaken" (RSV) carries with it the notion of surprise or suddenness. Is the person suddenly overtaken by a trespass ("on a sudden impulse," NEB), or is the person caught in the trespass suddenly overtaken by another member of the church? In either case, the responsibility of the community is clear: to restore such a person. The Greek verb rendered as "restore" is the same used in Mark 1:19 and Matt 4:21 for fishermen "mending" their nets. There is no punitive or retributive nuance at all, only remediation. Furthermore, the phrase "a spirit of gentleness" is likely a Semitism referring to the divine Spirit, whose fruit includes "gentleness" (5:23). Through the gentle Spirit, God promises to be present in the healing process within the community.

Paul alerts the readers to be aware of themselves as they engage in helping one another. In the middle of 6:1, addressed to "brothers and sisters" (poorly rendered in the NRSV as "my friends"), the switch comes from the plural "you" ("you who have received the Spirit") to the singular ("Look to yourself, lest you too be tempted," RSV). Each person is called to a self-awareness and (in 6:3-5) to a self-evaluation that helps to free the community in its work of restoration from being either judgmental or paternalistic.

Second, in 6:2 the imperative ("Bear one another's burdens") serves two purposes. On the one hand, it further defines the restoring of a fallen brother or a sister as a burden-bearing activity, that is, identifying with the colleague, sharing the pain of failure, assuming a portion of the judgment. On the other hand, bearing burdens fulfills "the law of Christ."

What is meant by "the law of Christ"? Commentators have offered a number of explanations of the phrase (the options are surveyed by Barclay 1988, 126-135). Since the word "law" (*nomos*) is used consistently in Galatians to denote the Torah or Mosaic law, it would seem strange to find it here meaning something else, especially in light of 5:14. The specification "of Christ," however, echoes all that has preceded in the letter regarding Christ's relation to the law. In 3:10-13 Christ is condemned by the Law, but in being accursed removes the law's curse "for us." In 4:5 he redeems those "under law" with the result that they receive adoption as God's children. In 5:1 Christ sets people free from slavery. In 3:16 Christ has completed the law's promises by being Abraham's "seed." Thus "the law of Christ" is not a new or abbreviated set of rules but the law as it has been acted on by Christ. It is the law Christ has restored to its original identity, no longer as "disciplinarian" (3:24, 25) and prison guard (3:23), but redefined by the death of Christ so that it can serve as the guide for the Galatian communities (5:13-14).

Third, the injunction to support teachers in 6:6 seems isolated from the other injunctions, and yet it need not be. Not enough about the teachers is written here to project a dire crisis among the readers over their support. What is said, however, is a recognition that there were teachers so engaged in the life of the congregations that they warranted support. The injunction is very much in line with Paul's statements elsewhere on the community's responsibility to its workers, despite his own personal desire to remain independent (1 Cor 9:3-14; 2 Cor 11:7-11; 1 Thess 2:5-9; Phil 4:10-18).

Fourth, the final injunction to persevere in doing good (6:9-10) is more eschatological in its orientation than most English translations acknowledge. One of the Greek words for "time" (*kairos*) appears twice in these verses, once appropriately rendered by the NRSV as "harvest-time" (6:9), but on the other occasion by "opportunity." The latter is misleading, as Furnish points out. "Thus, as we have opportunity does not mean: *Whenever*, from time to time, it may be possible to do good, we should do it. It means, rather, *as long as* this present eschatological time continues, it is in fact the time to love, and we should be obedient in love" (Furnish 1972, 101). While there is no limit on the scope of the "doing good," a certain priority is appropriately (in light of the unrest in the Galatian communities) given "the household of faith."

With these clarifications about the activity of the Spirit and the flesh and these few general injunctions to the readers, the body of the letter ends. Throughout the spotlight has been on the gospel and the pastoral context in Galatia. From the affirmation of the singularity of the message in the autobiographical section (1:10–2:21), through the statement of appeals and proofs (3:1–5:12), to the final section (5:13–6:10), Paul's argument has been vigorous and focused on the urgency of rejecting circumcision for Gentiles as a requirement for membership in the people of God. We shall see, in what turns out to be an unusual conclusion to the letter (6:11-18), he restates his case once more in hopes that the readers will be awakened from their spell cast by the agitators' message (3:1).

A Decisive Closing

(Galatians 6:11-18)

In several ways the ending of the letter to the Galatians stands out as distinctive when compared to the endings of other Pauline letters. The wish for peace (6:16) and the final blessing (6:18) are typical, but missing are a number of features that might be expected. Among these are the following:

- No commendations are made about or greetings sent to individuals in the receiving churches (as in Rom 16:1-16; 1 Cor 16:15-18; Phil 4:21a).
- No groups or individuals are mentioned as the senders of greetings (as in Rom 16:16, 21-23; 1 Cor 16:19-20; 2 Cor 13:12; Phil 4:21b-22; Phlm 23-24).
- No exhortation is made to share a "holy kiss" (as in Rom 16:16; 1 Cor 16:20; 2 Cor 13:12; 1 Thess 5:26).

These are conventions that serve in other letters to nurture the continued relationship between Paul and his readers, especially since he often intends to follow letters with visits.

Galatians, on the other hand, concludes with a return to the theological issue that caused Paul to write the letter in the first place. The ending provides the occasion to state once again the matter that separates him so sharply from the agitators, in the hope that the readers will rediscover the radical nature of the gospel of the crucified Christ. Other letters end with summarizing warnings or exhortations (as in Rom 16:17-20; 1 Cor 16:13-14; 2 Cor 13:11), but none so specific, direct, or related to the argument developed in the body of the letter as the conclusion to Galatians. The deviation from the usual Pauline pattern in both the opening (where the prayer of thanksgiving is replaced by a statement of astonishment, 1:6-10) and the closing of the letter calls attention to the urgency of the issue before the readers.

That Paul should take the pen from the secretary and add a concluding note is not surprising (6:11). The same feature can be found in other Pauline letters (1 Cor 16:21; Phlm 19). In fact, the writer of 2 Thessalonians, whether Paul or a later follower of Paul's, claims that the feature of a concluding autograph "is the mark in every letter of mine; it is the way I write" (2 Thess 3:17), a personal guarantee that the letter is really from Paul. In Galatians, however, mention is made of the "large letters" with which Paul writes, no doubt calling attention to the following sentences as singularly important. Burton compares the "large letters" to the modern practice of bold-faced type or italics (Burton 1928, 348). Thus 6:11 represents not only Paul's personal validation of the letter, but also his way of attaching particular significance to the concluding verses.

The structure of the bulk of the conclusion (6:12-17) is marked by contrast, something that Aristotle recommended as an appropriate way of summing up a speech (*The Art of Rhetoric*, III, 19, 6). The agitators are depicted in 6:12-13, and are rather boldly pitted against Paul himself (6:14-15, 17). The two differ on three basic matters: the necessity of circumcision for non-Jews (6:12, 15), vulnerability to suffering (6:12, 17), and the reason for "boasting" (6:13, 14). Each of the three disagreements, however, is an expression of the more fundamental opposition, namely that between "world" (6:14) and "new creation" (6:15).

A table of the oppositions looks like this:

Agitators	Paul
compel you to be circumcised (v. 12)	circumcision and uncircumcision do not matter (v. 15)
avoid persecution for the cross (v. 12)	bears the marks of Jesus (v. 17)
boast in your flesh (v. 13) (seek to make a good showing in the flesh, v. 12)	boasts only in the cross of Christ (v. 14)
↑	↑
World (v.14)	New Creation (v. 15)

The above table does not account for all the data in the passage (see Cousar 1990, 137-148). For example, the agitators are castigated in 6:13, when Paul charges those who are advocating circumcision for non-Jews with failing to obey the law themselves. The table, nevertheless, provides a schema for understanding the fundamental antithesis created by the inbreaking of the new creation in the crucified Christ and how such an event defines the differences between the agitators and Paul. The oppositions that have long characterized the community (Jew or Greek, slave or free, male or female) are abolished in light of the event of Christ, and a new set of antitheses are established (see Martyn 1985, 410-424).

First, a look at the agitators (6:12-13). How were they seeking "to make a good showing in the flesh," and how were they by urging circumcision avoiding persecution "for the cross of Christ"? Do these clauses reflect a desire on the part of the agitators to report to the church in Jerusalem their successes in gaining Gentile converts by circumcision? If so, the agitators could then claim that their mission to the Gentiles was producing Jewish proselytes. They might hope thereby to ward off reprisals from the hostile and zealous Jews in Judea, who were suspicious of their associations with non-Jews. This is the position of Robert Jewett (1971, 198-212). The problem, however, is that the distance between Jerusalem and Galatia is too far to make such an explanation plausible. One could understand how such a proselytizing mission in Judea or even in Galilee might ease the hostility of the Zealots, but Galatia seems too remote from Jerusalem to make much difference.

Instead, it may be that Paul is thinking theologically about the situation in Galatia in light of what he knows and believes about "the cross of Christ." Its proclamation invariably creates a crisis and usually evokes opposition from some group (5:11; 1 Cor 1:18-25; 4:9-13; 2 Cor 4:7-12; 11:23-29). From Paul's vantage point, advocating circumcision as a supplement to believing in Jesus as Messiah dilutes the message of the crucified Christ to such an extent that it no longer creates a crisis, no longer carries an offense, and is no longer vulnerable to persecution (5:11).

In contrast to the agitators who have avoided persecution and who bear on their bodies only the mark of circumcision, Paul mentions "the marks of Jesus" (*ta stigmata tou Iesou*), which he bears in his body (6:17). This is a reference to the scars received in his missionary activity from those who took offense at the gospel (2 Cor 1:8-9; 4:8-11; 6:4-10). The "marks" distinguish Paul from the agitators. They validate the message he preaches and commend him as credible voice.

Mention of the agitators' boasting "about your flesh" triggers for Paul an oath: "God forbid that I should boast of anything but the cross of our Lord Jesus Christ" (6:14, NEB). "Boasting" (whether as a verb or a noun) appears often in the Pauline letters. The Greek word means "to have confidence in" or "to take pride in." The word is used to great advantage in critiquing those who rely on the law (as in Rom 2:17 23), but at the same time it can express Paul's own personal commitments (as in Rom 5:2, 11). It is often used ironically. For example, Paul "boasts" in his weaknesses (2 Cor 11:30; 12:5, 9) and here "boasts" in the scandalous and provocative cross.

Three crucifixions are mentioned in 6:14—Christ's, the world's, and Paul's, the latter two secondary to and derivative of the former (see Minear 1979, 395-407). The verb used in connection with the latter two is in the perfect tense ("have been crucified"), indicating an action in past time that has lingering effects for the present (see also 2:20). The life of the apostle is continuously being shaped by the once-and-for-all crucifixion of Christ.

The context and its juxtaposition with "new creation" suggest that "world" is to be understood as that age in which distinctions such as circumcision and uncircumcision matter a great deal, where there is boasting "in the flesh," where one is protected against persecution, where the message of the cross is diluted. Elsewhere in the letter it is depicted as "this present evil age" (1:4), where people live under "the weak and beggarly elemental spirits" (4:9). This "world" and its security have been shattered in the crucifixion of Christ, and its authority over Paul has been and is being terminated.

The use of the christological designation, "our Lord Jesus Christ," is somewhat unusual, in that the title "Lord" appears in Galatians only three other times, twice in liturgical formulas (1:3; 6:18) and once in the designation of James as "the brother of the Lord" (1:19). Its presence in 6:14 indicates that the three crucifixions result in a changed loyalty, the transfer of allegiance for Paul to a new master, "our Lord Jesus Christ."

While verses 15 and 17 both employ the first person, singular pronoun and certainly reflect Paul's own experience, one must keep in mind that throughout this letter the autobiographical sections have played an important rhetorical function. Rather than merely reporting events that have happened to the apostle, their intent has been to serve as a paradigm for readers. For example, the recounting of his call and conversion in 1:11-24 focuses on the power of the gospel to transform persons in startling ways. Likewise, in 6:14 when Paul speaks of being crucified to the world and the world to him, he sets himself forward as an example of what happens to all believers united to Christ.

Verse 15 provides the rational for 6:14 . "For (*gar*) neither circumcision nor uncircumcision is anything; but a new creation is everything!"(NRSV). The "world," with its sacred categories of Jews and non-Jews, is now passé due to the arrival of the "new creation." The only other use of this expression in the Pauline letters comes in 2 Cor 5:17, where "new creation" depicts the community that is itself reconciled to God (5:18) and at the same time is an agent for the world's reconciliation (5:20). Several scribes in copying the Greek manuscripts added at the beginning of 6:15 the phrase "in Christ Jesus" to make the verse parallel to 5:6 and explicitly christological. The addition is not necessary since the christological focus of the "new creation" is already highlighted in the connection of 6:15 to 6:14.

The letter concludes with two blessings, one mentioning "peace" and "mercy" (6:16), the other mentioning "grace" (6:18). The first blessing, however, contains a very difficult exegetical problem: how to understand the phrase "the Israel of God." The problem is complicated by the fact that the expression is found no where else in Paul or in the New Testament or in the literature of second temple Judaism.

Two factors seem clear. First, "those who will follow this rule (*kanon*)" refers back to 6:14-15 and thus designates those who find their identity in the cross of Christ, who live in the new creation where neither circumcision nor uncircumcision matters. Second, in light of the whole thrust of the letter, it would seem unlikely that "the Israel of God" refers to another group different from "those who follow this rule," for example, to historic Israel or to the Jews of the first century. The letter has not dealt in anyway with historic Israel *per se* (as does Romans) or with Judaism, but with Paul's conflicts with a specific group of Jewish Christians. It would be unusual for either group to appear only in a concluding blessing.

Thus most likely "the Israel of God" designates those believers, whether Jews or Gentiles, who can identify with Paul's oath in 6:14 and who live in the new creation. The term could have initially been used by the agitators, and Paul is re-employing it here at the end of the letter, giving it a new twist. They could have contended that circumcision brought one into membership in "the Israel of God," in which case Paul is pronouncing a blessing on "the Israel of God" but implying that those who "follow this rule," that is, those who live in the new creation where neither circumcision nor uncircumcision count for anything are "the Israel of God."

Addressing the readers as "brothers and sisters," the letter appropriately ends with a traditional blessing using the word "grace" (see Rom 16:20; 1 Cor 16:23; Phil 4:23; 1 Thess 5:28; Phlm 25).

Though the conclusion omits many of the anticipated conventions of letter-writing, it stands as the most forceful closing of any of Paul's letters. He takes a final opportunity to lay before the Galatians the decisive character of the gospel, the radical history that the Christ-event has initiated, in which the old polarities such as circumcision and uncircumcision are replaced by a new creation. The closing is the key to the entire letter.

Philippians

Introduction

The Letter

The place to begin is with the text itself, with the fact that Philippians is written as a letter. Increasingly, the argument has been made that form cannot be separated from content. Both contribute to the meaning of any single passage and to a document as a whole. "Literary genres and forms are not simply neutral containers used as convenient ways to package various types of communication. They are social conventions that provide contextual meaning for the smaller units of language and text they enclose" (Aune 1987, 13). Paul did not write to the Philippians a gospel or a history, but a letter. Its arrangement of material and even its contents are shaped by the conventions of the letter form. At the same time, its subject matter forces certain modifications of the conventions.

While the most obvious reason for writing a letter in the ancient world was to communicate information, letters served a number of other functions, such as issuing orders, threatening or praising someone, mediating disputes, making requests, urging a particular style of behavior, or nurturing friendships. One ancient theorist writing under the pseudonym of Demetrius discusses twenty-one types of letters and provides samples to be followed (*Epistolary Types*; see Malherbe 1988, 30-41). A writer chooses one or another type of letter depending on his or her relationship to the recipient (whether writing to a person socially inferior, or to a social equal, or to a family member), on the current state of the relationship, and on the particular reason for writing (Stowers 1986, 51-57). Clarity with regard to the specific purpose of the letter is essential to effective communication. "Only the man who takes aim at the target in a properly measured manner hits it" (Pseudo Libanius, *Epistolary Styles*, 49).

Not every interpreter of Philippians, however, has determined that the letter has hit its target. In the mid-nineteenth century, F. C. Baur judged the letter not to have been written by Paul and gave as part of his evidence that it was "monotonously repetitious, lacking a profound coherence, expressing a certain poverty of ideas." "One fails to discover a motive or occasion for its composition not a definitely expressed objective" (Baur 1867, 59). Though Baur's judgment about Pauline authorship has been universally rejected, in certain respects he still has a group of disciples in the twentieth century. They understand that the repetition and the lack of cohesiveness are symptomatic of the piecing together of three letter-fragments into a single document (an issue to which we shall return shortly).

Many more interpreters have discerned coherence in the letter, but have acknowledged that the apostle had multiple reasons for writing, such as the following:

- Paul was expressing gratitude for a gift brought to him from the Philippians by Epaphroditus, who had become sick and was returning to Philippi as the bearer of the letter (4:10-20).
- Paul apparently thought it important to commend Epaphroditus for his labors and to urge the Philippians to receive him back with honor (2:25-30).
- Paul takes the occasion to warn the Philippians about a group or groups nearby, whom he labels "dogs, evil workers, those who mutilate the flesh" (3:2) and "enemies of the cross of Christ" (3:20).
- Paul urged the Philippians to "stand firm" and to maintain unity in the face of aggressive opposition (1:27-30) and internal disagreement (4:2-3).

A more recent approach to the letter concurs that there may have been more than one reason for writing, but argues that Paul has employed an ancient letter form as a model for Philippians and that its cohesiveness comes when it is understood as "a hortatory letter of friendship." This judgment is based on the premise that the genre and the cultural codes of the letter have to be clarified as the first step in the interpretive process and that Philippians is packed with the language and conventions of friendship (Stowers 1991, 107-114). Examples are: the presence-absence motif (1:19-26; 2:12), expressions of affection and the desire to be with the recipients (1:7-8; 4:1), the reciprocity between writer and readers (1:7, 30; 2:17-18; 4:14), the pattern of giving and receiving (4:10-20), the importance of mutual participation (koinonia, 1:5; 2:1; 3:10; 4:15), the stress of agreement and equality (1:27–2:4; 4:2), the need for a single mind (2:2, 5; 4:2), the sharing of common enemies (1:27-30; 3:2, 17-19). Moreover, Philippians is characterized by numerous injunctions to the community, nearly all couched in the language and categories of friendship (especially 1:27-2:18; 4:2-3).

The social institution of friendship in the ancient world differed markedly from modern-day relationships of personal friendship. Both Greek and Roman philosophers depicted friendship as the glue that held society together. Aristotle wrote of it as "the bond of the state; lawgivers seem to set more store by it than they do by justice, for to promote concord, which seems akin to friendship, is their chief aim, while faction, which is enmity, is what they are most anxious to banish. And if men are friends, there is no need of justice between them" (*Nichomachean Ethics* 8. i. 4). There are less permanent forms of friendship based on utility or pleasure, but the truest friendship is based on virtue, where friends have a common mind, wish the good for one another simply for the sake of the friend, and engage in reciprocal sharing of goods. "The proverb says, 'Friends' goods are common property,' and this is correct, since community [*koinōnia*] is the essence of friendship" (*Nichomachean Ethics* 8. ix.1. See the discussion of friendship in Saller 1982, 1-22; Marshall 1987, 1-34; Fitzgerald 1996; Konstan 1997.)

In this commentary we shall call attention to these literary conventions of friendship as they appear in the text. They are pervasive throughout the letter and critical for interpretation. It seems a bit confusing, however, to label Philippians "a hortatory letter of friendship." If the designation simply acknowledges the friendship motifs, all well and good. On the other hand, if one assumes that Philippians closely follows a specified letter form (*epistolē philikē*), then the term is used inaccurately. For one thing, Paul always demonstrated creativity and invention in the composition of his letters. None fits neatly into a rhetorical or epistolary mold. (See the debate over the rhetoric of Galatians.) Philippians markedly differs from the examples of friendship letters in the ancient theorists.

For another thing, the prominence of the figure of Christ in the letter must be taken into account. Christ transforms the social reciprocity between writer and readers into a three-way relationship——Paul, the Philippians, and Christ. It is a mutual sharing in the gospel that binds writer and readers together and undergirds the exhortations to unity and community. Groups become common enemies of Paul and the Philippians because in various ways they are in opposition to the gospel. Just as the conventions of friendship shape and structure the document, so this strong christocentric focus expands and modifies the conventions. (See Fee 1995, 12-14. Fee labels Philippians "a hortatory letter of friendship" but with this caveat.)

Authorship

Little needs to said about the authorship of Philippians. It bears Paul's name as author, and from the early second-century echoes from the letter can be heard in patristic writings. It appears in the canonical lists of Marcion and the Muratorian fragment, and consistently the letter is attributed to Paul the apostle. Only in the mid-nineteenth century does one find a sustained argument for non-Pauline authorship (Baur), but the scholarly community, almost unanimously, has rejected the proposal of pseudonymity. Serious questions have been raised about the number of letter-fragments contained within the canonical letter, but with confidence they are all ascribed to Paul.

One piece of the letter warrants special comment. 2:6-11 contains what is loosely referred to as a hymn, a section fairly rhythmical in style and having a high degree of parallelism. The obvious poetic flavor of the passage has stimulated a number of efforts to set it out in strophes and lines. Is this a poetic creation of the apostle himself, or is he quoting (as he does in other places) from the creedal and liturgical tradition of the early church? (There is no evidence, manuscript or otherwise, that it was a later interpolation into the letter.) Do we attribute this centerpiece of the letter to Paul or to predecessors or perhaps contemporaries in the faith, whom he quotes? (Nothing similar to modern quotation marks were in use in the first century.)

Regarding matters of literary form, language, and theology, the arguments are finely balanced on both sides of the issue. Paul is certainly capable of writing in a highly exalted and poetic style (for example, Rom 8:31-39), and a judgment based on literary genre alone is impossible. It is in matters other than form and style that the scales are slightly tipped in favor of an origin for the hymn that predates Paul. For example, a number of important Greek words occur in the passage that are not found elsewhere in the Pauline letters (e.g., "form," "equal to," "highly exalted," "something to be taken advantage of") or that are used in unusual ways (e.g., "he emptied himself"). More significant is the second movement of the hymn (2:9-11) that speaks of Christ's exaltation without mention of his resurrection and/or return, which are characteristically Pauline themes. (For the arguments for a pre-Pauline hymn, see Martin 1983; for the arguments for Pauline authorship, see Caird 1976, 100-104.)

However one decides the matter of the origin of the hymn, it is clear from the letter that Paul has made the hymn his own. It does not function as an alien citation he critiques (as, for example, some of the slogans of the Corinthians, which Paul quotes and then qualifies; see 1 Cor 8:1-13; 10:23-11:1). Instead, the hymn generates the language and the themes that dominate the letter. It provides the fundamental rationale for his appeal to the Philippians that they live worthy of the gospel and demonstrate unity, courage, and humility in the face of opposition. Because the hymn and its themes are so carefully woven into the fabric of the letter, the question of whether or not the hymn comes from the pre-Pauline community carries no major significance in the interpretation of the letter.

Integrity of the Letter

In recent years a number of scholars have detected in Philippians clues that lead them to argue that the canonical letter is actually a composite of three letters. Written by Paul over a fairly brief period of time, the three have been woven together at a later time into a single document, leaving uneven seams that expose the patchwork. (The most influential advocates of the composite theory are Beare 1959, 1-5; Rahtjen 1959-60, 167-173; Koester 1961-61, 317-332; and Collange 1979, 3-19.) The first uneven seam is found at 3:2. Here an abrupt change is made from an irenic mood of rejoicing (3:1) to an apparently sharp denunciation of "the dogs," "the evil workers," and "those who mutilate the flesh" (3:2). Nothing in the previous two chapters prepares the reader for such a scathing attack. Moreover, the "finally" of 3:1 suggests that the letter is coming to an end, which of course the canonical letter does not do. Since 4:4 picks up again the theme of rejoicing, the case is made that 3:2–4:3 is a fragment of another letter spliced in at this point.

The second uneven seam emerges with the thanksgiving (4:10-20) that comes so late in the letter that it appears to be an afterthought. Furthermore, why did Paul wait so long after Epaphroditus arrived with the gift to express his gratitude to the givers? Surely, 4:10-20 must be a separate and early fragment of a letter that has found its place here in the compilation. The uneven seams thus expose three letters: Letter A (4:10-20); Letter B (1:1-3:1; 4:4-9, 21-23); Letter C (3:2–4:3).

Several features militate against this composite theory and in favor of the integrity of the letter. First, the uneven seam at 3:2 presents problems, some of which will be dealt with in the following commentary. Efforts to explain the abrupt shift between 3:1 and 3:2 on psychological grounds (e.g., Paul is in prison, and his thoughts come and go) or on circumstantial grounds (e.g., Paul has received new and disturbing information about the Philippians) are imaginative but unconvincing. It is possible that Paul's apology for repeating himself in 3:1b is an allusion to the oral messages brought by Epaphroditus and Timothy (Furnish 1963–64, 86-88), though it is more likely that the apology serves as a conventional introduction to the exhortations that follow.

One of the characteristics of hortatory material is the assurance to the readers that they are not ignorant and that what is written is nothing that they do not already know (Stowers 1991, 115-116). We shall argue (in the commentary at 3:2) that the reference to the dogs, evil workers, and mutilators of the flesh is not so much a warning about a group threatening the Philippian community as it is the presentation of a negative example from whom the readers can learn and against which Paul can tell his own story.

In light of the above, it makes more sense to take 3:1 as the prelude to a section of contrasting models than it does to project an entirely separate letter. Since the "finally" in 3:1 can be translated as an inferential or transitional word ("therefore," "moreover," "as for the rest"), the notion that 3:1 is the conclusion of a fragment is not finally persuasive.

Second, the argument that the thanksgiving (4:10-20) comes too late in the letter and thus must be a separate fragment ignores the comment at the beginning of the letter where Paul thanks God "because of your sharing in the gospel from the first day until now" (1:5) and the extensive paragraph commending Epaphroditus, who risked his life to bring the Philippians' gift (2:25-30).

The location of 4:10-20 toward the end of the letter may reflect some ambivalence on Paul's part about the gifts. Lohmeyer referred to it as a "thankless thanks" (Loymeyer 1953, 178). On the one hand, Paul acknowledges the Philippians' peculiar generosity in sending gifts; but on the other hand, he asserts his sufficiency in Christ and makes a point to say that he did not ask for the gifts. More likely, however, 4:10-20 is to be read as another expression of the friendship that exists between Paul and the readers, of which the matter of giving and receiving is an essential ingredient (see the commentary at 4:10-20). If 4:10-20 were a separate thank-you note, then it certainly is an odd one, isolated from the many expressions of friendship found in the letter and reporting nothing of Paul's circumstances in prison.

Third, the most cogent argument in favor of the integrity of the letter and against the composite theory is the cohesiveness of the various pieces of the letter. The prayer of thanksgiving (1:3-11) introduces topics that run throughout all of the so-called three letters. Furthermore, several recurring themes pervade the various "fragments," making them not so fragmentary—themes such as joy, Paul's contentment in the face of his trial, his confidence that the Philippians will endure their trials, the importance of unity, and the mutual sharing in sufferings.

Despite the uneven seams, there is more reason to read Philippians as a single letter, written at one time, than to treat it as a compilation of fragmentary patches rather inelegantly spliced together by a later editor. In the final analysis, the composite theory leaves as many, if not more, dangling threads than does the present canonical form of the letter. (For a full discussion of the issue, see Garland 1985, 141-173.)

Paul and the Philippian Church

Philippi is located in northeastern Greece, in the territory called Macedonia. In 356 BCE Philip of Macedon took over the existing city of Krenides, renamed it, and made it a base of operations. Apparently the gold and silver deposits at nearby Mount Pangaion provided resources for his Macedonian expansion. Later, during the Roman occupation, Macedonia became a Roman province, with Thessalonica as its capital city. Philippi remained a relatively unimportant provincial town until the Roman flavor of the city was strengthened in 42 BCE following the battles fought nearby, in which Octavian and Antony avenged the death of Julius Caesar by defeating Brutus and Cassius. Philippi was made a Roman military colony, and many veterans of the war settled there. Octavian's defeat of Antony at Actium in 30 BCE led to a further influx of Roman soldiers.

Two important avenues of travel made Philippi strategic for communications and commerce. The Via Egnatia, which stretched from the west coast of Greece all the way to Byzantium, came by the city, giving it an east-west route (though often in need of repair), whereas the seaport, Neapolis, was ten miles southeast of Philippi and provided access to the Aegean Sea. (For a further description of Philippi, see Hendrix, 313-317).

It was by the sea route from Troas to Neapolis that Paul first came to Philippi (with his companions Silas, Timothy, and possibly Luke; Acts 16:11-12). The letter itself gives no details of the visit, leaving us only with the narrative of events found in Acts 16:11-40—the baptism of Lydia and her household, the healing of a girl with a spirit of divination, the arrest of Paul and Silas, the earthquake at the jail, the conversion of the jailer and his household, the apology of the police, and the departure of Paul and his friends to Thessalonica. The arrest by the authorities is confirmed in 1 Thess 2:2, where Paul writes of suffering and "being shamefully mistreated at Philippi." The date for the initial visit was approximately 49 or 50 CE.

It is interesting that three of the four names mentioned in connection with the Philippian church are women—Lydia, Euodia, and Syntyche (Clement being the fourth). Lydia's house became the hub of activity for the community (Acts 16:15, 40), and Euodia and Syntyche are identified as courageous leaders who have struggled with Paul "in the work of the gospel" (Phil 4:3). They were the God-fearing women who gathered by the river on the Sabbath for prayer and whom Paul and his companions joined (Acts 16:13-15). There is good reason to think of Lydia as a patroness, the head of a household, likely a businesswomen, who would have been amply qualified for leadership in the church (see Torjesen 1993, 14-16, 53-56).

Following the initial visit, the Philippian church maintained ties with Paul through the sending of gifts—when he was in Thessalonica (Phil 4:16), in Corinth (2 Cor 11:9), and in the imprisonment from which he writes (Phil 4:10-20). Paul understood the gifts as their sharing in the work of the gospel, their partnership with him in his missionary endeavors. From his side, Paul reciprocated by sending Timothy and Erastus to Macedonia with messages for the churches (Acts 19:22) and visits there himself (2 Cor 2:13; 7:5), though whether his visit came before or after the letter depends on the decision where he was located at the time of writing (in Rome or Ephesus; see below). He notes in the letter that he anticipates sending Timothy again (Phil 3:19-23) and hopes to come himself (Phil 2:24).

Moreover, Paul makes an unusual tribute to the Macedonian churches in 2 Cor 8:1-5 because of their generous participation in the offering for the Jerusalem church, despite "a severe ordeal of affliction" and "their extreme poverty." Undoubtedly a special bond exists between Paul and the Philippians, confirming the genuineness of the language of friendship in the letter.

The imprisonment gift sent by the Philippians was carried by Epaphroditus, who either in traveling or after arrival became critically ill. Due to his illness and apparent homesickness, Paul thought it wise for him to return to Philippi and sent along with him the letter (Phil 2:25-30).

Where was Paul imprisoned when Ephraphoditus visited him and when he wrote the letter? Three locations have been proposed. The more traditional option is Rome. Acts closes with Paul under house arrest there (Acts 28:18-31), and the references in Philippians to the praetorian soldiers ("the whole imperial guard," 1:13) and Caesar's household ("the emperor's household," 4:22) fit the context nicely (though these groups could also be found in other Roman-controlled cities). Whether or not the necessary communications between Rome and Philippi could have occurred as quickly as the letter presumes, given the distance between the cities, is a matter of dispute. More problematic is the change of plans that would have been necessary. When writing Romans, Paul anticipates going to Jerusalem, visiting Rome, and then "with no further work" for him in the eastern regions turning his attention westward to Spain (Rom 15:22-29). If, however, he writes to the Philippians from Rome and anticipates coming to them soon, then he has apparently scuttled his plans to carry out a mission in Spain and intends to head back to Macedonia.

Caesarea is another proposed location of Paul's imprisonment. Though there is no mention of a Caesarean imprisonment in Paul's letters, Acts records an imprisonment there (23:23-26:32) just before the voyage to Rome. Paul could possibly expect to visit Philippi on his way to Rome, which would not disrupt the travel plans laid out in Romans 15. While the distance between Caesarea and Philippi is the greatest of any of the three options, Paul is possibly confined long enough in Caesarea to allow for the journeys back and forth that are presumed in the letter. The problem, however, is that there seems to be no imminent threat of death during the Caesarean imprisonment and no anticipation of an upcoming verdict (as is reflected in Phil 1:20-26).

The third possible location for the imprisonment is Ephesus. It has become an increasingly popular choice among commentators, though ironically no mention of a specific imprisonment in Ephesus can be found in either Acts or the letters of Paul. Paul indicates, however, that he has been imprisoned many times (2 Cor 6:5; 11:23), and particularly speaks of an imprisonment in Asia (2 Cor 1:8-10). The comment "We despaired of life itself. Indeed, we felt that we had received the sentence of death" (2 Cor 1:8-9) coheres with the mood of Philippians 1. Of the three options, Ephesus is the closest to Philippi and would easily allow for the coming and going the letter suggests. If the letter is written from an Ephesian imprisonment, then the travel intentions set out in Romans 15 would not need to be changed. Finally, there is no hint in the letter that Paul has been back to visit Philippi since his initial trip mentioned in Acts 16. If this is the case, then Ephesus becomes the only one of the locations that would fit the circumstances.

Any choice made between the three cities leaves unanswered questions. Rome and Ephesus seem more likely than Caesarea, and among commentators on the letter advocates of the two locations are about equally divided. The primary issue is the decision about the date of the letter (if Ephesus, then sometime during the three-year stay there, 53–56; if Rome, then between 58 and 62) and the letter's place in the chronological sequence of Paul's letters.

The Opponents

At four places in Philippians reference is made to groups that in some measure stand in opposition to Paul, the addressees, or the gospel.

In 1:15-18 some preach Christ out of "false motives," "from envy and rivalry," "not genuinely, but meaning to increase my suffering in my imprisonment." Paul takes a tolerant attitude toward this group, giving them credit for preaching Christ, but contrasts them with others whose preaching grows out of "goodwill." While the location of these insincere preachers is not specified, they are mentioned in the section in which Paul reports his own present circumstances, and thus they seem to operate at the place of his imprisonment rather than in Philippi. It is impossible to connect them to other opponents reported in the letter.

In 1:28-30 "opponents" of the addressees are designated, who apparently are the cause of the suffering the Philippians are currently undergoing or are about to undergo. The connection between the writer's and the readers' struggles in 1:30 suggests that both are suffering for the cause of the gospel and at the hands of the Roman authorities. This is certainly true of Paul and would be equally plausible for the readers in such a Roman-oriented city as Philippi. Paul's own persecution at Philippi recorded in Acts 16:19-24, while provoked by the merchants who "owned" the slave girl with the spirit of divination, was actually carried out by the "magistrates" (Fee 1995, 29-32).

Chapter 3 calls attention to "the dogs," "the evil workers," and "those who mutilate the flesh" (v. 2). In light of the contrasting statement in 3:3 ("For it is we who are the circumcision"), these people are evidently Jewish. But are they Christian or non-Christian Jews? The term "circumcision" is most regularly used by Paul to designate Jews, but why in a city that apparently had no synagogue would Jews be cause for attention? If they were Jewish Christians, they would likely have been itinerant teachers advocating (as Jewish Christians did in Galatia) that circumcision was a necessary mark of the people of God. Whether or not they actually reside in Philippi is not stated. The Philippians were likely cognizant of the group (since no further details are given), and in the rhetoric of the letter they become negative models for the readers.

Chapter 3 identifies people as "enemies of the cross of Christ" (vv. 18-19). "Their end is destruction; their god is the belly; and their glory is their shame; their minds are set on earthly things (NRSV)." Beyond the enigmatic description, this group becomes difficult to identify. Are these people the same group as is mentioned in 3:2? If so, there are several possibilities.

The enemies could be Jewish Christian missionaries who want Gentile Christians to adopt Jewish practices. (The reference to "the belly" in 3:19 would then be a metonym for the male sexual organ [circumcision] or would refer to the preoccupation with food laws and the like [O'Brien 1991, 33-35].) Or the enemies could be Jewish Christians who boast of their spiritual qualities, have completely fulfilled the law, and interpret circumcision as the unique sign of such fulfillment (Koester 1961-62, 317-332; Holladay, 77-90). Again, the enemies could be Jewish Christians of Gnostic persuasion. In this case, rather than being law-perfectionists, they are antinomians. As those who have already been raised with Christ, they are libertines who deem themselves free from any kind of ethical restriction. Paul's indictment that "their god is the belly" would then refer to their unchecked lifestyle, particularly in the areas of food and sex (Schmithals 1972, 65-122).

But is the group in 3:18-19 to be identified in one way or another with the group in 3:2 in the first place? Could Paul be calling attention to two different movements known by the Philippians, one a Jewish Christian group advocating circumcision and another group of "heretical libertinists with Gnostic tendencies," who in their exalted self-consciousness believed they had already achieved salvation (Jewett 1970, 382)?

The array of possibilities posed by the above survey may overwhelm the modern reader of the letter. Each option has some feature to commend it, offering an explanation of a detail in the text that makes sense. Yet each option can and has been critiqued as failing to explain the whole text. It seems clear that the writer and the initial readers understood what particular groups were being depicted, but the letter does not give enough specific information for modern readers, who are removed from the actual setting, to make definitive judgments.

The text does enable us to identify the "opponents" in 1:28 as public officials subjecting the readers to suffering. The group in 3:2 are certainly Jewish Christians, who advocate circumcision. But much remains uncertain, especially about the group mentioned in 3:18-20.

More important than the full identification of these opponents is their rhetorical function, that is, why the groups are mentioned in the letter in the first place. Aside from the public officials in 1:28, none of the groups seems to represent a serious threat to the readers. Apparently the groups are not making converts among the Philippian Christians, nor are they the cause for unrest in the community. While the element of warning is not entirely absent, the groups primarily serve as negative models to the readers, examples of those who have misunderstood the faith and whose interpretations are to be avoided. What is critical for the interpretation of the letter is not their historical identification, but what the text explicitly says about them as negative models. We will return to this issue later.

Structure of the Letter

Two features of Philippians determine its structure. The first is its similarity to a letter of friendship. Loveday Alexander has examined the structure of ancient letters to family members, which are analogous to letters of friendship, and has noted several characteristics that are relevant for the study of Philippians (Alexander 1989, 87-101). In familial letters, following the opening address and the prayer for the recipients, the writer reassures the readers about his or her own situation ("I am in good health and prospering, though I do not know where I shall be going from here") and then requests reassurance about their welfare ("Please send word about your welfare. Take care of yourself."). Philippians follows just this pattern in that, after the address and the prayer of thanksgiving, Paul reports realistically but optimistically on his circumstances in prison (1:12-26) and then turns to the situation of the readers (1:27–2:18).

The importance of this exchange of news is further highlighted by the presence of the disclosure formula at 1:12 ("I want you to know . . ."). The formula is Paul's characteristic way of introducing the body of his letters (see Romans, 2 Corinthians, Galatians, 1 Thessalonians), where he gets to the major reason for writing. The report of his situation in prison and his concern for his readers then turn out to be not preliminary niceties or conventional courtesies, but the primary business of the letter. The sharing of news is a critical ingredient in the nurturing of friendship. In addition, as we shall see in the commentary, other passages make more sense when read in light of the conventions of friendship (e.g., the thanksgiving for the Philippian gifts in 4:10-20).

The second feature of Philippians that influences its structure is its character as a *hortatory* letter. Many specific words of injunction are directed to the readers throughout the letter (such as 1:27; 2:2-4, 12-15; 4:4-6, 8-9), but the peculiar pattern of exhortation in Philippians is the use of models, both positive and negative, to persuade readers to follow the specific injunctions. Ancient rhetorical theory stressed the use of models. Pseudo Libanius offers the following as a sample of a hortatory letter: "Always be an emulator, dear friend, of virtuous men. For it is better to be well spoken of when imitating good men than to be reproached by all men when following evil men" (*Epistolary Styles*, 52). Examples of models abound in the hortatory letters of Seneca, Pliny, Isocrates, and the Socratics (For examples, see Johnson 1978, 1-24; Fiore 1986, 79-163; Kurz 1985, 103-126).

The reader of Philippians finds positive models in the mention of those who preach Christ out of goodwill (1:15-16), in the hymn of the humiliation and exaltation of Christ (2:6-11), in the commendations of Timothy (2:19:23) and of Epaphroditus (2:25-30), in Paul's autobiography (3:4-14), and in the statements about the nature of the church (3:2-3, 20-21). Negative models are those who preach the gospel out of false motives (1:15-18), an unnamed group who seek their own interests (2:21), the "dogs"

(3:2), and those who live as "enemies of the cross of Christ" (3:18-19). The rhetorical impact is accentuated when a positive and a negative model are juxtaposed to one another (so 1:15-18; 2:21-22; 3:2-3, 4; 18-20).

The brief analysis of the letter below reflects both the structural parallels with the familial letters and the prominence of models as a means of exhortation.

I. Introduction (1:1-11)
   A. Salutation (1:1-2)
   B. Prayer for the recipients (1:3-11)
      1. Thanksgiving (1:3-8)
      2. Petition (1:9-11)
II. Reassurance about the sender (1:12-26)
   A. Paul's imprisonment; spread of the gospel   (1:12-14)
   B. Contrasting preachers of the gospel (1:14-18a)
   C. Paul's anticipated deliverance (1:18b-26)
III. Concern for the recipients (1:27–2:18)
   A. To express unity and courage in the face of opposition (1:27-30)
   B. To manifest unity and humility after the manner of the Christ-event (2:1-11)
   C. To work for wholeness and faithfulness as a community (2:14-18)
IV. Travel plans and Christ-like examples (2:19-30)
   A. The coming of Timothy (2:19-23)
   B. The coming of Paul (2:24)
   C. The coming of Epaphroditus (2:25-30)
V. Further exhortation through contrasting models (3:1–4:3)
   A. The call to rejoice (3:1a)
   B. The dogs, evil workers, and mutilators of the flesh (3:1b-2)
   C The church as the circumcision (3:3)
   D. Paul (3:4-17)
   E. Enemies of the cross (3:18-19)
   F. The church's heavenly citizenship (3:20-21)
   G. Appeals to steadfastness and unity (4:1-3)
VI. Closing (4:4-23)
   A. Final exhortations (4:4-9)
   B. The matter of giving and receiving (4:10-20)
   C. Greetings (4:21-22)
   D. Benediction (4:23)

Message of the Letter

As a community-building document, Philippians is written to shape the thinking of the readers, to mold their sensitivities in a distinctively Christian way. The verb *phroneō* ("think," in the sense of practical reasoning) occurs an inordinately high number of times in the letter, indicating that Paul is seeking to fashion the mind of the community in such a way that it will conform its life to Christ's death. (See the development of this in Meeks 1991, 329-336). What are the features of this distinctively Christian mindset Paul is urging?

From the beginning of the letter a story is told that reaches back to the "first day" when the readers heard and responded to the gospel (1:5), includes the present period of suffering, and looks forward to the "day of Christ" (1:6, 10; 2:16). The story immediately orients the readers to the eschatological context in which they are living, a context to be viewed positively since God is at work, actively bringing to completion the "good work" begun among the Philippians (1:6; 2:13). As the readers face suffering (1:29-30) and seek to be "children of God without blemish in the midst of a crooked and perverse generation" (2:15), their focus is toward the future. The citizenship of the community is "in heaven" (3:20). Rather than being preoccupied with "earthly things" (3:19), its mind is to be fashioned by Christ, whose arrival it now eagerly awaits (3:20-21; 4:5).

This eschatological orientation takes on an existential relevance in the apostle's autobiographical statement (3:10-14). His present knowledge of Christ and the power of his resurrection is experienced, ironically, in the sharing of Christ's sufferings and conformity to his death. Resurrection itself lies in the future, a goal to be aimed at, a prize to be sought. The present is not a time of arrival, but of "pressing on" and of "straining forward." What can be anticipated at Christ's coming is the transformation of the body of humiliation to the body of divine glory (3:21).

The eschatological stress of the letter functions as both an encouragement and a brake. It provides the community under duress with a renewed hope in the final triumph of God, when all things will be subject to Christ (2:9-11; 3:21). But its "not-yetness" warns against premature celebrations of the end, something in which the "enemies of the cross" may have engaged. (See a further discussion of eschatology in the commentary at 1:21-24.)

The primary character in this eschatological framework is Christ, who is mentioned in almost every paragraph of the letter. The hymn in 2:6-11 relates Christ's own story, who did not cling to his divine status but became incarnate, accepting the form of a slave, and who as a human was obedient to the point of death on a cross. In the light of such obedience, God exalted Christ, who as Lord bears the name to be universally honored.

The Christ-story in turn plays both a direct and an indirect role in the letter. Directly, readers are urged to let the story be the foundation for their practical thinking (2:5). The text does not ask that some extraordinary virtue be abstracted from the story and copied, but that the whole story itself take on a mind-shaping function for the community. Indirectly, the story provides the language for the other models called upon in the letter—Paul (sharing Christ's sufferings by conformity to his death, 3:10), Epaphroditus (coming close to death for the work of Christ, risking his life, 2:30), and, to a lesser extent, Timothy (seeking not his own interests but the interests of others, 2:20-21). The hymn detailing the career of Christ presents a "master model," " a generative image" that sets the terms for the thinking and acting of the Philippian community (Meeks 1991, 335-336).

In two other places in the letter Christ becomes the focus for Paul's self-reflection. In 1:21-22 as he faces trial and the prospects of either release or conviction, his musings are highly christocentric. If he is delivered, then "living is Christ" (1:21), but if he dies, that means being "with Christ" (1:22). Then in 4:10-13 Paul declares his "contentment" (*autarkēs*) with whatever economic situation he faces. "In any and all circumstances, I have learned the secret of being well-fed and going hungry, of having plenty and of being in need (NRSV)." The enabling power for this perspective is Christ. (Though the text does not mention "Christ" in 4:13, scribes added it in several manuscript traditions to clarify precisely who was the one strengthening Paul.)

The christocentric focus of the letter is not speculative or philosophical. There is no suggestion that among the readers were those whose understanding of the nature of Christ was misguided or defective and needed correcting. The more pressing issue lies in the *significance* of Christ, the meaning of his story for the life of the community and its members.

The eschatological framework and the prominent Christ-story are to inform and form an actual *koinōnia* that reflects the heavenly citizenship of its members. Three characteristics of such a *koinōnia* recur throughout the letter: unity (1:28; 2:1-2; 4:2), humility (2:3-4), and steadfastness amid opposition (1:27-28; 4:1). Whatever conflicts existed, either actually or potentially, in the Philippian community are to be transcended in light of the mutuality shared in the gospel.

Paul's nurturing of this *koinōnia* among the readers is not problem-specific (as is 1 Corinthians). The division between Euodia and Syntyche in 4:2 is the only concrete example mentioned in the letter, and it is reported in such a cryptic fashion that modern readers can only guess at the cause of their conflict. In writing a letter to friends, Paul is able to draw on the past relationships with the readers to address the community in a positive, rather than a negative fashion. For example, the Philippian gifts sent to Paul express the sharing (*sugkoinōnēsantes* and *ekoinōnēsen*) that distinguishes the community and also embraces him (4:14-15).

The key to the development of *koinonia* lies in the active relationship with Christ and in participation in Christ's mission in and beyond the community. The three uses of the noun in the letter denote not so much a fellowship experienced among the members as their involved participation—in the gospel (1:5), in the Spirit (2:1), and in the sufferings of Christ (3:10). The community that demonstrates unity, humility, and steadfastness does so out of its engagement with and in behalf of the gospel.

Finally, the mindset the letter seeks to foster among the readers is marked by joy. Sixteen times the noun *chara* ("joy") and its cognates occur in Philippians, a number far out of proportion to the size of the letter. Awareness of the historical context of the imprisoned writer and persecuted readers is critical to the nuanced presentation of this theme. What is both affirmed and urged among the readers should not be taken as a superficial, Pollyanna spirituality, but the deep celebration of God's presence experienced amid distress and pain.

Joy expresses the feeling Paul has for the readers at their participation in the gospel (1:4; 4:1, 10), the experience they can have in the return of Epaphroditus (2:28-29), the delight one relishes in the spread of the gospel (1:18), and, most strikingly, the stance both Paul and the Philippians can share in the face of suffering (2:17-18). The second of the three injunctions to "rejoice in the Lord" (3:1; 4:4 [twice]) includes the adverb "always," no doubt specifying that occasions of gladness at the divine presence are not limited to times of prosperity, plenty, and being well-fed (cf. 4:11-13). (See the further discussion of "joy" in the commentary at 4:4.)

Genuine Friendship

(Philippians 1:1-11)

The letter to the Philippians opens in the fashion of Greco-Roman letters, following the practice of ancient letter-writing. First comes the sender's name (1:1a), then the designated readers (1:1b), then a word of greeting (1:2), then a prayer for the welfare of the recipients (1:3-11). Yet in Paul's hands these typical forms are rich with theological meaning, peculiarly reflective of the warm relationship between the writer and the initial readers, and indicating the tone and content of what is to follow in the body of the letter.

In the initial salutation, three features stand out. First, the inclusion of Timothy as co-author of the letter (1:1a) is a departure from the convention of the letter form, but not unusual for a Pauline letter (six other letters in the Pauline corpus are said to be co-written). Since the first person singular pronoun is predominate through the letter and Paul is obviously the actual author, why is Timothy mentioned here (even sharing with Paul the title "servants of Christ Jesus")? It may be that Timothy was Paul's amanuensis (the secretary who took his dictation) and thus partially responsible for the letter. More important, however, is the fact that Timothy, who would have been known to the Philippians (cf. Acts 16:1-5, 11-40), appears later in the letter as Paul's valued colleague in ministry and is designated as a special envoy to visit Philippi soon (2:19-23). His inclusion as co-author reinforces for the readers Timothy's significance as a key figure in the Pauline mission and as one whose message should be heeded.

Second, the title "servants of Christ Jesus" (1:1a) occurs in the salutation only here and in Rom 1:1 (among the undisputed letters of Paul). It is not surprising to find this title rather than the formal appellation "apostle of Jesus Christ," since Paul enjoyed a close and harmonious relationship with the Philippians. The interesting question, however, is what the title connoted, how the initial readers would have understood "servants (*douloi*, slaves) of Christ Jesus." The usual explanation locates the setting of the term *douloi* in the slave system of the first century and associates it with lowly service, humility, and unconditional obedience to a master. Paul and Timothy are indentured slaves of Christ, totally at his disposal (so O'Brien 1991, 45).

The title, however, was so widely used in early Christianity for recognized figures (e.g., Jas 1:1; 2 Pet 1:1; Jude 1) that it may have lost much of its connection with the slave system. Dale Martin's judgment is that "Christians had used the term for so long as a title for their leaders that any connotations of humility, if there ever were any, would have long worn off" (Martin 1990, 54). Moreover, in the Old Testament, God's chosen and authorized leaders are often called "servants of God," reinforcing the impression that in 1:1a the title would likely suggest to the initial readers the divinely given authority of Paul and Timothy to speak and act in God's name (so, Martin 1976, 60-61). At the same time, one cannot ignore that the only other use of *doulos* in Philippians occurs in the Christ-hymn (2:7, "taking the form of a slave"), which generates much of the language used throughout the letter. Members of the Philippian congregation, listening to the letter read in their midst, might initially associate the title with the role of Paul and Timothy as divinely commissioned messengers. After hearing 2:7, however, they are more likely to associate it with the incarnation and humiliation of Christ.

Third, the letter is sent "to all the saints in Christ Jesus who are in Philippi, with the bishops and deacons" (1:1b). Though the whole community is addressed, the reference to bishops and deacons stands out, since this is the only occurrence of the Greek term *episkopos* ("bishop" or "overseer") in the undisputed letters of Paul, and nowhere else is information given about the organizational structure or offices of the various Pauline churches. Most likely the reference here is to people who regularly perform functions for the worship and activity of the Philippian community (oversight and service) and not to well-defined offices to which they may have been specially chosen, as occurs later in 1 Tim 3:1-12. It may even be that the juxtaposing of the terms had significance for the readers, the second explanatory of the first. Paul possibly "wanted to make it clear that the function of oversight was of value only as a *service* for the building up of the community and that therefore it would require much humility" (Collange 1979, 40).

The prayer for the recipients that follows the salutation is neatly divided into two parts. The former is an expression of thanksgiving for the Philippians (1:3-8) and the latter a word of petition for their spiritual well-being (1:9-11). The two parts together highlight the friendly relationship that exists between Paul and the Philippians and also introduce topics that are addressed later in the letter.

In his prayers Paul always remembers these particular readers with fondness. Three specific items are mentioned as a cause for joy. First, from the beginning the Philippians have participated in the gospel (1:5). While their participation is concretely expressed in the gifts sent to undergird Paul and his ministry (4:10-20), there is no hint that it is limited to benevolence. The specific comment later in the letter that Euodia, Syntyche, and Clement "have struggled" with him and his co-workers in the work of the gospel indicates that their involvement has gone beyond gift-giving (4:3). Second, Paul is thankful not only for the Philippians themselves, but also for the activity of God, who has begun a good work among them and will see it to completion (1:6; cf. 2:13). Paul's confidence in the reliability of God is particularly appropriate in light of the current (or impending) suffering the readers are undergoing (1:29). In their anxiety they are reassured that God leaves no buildings unfinished, no battles in doubt, no chaos unresolved. Third, Paul has reason for thanksgiving because of the mutuality and intimacy that exists between the Philippians and himself (1:7-8). They hold him in their hearts while he is imprisoned, and he vows before God that he yearns for them. The expression "with the compassion of Jesus Christ" is striking and gives reason once again for seeing the mutuality between Paul and the Philippians as a three-way relationship. What draws writer and readers together in this mutual affection is their common connectedness to Christ. "All of you share in God's grace with me" (1:7).

The prayer, both the thanksgiving and petition sections, telegraphs for the readers several topics that reappear through the letter (Schubert 1939, 71-82). Following is a partial list:

• joy (1:4, 18, 25; 2:2, 17-18, 28; 3:1; 4:1, 4)
• sharing/participation (1:5, 7; 2:1; 3:10; 4:14)
• gospel (1:5, 7, 12, 16, 27; 2:22; 4:3, 15)
• thinking/mind (1:7; 2:2, 5; 3:15, 19; 4:2, 8)
• imprisonment (1:7,12-14, 16-17, 19-26, 30; 2:17; 4:14)
• compassion/love (1:8, 9, 16; 2:1-2, 12; 4:1).

Further, the specific petitions in 1:9-11 have about them a hortatory dimension that particularly prepares the way for the injunctions that occur later in the letter. Paul asks in behalf of the Philippians that their love abound more and more with knowledge and all insight (1:9), that they be able to discern what really matters (1:10), that they be sincere and blameless in the day of Christ (1:10), and that they produce a harvest of righteousness that ultimately glorifies God (1:11). The petitions disclose the intent of the letter: to enable the readers to think and live in such a way that their common mind and life become a visible sign of the coming salvation, even in the face of suffering (1:28-29).

An important ingredient is the power of discernment (1:10) that enables the readers to sort out the good from the bad, the relevant from the irrelevant, the significant from the trivial. It is the kind of discernment mentioned in Rom 12:2 ("Be transformed by the renewing of the mind, so that you may discern what is the will of God—what is good and acceptable and perfect"). A love informed by "knowledge and full insight" produces such discernment, which in turn issues in fruitful and faithful lives.

Another feature of the prayer underscores a further theme of the letter. The word "day" occurs three times (1:5, 6, 10) and situates the Philippians in terms of the divine reckoning of time. They live between "the first day," when the gospel was declared and received in their midst, and "the day of Christ," when their progress will be complete. The use of "day" as an eschatological symbol goes back at least as far as the time of Amos, who warns a presumptuous Israel that "the day of the Lord" can turn out to be darkness and not light (Amos 5:18-20). Hearing the gospel and sharing with others in its power is like Eden all over again ("the first day"), the initiation of something entirely new. The final day toward which life is aimed is the day of Jesus' return, when the veil will be lifted and the good beginnings will be fully consummated. The readers live between the two days. They are not to confuse the first day with the last (as did some members of the Corinthian church), assume that it has already arrived, and thus ignore the moral ambiguities that face those who live between the days. Instead, because of "the first day" they are to have confidence in God's promise about "the day of Christ" and in the meantime to grow in love and discernment.

Though the letter does not provide sufficient information to say conclusively, this locating of the readers in a time between "the first day" and "the day of Christ" may suggest that some Philippians were confused about eschatological matters. In 3:12-14 Paul states that he has not yet reached the resurrection of the dead but, like a runner in a race, presses forward toward the goal. He urges readers to adopt a similar stance (3:17) and then pictures the church as a group whose citizenship is heavenly and who live in anticipation of Jesus' coming from heaven to earth (3:20-21). Whether there were those in Philippi who thought the goal had already been reached or who had given up hope that Jesus would return is hard to say. In any case, the awareness that one lives between the "first day" and "the day of Christ" is essential.

The prayer of thanksgiving (1:3-11), then, builds an important bridge to the readers and sets the tone for the rest of the letter. If they did not already know it, the Philippians hear now of the special place they have in Paul's thoughts and prayers. The expressions of their support of him are acknowledged, and through the petitions he offers to God on their behalf they learn of his continued concern for them.

Progress of the Gospel

(Philippians 1:12-26)

Two features of 1:12 mark it as the beginning of the body of the letter. First, the disclosure formula, coupled with the familiar direct address, typically functions in the undisputed letters of Paul as a transition from the introduction to the body of the letter ("I want you to know, brothers and sisters . . ." The NRSV's rendering of *adelphoi* as "beloved" unfortunately misses the familial imagery.) Rom 1:13; 2 Cor 1:8; Gal 1:11; 1 Thess 2:1 have like-worded expressions that signal the shift to the major business of writing (Mullins 1964, 44-50; White 1971,: 91-97).

Second, letters of friendship, like familial letters, are generally structured so that following the opening conventions the writer reports on his or her own circumstances, reassuring the readers that things are going well, before turning to inquire about the situation of the readers. Paul follows just this pattern in telling of his own status in prison in 1:12-26 before focusing on the readers in 1:27-2:18. Having reestablished the ties of friendship in the prayer for the recipients (1:3-11), he reflects on his own situation and the upcoming trial. It is the first business of the letter.

This autobiographical section is divided into three paragraphs:

Paul's imprisonment and the progress of the gospel (1:12-14)
Contrasting preachers of the gospel (1:15-18a)
Paul's immediate future (1:18b-26)

Paul's Imprisonment
(1:12-14)

Rather than providing details about the nature of his imprisonment, Paul's initial and primary point is that the imprisonment has resulted not in impeding the gospel but in advancing it. The Greek noun *prokopē* ("spread," "progress") appears in 1:12 and 1:25 and serves as an *inclusio* for the entire

section. Paul's imprisonment has resulted in the spread of the gospel with
two particular groups. First, the word has gotten out among the soldiers of
the praetorian regiment and others related to his imprisonment that Paul is
confined not because of criminal activity but for the cause of Christ (literally,
"so that my chains have become plainly seen as being in Christ," 1:13). No
converts are indicated, but those outside the Christian community have had
the occasion to hear the gospel. (Later mention is made of "saints" among
"the emperor's household," 4:22.) Second, members of the church ("brothers
and sisters") have been stirred to a more courageous and open witness to
Christ because of Paul's imprisonment. Rather than being intimidated or
discouraged, they have been invigorated in declaring the gospel.

It may be that for some of his initial readers Paul's imprisonment had
raised doubts about the future of the gospel, whether in the long run it
would amount to much. While modern readers can look on the imprisonment as courageous and heroic, this was not necessarily the reaction of first-
century Christians. The confinement of the leader of the fledging church
could put a quietus on the enthusiasm and optimism of the group. Though
there is no indication that Paul's apostleship was being challenged in
Philippi, it was certainly called into question in Corinth precisely because
Paul's ministry had so many setbacks and did not evidence a flamboyant and
success-filled spirituality (2 Cor 10–13). He defended himself to the
Corinthians by using a rhetorically powerful self-parody, in which his hardships (including imprisonments) are ironically enumerated. It could be that
certain of the Philippians had similar problems with Paul's incarceration. In
any case, 1:12-14 makes it clear that his imprisonment is not to be equated
with failure or with the hindrance of the gospel, but with its progress.

Contrasting Preachers of the Gospel
(1:15-18a)

The mention of the boldness with which some preach the gospel leads to the
second paragraph and to an intriguing contrast between two groups of
preachers (1:15-18a). They are depicted in a forceful chiastic structure:

A. Some preach Christ from envy and rivalry (1:15).
   B. Others from goodwill (1:15).
   B'. These out of love, knowing I am put here for the defense of the
   gospel (1:16).
A'. Others out of selfish ambition, not sincerely, intending to increase my
suffering in my imprisonment (1:17).

Two questions arise about these groups: Who are they, and why does Paul take such an accepting stance toward those who preach from insincere motives?

Both groups are Christians and apparently are located at the place of Paul's imprisonment rather than at Philippi (since they are mentioned in connection with the autobiographical section). Aside from their contrasting motivations, they are distinguished by their attitudes toward Paul's imprisonment. One group preaches, "knowing" that his confinement involves the defense of the gospel, and in some way this knowledge relates to their motives of goodwill and love toward Paul. They are certainly like, if not the same as, those who in 1:14 who are emboldened to speak with courage because of his imprisonment.

The other group operates with selfish ambitions and insincere motives "intending [better, supposing or imagining] to increase my suffering in my imprisonment" (1:17). With both groups, motives for preaching are linked to perspectives on Paul's imprisonment, but how are they linked? How could Paul's confinement have stirred up in them "envy and rivalry"? Is the issue personal animosity, anti-imperial politics, or theological differences? Numerous proposals have been made particularly about the identification of this second group (see the survey by O'Brien 1991, 100-105), but because the text does not offer specific details, none of the proposals is thoroughly convincing. We are left with two undefined clusters of preachers, one acting out of goodwill and love, the other acting from a competitive spirit.

Why is Paul so accepting of the second group? ("What does it matter? Just this, that Christ is proclaimed in every way, whether out of false motives or true; and in that I rejoice" 1:18a). When one considers the uncompromising stance taken toward the itinerant teachers in Galatia, Paul's indifference toward the personal ill will directed at him by these preachers is astonishing. He supports the message they declare, but acknowledges problems with the reasons why they declare it. It becomes clear that "the motives of the proclamation of the gospel are subordinate to the fact of its proclamation and then regarded as secondary" (Schütz 1975, 161.) The overriding message of the gospel is what matters. It serves as the norm for judging the motives of all sorts of preachers, not vice versa. Thus the gospel can be served by those whose impulses are less than pure and by those who do not honor Paul. It turns out to be ironic, however, that this second group, while motivated by antagonism toward Paul, actually furthers his interests and gives him a reason to rejoice.

Paul's Immediate Future
(1:18b-26)

The third paragraph (1:18b-26) of this section provides a profound reflection on Paul's immediate future, his trial, and the alternatives of life and death. It is important to note that the subsection begins with a word of rejoicing (1:18b) and concludes with an anticipated joy Paul will share with the Philippians (1:25-26). Otherwise the statement "to depart and be with Christ is far better" could be taken (and has been) as a death-wish on Paul's part. Such a reading ignores the positive mood of the context. Verse 23 is no indecisive or depressing "to-be-or-not-to-be" soliloquy.

Paul's reflections are aided in 1:19 by a fleeting echo of Job 13:16 (LXX): "Even this will turn out for my deliverance, for deceit shall not enter in before him." Readers nurtured on the Septuagint could discern Paul's association with Job, the ancient sufferer, who rejects the argument of one of his "comforters" that his troubles must be divine punishment for his evil ways. Just as Job in response expresses the confidence that he will be vindicated for the trust he has put in God, so Paul affirms that however the trial turns out, his defense of the gospel will be confirmed by God (see Hays 1989, 21-24). The "deliverance" (*sotēria*) Paul expects is neither release from jail nor eternal salvation, but God's vindication of his stand for the gospel. The prayers of the Philippians and the supply of the Spirit give him assurance about this.

The trial that Paul awaits becomes a matter of urgency (1:20). He expects to be given a voice, to be afforded the opportunity to defend and confirm the gospel. It is conceivable in such circumstances that he could falter and be disgraced before the Roman authorities. To "be put to shame in any way" does not mean losing the case and thus losing his life, but in some manner failing to speak the gospel faithfully. The trial becomes an occasion for the magnifying of Christ in his physical presence, that is, by his speaking "with all boldness."

That Paul could honor Christ "whether by life or by death" triggers an interesting consideration of the potential alternatives before him (1:21-26). In a sense, the alternatives are purely hypothetical since Paul is convinced that he will be vindicated, released from jail, and freed for further ministry among the Philippians (1:25-26). And yet the alternatives raise the more urgent questions of human existence "beside which the outcome of Paul's trial, which is supposed to be the real topic of conversation, appears the merest shadow" (Barth 1962, 36).

The alternating patterns of 1:21-24 enhance the rhetorical impact.

A. Living is Christ (1:21a)
B. Dying is gain (1:21b)
A. To live in the flesh means fruitful labor (1:22)
B. To depart and to be with Christ is far better (1:23)
A. To remain in the flesh is more necessary for you (1:24)

Though Paul is confident of deliverance, what if the verdict goes against him? What if the decision of the Roman tribunal leads to execution rather than release? Paul of course has no choice in the matter. It won't be his decision to make. But which alternative would he prefer? Living means Christ, knowing him, "the power of his resurrection and the sharing of his sufferings" (3:10); it means significant work (1:22) and continued involvement with the Philippians (1:25). Dying means gain, the enlargement of the relationship with Christ. Death seems a far better alternative, but Paul does not linger with the prospect because he is convinced that the result of the trial will be deliverance and the necessary work that needs to be accomplished.

Clayton Croy (1996) is no doubt correct in noting that Paul in 1:19-26 employs a rhetorical trope known as "feigned perplexity" (Greek: *aporia* and *diaporesis*; Latin: *dubitatio* or *addubitatio*). The technique involves a rhetorical pretense of uncertainty and the posing of a question as a way of strengthening or dramatizing an argument. Paul is not in mortal jeopardy due to alleged crimes, nor is he so despondent that he is contemplating suicide. In his own mind he knows that he will remain and will continue in the service of the Philippians (as he finally says in 1:25), but he does not present it as such. He is hard pressed and is torn between the alternatives, with the result that his ultimate choice dramatically demonstrates his commitment to the readers.

This passage raises a notoriously difficult issue regarding Paul's eschatology. To put it in the language of the text, if "living is Christ," in what sense is death "gain"? What is intended by the expression "to depart and be with Christ" (1:23)? Has Paul abandoned his earlier eschatological perspective where he taught that believers who die remain in an intermediate state of sleep until the return of Christ, when they will be transformed and clothed with immortality (1 Thess 4:13-5:10; 1 Cor 15: 35-55)? Is he now saying that at death believers go immediately to be with Christ? The possibility of a change in Paul's perspective seems remote since this very letter is replete with eschatological references that suggest a future resurrection (1:6, 10; 2:16; 3:11, 14, 20-21), but the problem remains.

Numerous proposals have been made about 1:21, 23, and a consideration of some of them can shed light on the text. First, Barth argues that the question of life beyond death is actually secondary in the passage and that the "gain," which is "being with Christ," refers to Paul's death. If Christ is magnified "in his body" by death (1:22), this is "the final consummate act" (so 3:10), bringing a closer identification with Christ than is possible in life (Barth 1962, 38-41). Barth's position is not far from that of Lohmeyer, who interprets the entire letter as a reflection on martyrdom. Here Paul muses on the potentiality of being a martyr himself and thus at his death of being with Christ, something that for ordinary believers would come only at the return of Christ (Lohmeyer 1953, 59-70).

Second, a number of interpreters argue that Paul in Philippians is in fact not inconsistent with his previously stated understanding (that believers who die remain in an intermediate state until the return of Christ and the consummation of the created order) and that what is being said in 1:21 and 23 is that the intermediate state involves not a break in the relationship with Christ but an enriching of it (cf. 2 Cor 5:6-8). Death for believers brings a deeper union with Christ. "It is clear from a comparison of Phil 1:23 with 3:20, 21 that the state into which Paul will enter at death is far better, bringing with it a greater closeness of communion with Christ, and yet that it is still a state of expectation, less than the fullness of redemption described in 3:20f" (Lincoln 1981, 106).

Third, Caird finds the second explanation somewhat unintelligible since "those who sleep in the grave cannot be said to be *with Christ* who has left it." Instead, he proposes that since Paul often employs "sleep" as a metaphor for death (1 Cor 7:39; 11:30; 15:6, 18, 20, 51; 1 Thess 4:13-15), he means it as a real analogy. Sleep negates the passage of time. When persons fall asleep, the next thing they are conscious of is waking. When believers fall asleep in death, the next thing they are conscious of is the day of Christ's return. Paul is not expressing a changed eschatology in 1:23. He simply takes into account the matter of consciousness when he links "departing" and being "with Christ" (Caird 1976, 113-114).

The problem with the Barth and Lohmeyer position is that exalting martyrdom to such a high place, thus isolating Paul as a potential martyr (and a special case), and thereby separating him from his fellow believers in Philippi, seems highly problematic in this letter. Too often Paul links his situation with that of his readers (e.g., 1:30) to make such a proposal plausible. Caird's argument that Paul is really concerned with the issue of human consciousness makes sense, except that the metaphor of sleep does not appear in

Philippians at all and the initial readers, who would not have access to Paul's other letters, could hardly be expected to assume its presence here.

The second alternative seems the most probable of the three, with two provisos. First, Paul's intent here is "exclusively christocentric" (Collange 1979, 69). The text provides no details about an intermediate state between death and the final resurrection. While modern interpreters *assume* such an interim in order to reconcile this passage with others, the one and only point of 1:21, 23 is that death brings an enlarged experience of Christ, making it the preferred alternative. Second, Paul's reticence in dealing with the specifics of life after death is no doubt occasioned by the shroud of mystery that necessarily hangs over the whole issue. Human beings (including Paul) do not have the conceptual and linguistic capacity to deal with the complexities of existence beyond this world of time and space, and Paul makes no attempt to speculate about them. What causes rejoicing for him is that nothing in life or death, or whatever lies beyond death, can separate him from the presence of Christ (Fee 1995, 149).

Paul's concluding word in reporting his circumstances to the Philippians is an expression of delight in their anticipated growth in the faith. Just as the gospel has progressed in the midst of his imprisonment, so he is confident that they will progress, making his upcoming visit to Philippi a happily anticipated event (1:25-26).

Living as Citizens Worthy of the Gospel

(Philippians 1:27–2:18)

The body of the letter in the Greco-Roman period defies rigid formal analysis, since it tends to be flexible and adaptable from situation to situation and from topic to topic. The conventional features that are easy to identify in the openings and closings of letters disappear in the body. It is in the body of the letter that the writer gets to the real reason for writing, and hard and fast laws are inappropriate. Nevertheless, while there are few rules in this game, "there are patterns to be observed" (Alexander 1989, 90). One of the patterns observed in the body of the familial letter is that it begins with reassurances from the sender about his or her circumstances and then seeks reassurance from the addressees about theirs ("I want to hear good news about you").

This twofold pattern is precisely reproduced in the body of the letter to the Philippians. Paul says about himself that his imprisonment has resulted in the growth of the gospel, that he anticipates vindication at his upcoming trial, and that he looks forward to a happy visit with the Philippians in the near future (1:12-26). Then he turns to the recipients, saying that he wants to see or hear about them (literally, "about your affairs," "about the things concerning you," 1:27). That Paul wants to learn about their spiritual rather than their physical welfare does not detract from the formal parallel to other letters of friendship. But rather then being merely solicitous, Paul spells out what he wants to see or hear from the Philippians: how they are unified in their advocacy of the gospel in the face of opposition. The manner in which this concern for the readers is expressed reminds us of the strong note of exhortation. More is at stake in the letter than merely the cultivating of a friendship.

Fee (1995, 156-157) notes a chiastic structure, linking the various parts of this section:

A. Appeal to steadfastness and unity in the face of opposition (1:27-30)
   B The appeal to unity, based on their common life in Christ (2:1-4)
      C The appeal to Christ's example (2:5-11)
   B' Application of the appeal, based on mutual relationship (2:12-13)
A' Further application: unity in the face of opposition (2:14-16)

In the final two verses of the unit (2:17-18) Paul returns to his own situation in jail and prepares for the next section, which deals not only with his visit to Philippi but also with the visits of Timothy and Epaphroditus (2:19-30).

Appeal to Steadfastness

(1:27-30)

The initial exhortation is nuanced in a way that does not always show up in English translations (1:27). "Just one thing! Live as citizens worthy of the gospel of Christ, so that whether I come to you myself or not, I might hear about your affairs: that you stand firm like soldiers in the one Spirit, contending side by side for the faith of the gospel as good athletes do." Three images are used for the readers: citizens, soldiers, and athletes (Caird 1976, 115).

The image of citizens is particularly striking for an audience in a colony like Philippi where people qualified for Roman citizenship. On the surface, the exhortation simply urges the readers to take their civic and political obligations seriously, except that in 3:20 they are reminded that their primary citizenship is not in Rome but in heaven. They are thus enjoined in 1:27 to live in Philippi *not* like every other Roman citizen, but as those whose distinctive guide and standard for life is the gospel. The image vividly conveys the struggle of believers to be in but not of the world.

The image of soldiers anticipates both the theme of conflict that appears in 1:28-30 and the theme of unity that appears in 2:2. The Greek verb translated "stand firm" (*stēkete*), together with its cognates, was regularly used in ancient literature "to indicate the duty of the soldier in battle, or to describe the taking of a position vis-à-vis that of an adversary" (Geoffrion 1993, 55). Like soldiers who refuse to break ranks and retreat in the face of fierce opposition, the community is to remain steadfast, united in the one Spirit of God. In light of Paul's use of the word "spirit" in 2:1 and in passages such as 1 Cor 12:13 (cf. Eph 2:18; 4:4) and in light of the fact that the Greek word for "spirit" (*pneuma*) is used in the New Testament to refer to the temperament or mood of a group (as in "*esprit de corps*"), it makes better sense here to think of the divine Presence rather than the human spirit (as in the

NRSV). God's gift of the Spirit fortifies the community for steadfastness and binds them together as one.

If the phrase "stand firm" seems a defensive term, the picture of athletes struggling together as one team (*sunathlountes*), engaged side by side for the cause of the gospel, is a much more aggressive image, like the struggle (*agōena*) in which Paul is engaged (1:30). The community reflected in the metaphor here is on the move "in the work of the gospel," as also Euodia, Syntyche, Clement, and the others were (4:2-3).

The images of citizens, soldiers, and athletes remind the readers who they are and encourage them as they face opposition. If they are not cowered by the threat posed against them, this will be an omen both of their opponents' "destruction" and of their own "salvation." Though the Greek of 1:28 is somewhat ambiguous, the intent of the verse is not to determine who is ultimately lost and who is ultimately saved, but to inform the Philippian community that how they respond to opposition has public implications. The evidence will be plain. Their courage will mark them as "children of God without blemish in the midst of a crooked and perverse generation, in which you shine like stars in the world" (2:15). Since this is a heavy burden for the community to bear, the concluding word is apt: "And this is God's doing" (1:28). The Philippians are not alone in their stance against their oppressors.

Who are these opponents of the Philippians? There is no reason in the text to connect them with other groups mentioned in the letter (such as those in 3:2 or 3:17). The most telling piece of information comes in 1:30 when Paul connects his struggles with the struggles of the readers. If the parallel is to be taken seriously, then he is imprisoned by Roman authorities for his preaching of the gospel, and most likely the Philippians are under threat from a similar group for the same reason. Since there was not a strong indigenous group of Jews in Philippi and since the city was a Roman colony, we may conclude that the opposition comes from the civil authorities. They may have been in some way offended by the life and witness of the Christian community or they may be the pawns of other power groups in the community. The scenario in Acts 16:16-24 envisages frustrated commercial interests who pressure the local authorities into incarcerating Paul and Silas.

The arresting feature of this paragraph comes in the way in which the mention of suffering is described. An accurate translation of 1:29 reads: "For it has been graciously given to you, in behalf of Christ, not only to believe on him but also to suffer in his behalf." Suffering for Christ is not depicted as a tragedy or a miscarriage of justice, but as a divine gift of grace. A special privilege is bestowed on the Philippians, both to believers and to sufferers.

To Western ears this depiction of suffering sounds morbid. Three features of Paul's attitude toward suffering warrant mention here. First, the suffering spoken of in the text is not the tragic and often meaningless suffering caused by ravaging diseases, natural disasters, or the premature ending or dehumanizing prolongation of life. Such occasions of suffering are taken into account in Rom 8:18-25, when Paul refers to the groanings of an incomplete creation, awaiting redemption. But apart from this instance, by "suffering" Paul means the variety of physical trials and tribulations, mental stresses, and violent rejections incurred in the service of the gospel. In a sense, these are sufferings that could have been avoided had one chosen not to follow the crucified Christ. Paul provides in other letters catalogs of such hardships that have happened to him (e.g., 1 Cor 4:9-13; 2 Cor 4:7-12; 6:4-10; 11:23-29).

Second, Paul is never surprised by such suffering, nor does he stop to query God why it occurs. He knows why. He knows that the gospel is to be lived out and preached in a world that is invariably offended by the message of the gospel and that cannot tolerate its character as grace (cf. 1 Cor 1:18-2:5). Religion in general may be accepted or even revered by society, but the word of the cross evokes rejection. As Käsemann put it, "Hostility to the cross is the leading characteristic of the world" (Käsemann 1971, 37). Suffering for faithfulness to the gospel never comes unexpectedly.

Third, such suffering can be spoken of as a gracious gift, because it binds one to the crucified Christ. In 3:10 Paul writes of wanting to know "the sharing (*koinonia*) of his sufferings by becoming like him in his death," a component of knowing "the power of his resurrection." In 2 Cor 4:10-11 he speaks of "carrying in the body the death of Jesus" and of "always being given up to death for Jesus' sake," to the end that the life of the risen Jesus also "may be made visible in our mortal flesh." Paul is not masochistically seeking for himself or for the Philippians opportunities to be persecuted nor is there any lust for martyrdom to authenticate his or their discipleship (as is seen, for example, in Ignatius of Antioch [*To the Romans*, 4:1-3]). Instead, hardships endured for the gospel become occasions for God's power to be experienced (2 Cor 12:9-10), as it was in the crucifixion and exaltation of Jesus (Phil 2:6-11). Suffering for Paul then comes as an inevitable consequence of fidelity to the gospel and becomes a means of fellowship with the crucified Christ. That is why he writes to the Philippians that they are a gift of grace.

The word "gospel" appears six times in critical locations in Philippians 1 (vv. 5, 7, 12, 16, and twice in 27). It is the glue that holds the chapter together, or perhaps it is more accurate to say that the gospel is the glue that holds Paul and his readers together. Whether fostering his ties with the Philippians or reassuring them about his own predicament in prison or exhorting them to a faithful response to their opponents, Paul's primary focus is the message in which both share and for which both vigorously contend.

Appeal to Unity

(2:1-4)

Chapter 2 continues the exhortation to unity begun at 1:27, with two modifications. First, 2:1-4 is more highly structured, giving considerable force to the specific injunctions. Verse 1 lists four reasons for unity: encouragement in Christ, comfort from love, sharing in the Spirit, compassion and sympathy. Verse 2 presents the exhortations in a neat chiastic structure:

A Be of the same mind
  B Have the same love
  B' Be of one accord
A' Be of the same mind

Verses 3-4 continue the exhortations in an alternating pattern of contrasts: *not* from selfish ambition or conceit *but* in humility; *not* to one's own interests *but* to the interests of others.

Second, whereas the previous section (1:27-30) highlighted the need for unity and courage in the face of external opposition, with a focus on the community's public witness, 2:1-4 is directed more to the relationships *within* the community. For example, the exhortations in 2:3-4 go beyond the matter of unity to the need for humility. "Do nothing from selfish ambition or conceit, but in humility regard others as better than yourselves" (2:3).

Humility is a prominent theme in Philippians, occurring in various forms four times (2:3, 8; 3:21; 4:12; see the discussion of humility by Grundmann 1988, 1-60). As a virtue, it no doubt seemed odd in the Greco-Roman culture that found it totally alien to its ethical system. Humility signified that which is lowly, mean, insignificant, weak, and trivial. Even with respect to the spiritual state of a person, it was used disparagingly. A person who lives in poor and petty circumstances takes on a servile disposition and becomes an obsequious flatterer. People of position are to show pity toward the humble since it "is easy to outdo the lowly" (Aristotle, *Nicomachean Ethics* IV, 3, 26).

In contrast, Jewish and Christian writings (LXX, the Dead Sea scrolls, rabbinical literature, and the New Testament) present a positive approach to humility, both in relation to God and to other people. In the first place, humility depicts the proper response to God, to whom service and obedience are owed. It is often associated with fasting, expressing abasement before God (e.g., Lev 16:29, 31; Isa 58:3,5). The people of Qumran even referred to themselves as "the poor," "the lowly," and "the afflicted" to express their dependence on divine mercy and their desire to be the faithful in Israel (e.g., 1QH V, 13-22; 4QpPs 37 II, 8f; III, 9f). Jesus spoke of himself as "gentle and humble in heart" (Matt 11:29).

But in the second place, humility also describes a right relationship to other people. Wengst has argued that the difference between the Greco-Roman writings and the Jewish and Christian writings with respect to humility lies in the perspectives from which each is written. The literature of the former comes from a high position that looks down on the socially infe-rior, who invariably appear lowly, subservient, and humble. The Old Testament, however, speaks from the perspective of insignificant people and in fact takes the side of those who are downtrodden and humiliated, because God is on their side. Humility denotes "the solidarity of the humiliated" (Wengst 1988, 1-60).

In the third place, the christocentric orientation of Philippians' humility unites Christian humility in relation to God and to other people. It becomes a prominent and advocated characteristic for members of the community because of the Christ who "humbled himself and became obedient to the point of death" (2:8). In practical terms, it involves moving beyond a preoccupation with one's own affairs to a concern for the interests of others (2:3). Such two-directional humility is essential for the Christian community. Barth writes,

> The reason why we are to see the other's point of view, to let ourselves be enticed out of our own hut and over into his, is not that that were suppos-edly a holy place, but that it is only when men [and women] thus come together, when they take a joint view of things, when they bow jointly before him who is greater than both my neighbor and myself—it is only then that the really holy, true, and helpful One comes into my field of vision at all. It is not until I see the other's point of view that I myself really see. . . . Always my neighbor is the barrier, but also the door. There is no road that passes him by. (1962, 59)

Appeal to Christ's Example
(2:5-11)

Verse 5 introduces the so-called Christ-hymn (2:6-11) that serves as the cen-terpiece for the letter. The complexity of the issues regarding the passage has resulted in an enormous number of books and articles dealing with its origin and sources, literary form, authorship, possible reflection of pre-Pauline Christianity, translation and exegetical details, christology, connection to later christological symbols, and contextual use. (For a survey of the research up until the early-eighties, see Martin 1983.) In line with the purposes of this commentary, we shall confine ourselves to three areas of investigation about the passage: its literary form, content, and function in the immediate context. (On the hymn's origin, see the Introduction.)

Literary Form

Two literary features of this passage are important. First, there is general agreement among scholars that 2:6-11 represents a poetic piece of some sort, perhaps a hymn or a creedal statement. It evidences (more in the Greek than in the English translation) a stately, rhythmical pattern, marked by striking parallelisms that are sometimes complementary and sometimes contrasting. We use the term "hymn" throughout the discussion, but in a very general sense, without any suggestion that it was sung or that it reflects an established literary form.

Can the passage be arranged according to its rhythmic structure, with strophes and lines? The scholarly answer is, "Yes," but then the options are numerous. Proposals have included the following: six strophes of three lines each; three strophes of four lines each; six strophes of two lines each; and four strophes of three lines each. The multiplicity of suggestions confirms the poetic nature of the passage, but also indicates the difficulty in finding a stylistic structure that honors both form and content.

The proposal that comes the closest to acknowledging the hymn's literary form and its subject matter treats the passage as a chiasm of four strophes, the first and last of which are of six lines each, while the second and third are of four lines each (Hooker *Adam* 1990, 94-95). Since the decision of the hymn's structure must be based on the Greek text, a literal translation is provided:

A   who, being in the form of God,
                   did not regard it as a something to be taken advantage of
                            to be equal with God,
          but emptied himself,
                   taking the form of a slave,
                            being born in human likeness.
B   And having been found in form as a human,
                   he humbled himself
          becoming obedient unto death—
                   even death on a cross.

B'   Therefore God also
            highly exalted him
      and gave him the name
            that is above every name,
A'   so that at the name of Jesus
            every knee should bend,
                  in heaven and on earth and under the earth,
      and every tongue should confess
            that Jesus Christ is Lord,
                  to the glory of God the Father.

The initial six-line strophe (A) relates the story of the incarnation, followed by a four-line strophe (B) that expands the narrative in terms of Christ's life on earth, including his obedience unto death. The second half of the hymn reverses the form and the content. B' states Christ's exaltation and receipt of a name, while A' develops the exaltation theme further.

The second literary characteristic of the passage is its narrative quality. It relates the story of Christ, from his being in the form of God and deciding that equality with God was not something to be taken advantage of, his self-emptying, and taking the form of a slave in the likeness of human beings, to his obedience unto death. The career is continued in 2:9-11 but with God as the primary actor, exalting Christ and giving him the supreme name. Interestingly, no specific mention is made either of Christ's resurrection or his return, two points in his career that are very prominent elsewhere in the other Pauline letters.

The fact that the passage has both a poetic and a narrative quality suggests a certain wariness in approaching the matter of content. Both genres tend to be evocative rather than didactic, to spur the imagination rather than to instruct. While both are appropriate forms for "doing" theology, neither produces as tidy a result as analytical prose. Since expressions occur in the passage such as "in the form of God," "equality with God," "he emptied himself," "in likeness of human beings," the reader is tempted to ignore the poetic and narrative nature of the text and to interpret it more as a philosophical treatise, having to do with Christ's nature and essence. Its literary character, however, cannot be bypassed in the move to theology.

Content

The narrative of Christ's career has two major movements: humiliation (2:6-8) and exaltation (2:9-11). There are three possible interpretations of the first movement:

The traditional interpretation of the first movement begins the story with the preexistence of Christ, who though he was in the form of God did not consider equality with God as something to be clutched or taken advantage of, but "emptied himself"; that is, he became incarnate as a human being. His obedience to God carried him to a shameful death on a cross. "The form of God," left behind in the incarnation, was not his deity as such, but his sharing of the divine glory and splendor and living in the visible manifestation of God's majesty. Christ's movement within the hymn, then, follows the course of a parabola—from heavenly divine glory through humiliation and death to exaltation and universal recognition as Lord (cf. Barth 1962, 60-68; O'Brien 1991, 186-271).

A second interpretation of the first movement rejects the notion of preexistence in the hymn and instead sees it as the story of the earthly Christ, in contrast to Adam in Genesis (1:26-27; 3:1-5). Adam was "in the image of God," but responded to the serpent's appeal by snatching at the opportunity to enhance his own status, to "be like God." His decision resulted in his losing what he had, in becoming a slave to corruption and death (cf. Wisd. Sol. 2:23-24). Christ is the Last Adam, who did not choose as Adam had, but instead freely accepted the consequences of Adam's choice. "He made himself powerless" (*ekenōsen*), for which God exalted him.

> The Christ of Phil 2:6-11 therefore is the man who undid Adam's wrong: confronted with the same choice, he rejected Adam's sin, but nevertheless freely followed Adam's course as fallen man to the bitter end of death; wherefore God bestowed on him the status not simply that Adam lost, but the status which Adam was intended to come to, God's final prototype, the last Adam. (Dunn 1980, 119; cf. Talbert 1967, 141-153)

The decisive issue for this second interpretation is the rendering of 2:6. How can it be said that Adam was "in the form of God"? The case is made that the Greek words *morphē* ("form") and *eikōn* ("image") are nearly synonymous in the Septuagint and that Adam is "in the form of God" in the sense of Gen 1:27 ("in the image of God he created them"). Furthermore, the word *harpagmos* (NRSV: "something to be exploited") is taken to be something not yet possessed, something to be grasped *de novo*. Thus Adam and the earthly Christ are both in the image of God. Adam heeds the serpent's invitation and seeks (grasps after) the likeness of God (Gen 3:5), but ends up a fallen creature, in human likeness and in the form of a slave (as people now are, after the fall). Christ, on the other hand, resists the temptation to grasp after equality with God and humbly takes on the lot of fallen humanity.

The problems with this interpretation are the linguistic assumptions made. "Form" (*morphē*) and "image" (*eikōn*) do not turn out to be quite so synonymous in the LXX as is suggested, nor does *harpagmos* likely denote something not yet possessed. Beyond the dubious linguistic data however, the association with Adam seems highly possible and in line with Paul's christology elsewhere.

A third (and the most plausible) interpretation understands 2:6-8 as the narrative of the incarnation, as with the first option, but at the same time discerns in these verses the story of Adam in Genesis 1-3, as with the second option. Rather than setting the previous interpretations over against each other, the two become mutually explanatory. The Adam-christology, evident elsewhere in the Pauline letters (e.g., Rom 5:12-21; 1 Cor 15:21-22, 45-49), highlights the self-giving character of both the preexistent *and* the earthly Jesus. Adam, who was not preexistent, and Christ, who was, are not paralleled in every way, but only at a single point. The contrast drawn is between Adam, who grasped at equality with God, a dignity to which he had no right, and Christ, who did not take advantage of a status to which he had every right but who humbled himself unto death on the cross. This third reading avoids some of the questionable linguistic assumptions of the second option, recognizes the presentation of both a preexistent and an earthly Christ, and enables the hymn to function more credibly in the context of exhortation set in 2:1-5 (cf. Caird 1976, 118-124; and especially, Wright 1992, 56-98).

In the second movement of the hymn (from humiliation to exaltation in 2:9-11), a dramatic reversal takes place, with God now becoming the acting subject to vindicate the humiliated Jesus. The focus falls on the "name" that is above every other name, before whom the spiritual powers of the universe bow, and whom every tongue gives public acclaim as Lord. In 2:11 echoes of Isa 45:23 can be heard, where a similar recognition ("every knee shall bow, every tongue shall swear") is given to God in light of God's universal power to save those who repent, from "all the ends of the earth" (cf. Rom 14:12). The comprehensive recognition Jesus receives is God's gift (2:9-11), and thus his lordship is "to the glory of God the Father."

Function

The question arises: how does this hymn, which is so thoroughly christological in content, function in the Philippian letter? The issue becomes particularly sharp when we recognize that there is no inadequate view of Christ among the readers that the hymn is meant to correct. In the history of research there have been numerous suggestions about the place of the hymn in the argument of the letter, but two are especially significant for our consideration in that they both seek to avoid the simplistic understanding of Jesus as a moral example.

One proposal contends that 2:5 should be translated something like the rendering in the NEB ("Let your bearing towards one another arise out of your life in Christ Jesus") and that the phrase "in Christ Jesus" should be understood as the realm or community of Christ Jesus. The hymn primarily narrates the drama of salvation, culminating in the affirmation of Jesus' lordship. How believers live and relate to one another in the community is determined by their belonging to Christ's rule. They are to be obedient to the humiliated and exalted Jesus, who is Lord of all. The hymn functions to tell the story of God's saving activity rather than to project a model for believers to imitate (cf. Käsemann 1968, 45-88; Martin 1976, 91-93).

By emphasizing the function of the hymn as a narrative of the salvation-event, this proposal has the advantage, first, of avoiding a naive ethical idealism that turns Jesus into an example to be followed, and, second, of providing a rationale for 2:9-11, which obviously cannot be part of an example to be imitated. The weakness of this proposal, however, is that it tends to isolate 2:5-11 from its immediate context (1:27–2:4), which is strongly hortatory in nature.

A second proposal acknowledges the danger of an ethical idealism, but maintains that the immediate context cannot be ignored. The exhortation to unity and particularly to a humility that attends to the interests of others before oneself is perfectly modeled in the story of the Christ, who by right could claim divine glory but instead "humbled himself and became obedient to the point of death" (2:8). It is hard to ignore that in some sense Jesus serves as a paradigm for the behavior of the readers. How can one acknowledge the exaltation motif in 2:9-11 and at the same time (without falling into idealism) acknowledge that the text presents Jesus as a model?

Stephen Fowl offers a solution by contending that the hymn should be taken not as a static model but as an "exemplar," a term he borrows from the philosopher T. S. Kuhn. Instead of being an abstract, law-like generalization, an exemplar is a concrete formulation, normative for a community (in Kuhn's case, a community of scientists), which can be extended by analogy to offer solutions to other particular problems. The story of Christ in 2:6-11 is a concrete description of the Lord in whom the Philippians believe. But in its context (1:27–2:18) appropriate analogies are drawn from it that are applicable to their situation. Christ's actions become the warrant as well as the paradigm for the actions Paul urges on his readers. Because God vindicates Christ's humiliation and death, readers can anticipate the same vindication if they remain strong in the face of opposition (Fowl 1990, 77-101; cf. also Hurtado 1984, 113-126).

This second proposal (and its variations) provides a better explanation for the hymn's functioning in the context of the letter than does the first. It makes possible a smooth and plausible connection with the exhortations begun in 1:27 and in turn gives them a christological authorization.

Another advantage of Fowl's understanding of Christ (in 2:6-11) as exemplar is that it can be extended to other problems facing the Philippian community. The hymn generates the language and concepts that shape much of the positive and negative modeling that occurs throughout the letter. For example, in 3:4-11 Paul tells his own story in contrast to the dogs, evil workers, and mutilators of the flesh (3:2). Whereas Jesus "did not regard" (ēgēsato) equality with God as something to be taken advantage of (2:6), Paul has come to "regard" (egemai) as loss his inherited and achieved status in Judaism (3:7-8). The critical point comes in his statement, "I want to know Christ and the power of his resurrection and the sharing of his sufferings by becoming like him in his death, if somehow I might attain the resurrection from the dead" (3:10-11). As Fowl comments, "Paul's view clearly conforms to the precedent provided by Christ presented in 2:6-11 in its refusal to separate humiliation and suffering from exaltation" (Fowl 1990, 99-100).

Again, in 3:18-21 the "enemies of the cross" (cf. 2:8) are set in contrast with believers, whose commonwealth is in heaven. They live now "in the body of humiliation" (cf. 2:8), awaiting the "Lord Jesus Christ" (cf. 2:11), but they will be "transformed" (cf. 2:7) and "conformed" (cf. 2:6, 7) to Christ's glorious (cf. 2:11) body. The pattern of vindication following humiliation reflects the movement of the hymn (2:6-11; cf. Hooker 1990, "Philippians 2:6-11," 92).

Having considered the hymn's literary form, content, and function within the letter, we conclude our study of it by examining its introduction in verse 5. The translation is problematic in part, because it contains a notorious ellipsis (the omission of a verb in the dependent clause) and because its rendering is usually determined by whether one takes the hymn to be a drama of the salvation-event (Käsemann, Martin) or an exemplar/paradigm for hortatory purposes (Fowl, Hurtado). The RSV covers the ellipse by adding "you have" to read, "Have this mind among yourselves that you have in Christ Jesus."

But more important than the translation of the ellipse is the initial verb in the imperative (phoneite). It occurs ten times in Philippians (1:7; 2:2

[twice], 5; 3:15 [twice], 19; 4:2, 10 [twice]) and refers to the practical (as opposed to theoretical) wisdom of the community. Meeks translates 2:5, "Base your practical reasoning on what you see in Christ Jesus" (Meeks 1991, 332). The text addresses the moral thinking of the readers, the process of discernment by which decisions are made, the distinction between what is more or less important and between the essential and the trivial. Coupled with the exhortation expressed in the opening prayer of thanksgiving (1:9-11), verse 5 exposes the letter's most comprehensive purpose—to shape in the readers a distinctively Christian mindset, a moral reasoning characterized by the humiliated, obedient, vindicated Christ. In 3:15 maturity is defined in terms of such practical thinking. It is the common mind the apostle seeks for the community (2:2; 4:2). No wonder then that this hymn (2:6-11) plays such a critical role in the argument of the letter.

Application of the Appeal
(2:12-18)

The two paragraphs that immediately follow the hymn (2:12-13, 14-18) are linked to it by a consequential particle ("therefore") and thus continue the hortatory section begun at 1:27. The community that has been exhorted to unity and harmony and to courage in the face of opposition is told to work out its own salvation and to live without argument and complaint.

Three features of 2:12-13 add new dimensions to the appeal being made to the Philippians. First, the word "salvation" is used for the task before the community. Some commentators persist in taking this as a word to the individual reader, having to do with personal salvation, with his or her inclusion in the eschatological salvation. But this interpretation violates the context and Paul's concern throughout the letter for the whole community. "Salvation" denotes not only the integrity, well-being, and hope of individual members of the congregation at Philippi, but also the integrity, well-being, and hope they are to exhibit *together*, as one body, even under duress. It is interesting that the text uses the loaded theological term "salvation" (as also in 1:28) to depict something the church is to "work out." The matter of unity, courage, and humility is not an option for Paul's readers, but has to do with the very heart of their Christian faith and life.

A second feature comes in the phrase "with fear and trembling" (2:12). In the three other occurrences of the expression in the Pauline corpus (1 Cor 2:3; 2 Cor 7:15; Eph 6:5), it is used to depict the healthy respect one has or should have for a human group with whom one is working, a respect also evident in the Old Testament pairing of these words (cf. Gen 9:2; Exod

15:16; Deut 2:25; 11:25). Barth calls this "startled humility, the consciousness of having nothing to assert in one's own favor and against the others"
(Barth 1962, 72). Since 2:12-13 makes God the ultimate actor in the working out of salvation, one also cannot rule out the elements of honor, rever-
ence, and even dread that people experience in the presence of God. Awe
before God and humility before one's brothers and sisters in Christ go
together.

The third interesting feature of the paragraph is the paradox between the
imperative "work out your own salvation" and the ensuing explanation
("for"), "it is God who is at work in you." On the one hand, the readers have
a responsibility to continue to struggle for the unity and integrity of the
community in its following of Christ. The second sentence does not lessen
the demands of the first. On the other hand, 2:13 affirms the exclusive effec-
tiveness of divine grace. God is the empowering presence, enabling in the
community both the will and the ability to accomplish God's good purpose.
In those moments when the Philippians stand firm and strive side by side for
the faith of the gospel, they can be assured that God, "the real Accomplisher
of all real salvation," is at work among them (Barth 1962, 73).

What negates the integrity of the community and endangers its salvation
are complaints and arguments (2:14). Paul knew of the grumbling of the
Israelites during their years in the wilderness (1 Cor 10:10), and he cites in
2:15 the accusing words of Moses in his farewell speech, "They have sinned;
they are not his children; they are blemished; they are a crooked and perverse
generation" (Deut 32:5, LXX). The Philippians text, however, affirms that if
the readers refrain from grumbling, they *will be* the children of God and
without blemish. The final phrase in the quote from Moses ("a crooked and
perverse generation") is now used to describe the surrounding society.

Why are "murmuring and arguing" singled out? They represent the
opposite of "fear and trembling," the antithesis of humility in relation to
one's neighbors and awe in the presence of God. Parallel to "selfish ambition"
and "conceit" (2:3), they reflect the very inversion of the practical reasoning
shaped by the Christ-hymn, and they can quickly divide the community.
One is tempted to mirror-read 2:13 and to assume that the readers either
were squabbling among themselves or questioning God's ways. This may
have been the case; however, apart from the oblique reference to Euodia and
Syntyche in 4:2, the letter seems intended more to stem the tide against
potential disagreements that often arise when groups are under pressure than
to chide the community for being contentious. In fact, the present imperative of 2:14 could be translated, "Continue to do all things without
complaints and arguments."

The image used for the community in 2:14 (stars shining in a dark sky) highlights the historical plight of the Philippians. Theirs is neither a separatist nor an idyllic situation. The surrounding society is characterized as "a crooked and perverse generation," both adjectives carrying the notion of an environment maliciously distorted. In such a context, the Christian community neither goes underground nor forsakes its calling, but remains visible and public. Not an easy assignment, but a possible one if it "clings to" the gospel ("the word of life"). The participle at the beginning of 2:16, which I have translated "clings to," is ambiguous and can be rendered either "holding fast to" or "holding forth." The latter translation would be particularly appropriate to the community's vocation to be stars shining in the world.

The paragraph closes with repeated mention of the mutuality that binds the apostle to the Philippians. First, Paul acknowledges his investment in their spiritual well-being (2:16). On the day of Christ their steadfastness will vindicate his labors in their behalf. Second, Paul's imprisonment, understood as a drink-offering made to God, is mingled with the suffering the Philippians are undergoing (2:17). In what is to us somewhat confusing cultic imagery, Paul's struggles for the gospel are linked with the similar struggles of the readers (as in 1:30). Third, the result of common suffering is a mutual rejoicing. "I am glad and rejoice with all of you—and in the same way you also must be glad and rejoice with me" (1:18).

This section (1:27–2:18) that begins as a request for reassurance about the circumstances of the addressees (1:27b) turns out to be a sustained plea for citizens to live in a manner worthy of the gospel—in unity, courage, and humility in the face of oppressors. The hortatory nature of the appeal is neither harsh nor judgmental but is rooted in the deep friendship linking writer and readers. Aristotle's comment that "community (*koinōnia*) is the essence of friendship" (*Nichomachean Ethics* 8.ix.1) finds its Christian expression in the mutuality of 2:16-18.

This friendship is not dependent on Paul's physical presence in Philippi. In 2:12 the Greek text does not contain the word "me" as the object of "obeyed," as does the NRSV ("as you have always obeyed *me*"). Paul's concern is for the readers' obedience to Christ, not to himself. The mention of friendship does, however, lead to a consideration not only of Paul's upcoming visit to Philippi but also the visits of Timothy and Epaphroditus (2:19-30).

Commendation of Two Christlike Models

(Philippians 2:19-30)

The so-called travelogue section of Philippians is composed of two rather extensive paragraphs, announcing the proposed visits of Timothy (2:19-23) and Paul (2:24) and commending Epaphroditus, who is apparently the bearer of the letter (2:25-30). Both paragraphs contain features of the letter of commendation, of which Pseudo Libanius gives a sample: "Receive this highly honored and much sought-after man, and do not hesitate to treat him hospitably, thus doing what behooves you and what pleases me" (*Epistolary Styles*, 55; cf. Marshall 1987, 96-129).

On the surface, the transition from the hortatory section (1:27-2:18) to the travelogue seems abrupt. What provokes the shift to Timothy's visit at 2:19, and why is Timothy mentioned before Epaphraditus, who presumably would be the first to arrive at Philippi? The answer to both questions can be found in the Greek phrase *ta peri humōn* (literally "the things concerning you," "your affairs"), translated in the NRSV as "news of you" (2:19) and "your welfare" (2:20). The same expression occurs at the beginning of the hortatory section in 1:27, where Paul expresses the desire to hear of "the things concerning you" or "your affairs" (NRSV: "about you"). Timothy then has a special role as messenger to convey to the Philippians Paul's "affairs" (2:23) and to report back to him about their "affairs." Rather than being an abrupt change of topic, mention of his visit flows somewhat naturally from the hortatory section, because he (and not Epaphroditus) is the means whereby Paul expects to be reassured about the well-being of the readers.

Often in the Pauline letters the inclusion of travel plans does more than provide interesting or necessary information. For example, Paul makes a case with Philemon that his slave Onesimus should be received back no longer as a slave but as a brother. The body of the brief letter then concludes: "One more thing—prepare a guest room for me, for I am hoping through your prayers to be restored to you" (Phlm 22). The mention of Paul's coming visit rhetorically functions as both a carrot and a stick, an enticement to

Philemon to do what he knows is right before the apostle's arrival and to serve notice that Paul intends to follow up on the matter at hand.

In an analogous fashion, mention of the visits of Timothy and Epaphroditus rhetorically serve more than a single purpose. At one level, they are included because Timothy is to be Paul's messenger bearing news back to him about the Philippians and Epaphroditus, their ambassador to Paul, who is returning home after a serious illness. And yet the way both are described indicates that they also serve as models to the readers, as examples of the very Christ-like practical reasoning that Paul has urged in 1:27–2:18.

The use of models in various types of writing is advocated by the ancient teachers of rhetoric and occurs throughout Greek and Latin literature. For example, Aristotle proposes the use of paradigms either as demonstration of some reality or as supporting witness to a statement being made (*On Rhetoric*, 2.20, 1393a, 1394a; see Introduction, p. 128). Here Timothy and Epaphraditus become examples to the readers, but in a particular rather than a general fashion.

Timothy is given high commendation. "I have no one like him who will be genuinely concerned for your welfare" (2:20). All of the others close to Paul in his imprisonment seek first their own interests, not those of Christ. Timothy, however, "has served" with Paul "like a son" (2:22). The Philippians would have known of Timothy's character since he was with Paul at the establishment of the church (Acts 16:1-3) and later visited there (Acts 19:22; 20:3-6). What is striking about the depiction of Timothy is that it echoes both 2:4 ("look not to your own interests, but to the interests of others") and 2:7 ("taking the form of a slave"). Timothy reflects the pattern of the central exemplar Christ and in that sense becomes himself a model for readers to imitate.

The same can be said for Epaphroditus, though not so much is known about him. His name would suggest that he was a Gentile whose parents had been devotees of Aphrodite, but he is mentioned nowhere else in the New Testament. He receives special attention as is fitting for one carrying the letter—"my brother and co-worker and fellow soldier, your apostle and minister to my need" (2:25). Epaphroditus has become critically ill either on the way to Paul or after he arrives and has also grown anxious because word has reached the Philippians of his situation. Whether or not 2:26 implies that Epaphroditus has been extremely homesick ("he has been longing for you all"), 2:27 at least acknowledges that Epaphroditus' regaining his health and returning to Philippi relieve Paul's anxiety about him (2:28). At the same time, Paul, worrying that his friends might not receive Epaphroditus back with open arms, urges a warm welcome, because "he came close to death for the work of Christ" (2:30). The Greek expression *mechri thanatou* ("to the point of death") is found only one other place in the Pauline letters—in 2:8. By risking his life in bearing the Philippians' gift to Paul, Epaphroditus, like Timothy, reflects the self-sacrifice of Christ and is presented as an example to the readers of what is needed in the community.

At one level the complimentary words written about Epaphroditus are meant to see that he receives an appropriate welcome when he returns home, that the community has a proper appreciation of what he has done in their behalf. The added phrase "and honor such people" (2:29), however, lifts him and others like him to an exemplary role (see Kurz 1985, 113).

We are beginning to see the extent to which the Christ-hymn of 2:6-11 pervades the whole letter and in a sense makes it possible for others like Timothy and Epaphroditus (as we shall see, like Paul also) to be secondary models. They are included as part of the appeal to the readers because their conduct proves that the story of Christ has shaped their manner of life. In specific ways, they (Timothy: genuinely seeking the welfare of others; Epaphroditus: risking his life to the point of death for the work of Christ) manifest what Paul exhorts in 2:5 ("Base your practical reasoning of what you see in Christ Jesus").

Conformity to the Cross

(Philippians 3:1–4:3)

From the travelogue, the text moves back to the readers and their immediate situation, to exhortations and further examples (3:1–4:3). The effect is to provide specificity to the basic intention of the letter—that the Philippians live as citizens worthy of the gospel even when under intense pressure and that they evidence in their community life a practical reasoning shaped by Christ's own story. A number of expressions in the section (e.g., "brothers and sisters" in 3:1, 17; 4:1) and the generally affectionate stance toward the readers (e.g., 4:1) remind us that the tone throughout remains that of friendship. The exhortations not only call for steadfastness (4:1) and unity (4:2), but are based on a mutuality of life together in Christ (3:1, 20-21; 4:1, 2).

The section fits together in light of its purpose, though on the surface it seems to be marked by stops and starts. Often the paragraphing used in English translations gives the impression of breaks that are not there. Chapter 3 begins with a general appeal to "rejoice in the Lord." It is a note that is sounded at critical junctures in the letter, sometimes concluding one section, sometimes beginning another (1:18; 2:18; 3:1; 4:4). The Greek word in 3:1a translated in the NRSV as "finally" is to be taken as another transition in the letter rather than as a conclusion (so a better translation: "therefore," "as for the rest," "moreover"). The apology for repetition that is included in the same verse (3:1b) likely refers to what follows, to the mention of the dogs in 3:2, thus suggesting a paragraph break between 3:1a and 3:1b (so NRSV; cf. Furnish 1963–64, 80-88).

The subsection beginning at 3:1b then is composed of a series of connecting issues that continue through 4:3. First, with an introductory "for" (*gar*) the dogs are contrasted with the writer and the readers ("we"), "who worship in the Spirit of God and boast in Christ Jesus and have no confidence in the flesh" (3:3). There is a sequence here that will recur later in the chapter:

• acknowledgment of repetition (3:1b)
• a negative example (3:2)
• a contrasting ("for") affirmation about the church (3:3)

The mention of "flesh" (3:4a) in turn triggers the long autobiographical reflection (3:4b-14), which concludes, logically, with an appeal to follow both the example of Paul and those who live like him (3:15-17).

Then the pattern of 3:1b-3 is repeated: acknowledgment of repetition (3:18), a negative example ("enemies of the cross," 3:18-19), and a contrasting statement ("for") about the church as those whose "citizenship is in heaven" (3:20-21). The exhortations at the close of the section (4:1-3) are tied in with the broader context in that they echo themes with which the earlier exhortation section began ("stand firm," 1:27; "the same mind," 1:27; struggling side by side in the work of the gospel, 1:27).

In a variety of ways, then, 3:1–4:3 holds together as a coherent appeal to the readers. Connecting words, repeated sequences, autobiography and imitation motifs, and recurring themes link "an uninterrupted composition" (Caird 1976, 131). Projecting psychological or circumstantial reasons to explain the apparent break at 3:2 is simply unnecessary to account for the flow of the text, nor is there any reason to assume that 3:1b or 3:2 begins a separate letter fragment sent to the Philippians at an occasion different from the rest of the letter. The text makes admirable sense as it stands. (See the discussion in the Introduction.)

Acknowledgment of Repetition
(3:1b)

Paul's acknowledgments in 3:1b and 3:18 that he repeats himself (perhaps referring to oral communications from Paul or Timothy or Epaphroditus) should not be too surprising. Malherbe has pointed to a standard feature of exhortation in friendly letters—the assurance to the readers that they are receiving nothing original, but traditional, time-tested counsel (cf. Isocrates, *Nicoles*, 40; Dio Chrysostom, *Orations*, 3, 25-26; 13, 14-15; Malherbe 1988, 280). Taking note that what is said is repetitive serves to arouse attention, to jog the memory, to force the readers to recall important lessons from the past. As Dio Chrysostom wrote,

> Since I observe that it is not our ignorance of the difference between good and evil that hurts us so much as it is our failure to heed the dictates of reason on these matters and to be true to our personal opinions, I consider it

most salutary to remind men of this without ceasing. (*Discourse* 17, 2; cf. Isocrates, *Nicoles* 12)

Thus Paul's words of reminder about heretical groups to be examined but not followed spark interest among the readers and set the stage for the positive affirmations to be made about the Christian community.

A Negative Model:
Dogs, Evil Workers, Mutilators of the Flesh
(3:2)

While "dogs" carries a variety of connotations and "evil workers" is a relatively general term, the expression "those who mutilate the flesh" (*katatome*) is very specific. The Greek term is an ironic play on the word "circumcision" (*peritomē*) and identifies the group mentioned in 3:2 as Jewish Christians, perhaps missionaries like Paul, but who advocate circumcision for Gentile believers. Why they advocate it is not so obvious. Most likely they either contend that circumcision is the essential badge for membership in the people of God and thus is necessary for Gentiles, or they argue that it symbolized a perfection that can be achieved in the religious life. In either case, the very term they cherish is snatched from them, spiritualized, and given to the church. In light of the pun on circumcision, then, "dogs" must also be given an ironic twist. It was occasionally used by Jews as a derisive label for unclean Gentiles (cf. Mark 7:27-28) and now is being turned back on its users.

Interestingly, no further comment is made at this point about the group itself, its activities or its theology, suggesting that it was unlikely to have held much of a threat for the Philippians nor to have had much success enticing Gentile believers to be circumcised (as was the case in Galatia). In fact, the Greek verb *(blepete)* rendered three times in the NRSV as "beware" might more properly be translated "consider" or "take note of." As Kilpatrick has pointed out, when followed by an accusative direct object (as it is in 3:2), this verb does not carry the note of impending danger (see 1 Cor 1:26; 10:18; 2 Cor 10:7; Kilpatrick 1968, 146-148). The intent is not to issue a warning about a troublesome menace so much as to call attention to a group's identity that clashes with the identity of the church, to provide "an admonitory example" (Caird 1976, 135). This is not to say that the text projects a phantom foe; the Philippians had certainly heard about, if not encountered, a group like this. The context, however, is more hortatory than polemical.

A Positive Model: "We"

(3:3-4a)

In contrast to the dogs, the "we" is given center stage. Inclusively, Paul and his Philippian audience, Jewish and Gentile believers, comprise "the circumcision." The highly ironical cast of the passage should not hide the significant redefinition of the people of God taking place in the text—from ethnic and cultic considerations to the three affirmations about the "we" that follow in 3:3. It is critical to note that an old Israel is not being replaced by a new Israel (categories Paul as a Jew would hardly understand); there is only one people of God. The contrast in the text is not between Jews (*per se*) and Christians (*per se*), but between a particular group (no doubt Jewish in origin) who want to require circumcision for Gentile believers and a group (composed of Jews and Gentiles) who see the rite as irrelevant for Christian identity. This means that in line with the promises of the Old Testament, the spiritual coinage of the people of God is being reminted, its self-understanding reconstituted. (The redefinition becomes even more prominent in the autobiographical section of 3:4b-14.)

Three activities mark the identity of the community:

- worshiping in the Spirit of God
- boasting in Christ Jesus
- taking no confidence in the flesh

The first two activities, in positive ways, highlight the community's initiating strength ("Spirit of God") and its ultimate orientation ("Christ Jesus"). The third confirms the former two by specifying where the confidence of the community does *not* lie ("in the flesh").

The word "flesh" turns out to be a critical term in the passage, since it leads to the extensive reflection on Paul's own experience. The Greek word has a broad semantic range in the Pauline letters. In each instance the context becomes the decisive factor in determining its meaning. It can denote simply being alive as a human being ("to remain in the flesh is more necessary for you," 1:24). Or it can designate humanness in its opposition to God, a humanness that ignores the presence of the Spirit (e.g., 1 Cor 15:50; 2 Cor 5:16; 11:18). At times, "flesh" even takes on an independent existence, a quasi-personal power to which one can orient his or her life, such as in the sentence, "To set the mind on the flesh is death" (Rom 8:6). While the "flesh" is not inherently evil, it becomes the occasion for sin, and a list of sins can be called "works of the flesh" (Gal 5:19-21). Bultmann makes a careful distinction when he says that "flesh" can denote the stage or possibilities for people's lives (as in 1:24) or it can become the determinative norm according to which people orient their lives and presume to discover meaning. While the former meaning has no evil connotations, the latter is the essence of sinful self-delusion (Bultmann 1952, 1:239).

"Flesh" often serves as a useful term in the letters, especially when the issue of circumcision is either in the forefront or lurking in the background of an argument (e.g., Gal 3:3; 6:12). To say in contrast to "the dogs" (the victims of a pun on circumcision) that we "have no confidence in the flesh" means that for the Gentile Christian community, circumcision carries no compelling legitimacy as a religious symbol. It commands no allegiance and can set no boundaries.

In 3:3-4 the elasticity of the term "flesh" becomes obvious. In 3:3 it designates the rite of circumcision, but in 3:4 is stretched to include not only circumcision, but a much longer list of religious credentials. In the following verses (3:4-11) Paul gives the reasons why he finds them inadequate.

A Positive Model: Paul
(3:4b-11)

In 3:5-6 Paul lists his credentials, first those inherited (3:5a-d) and then those achieved (3:5e-6). He can claim circumcision, even in the precise manner specified by the law, a characteristic highly valued by "the dogs." He is an Israelite by birth, from a preferred tribe, who speaks Aramaic as his native tongue. He chose to be a Pharisee (the only time this term is mentioned in the letters). His zeal for his religious traditions led him to harass the church. By the law's standard of righteousness, he was without reproach. In a remarkably matter-of-fact fashion, Paul depicts himself not as an outsider, but as a loyal Jew, both by heritage and by accomplishments.

The shift occurs at 3:7 with startling abruptness.

> Yet whatever for me were assets, these things I have counted as loss because of Christ; and what's more, I am counting all things as loss because of the surpassing value of knowing Christ Jesus my Lord. Because of him I have sustained the loss of all things and am counting them as rubbish, in order that I may gain Christ and be found incorporated into him, with no righteousness of my own, a righteousness based on law; rather with the righteousness that comes through the faith(fulness) of Christ, a righteousness from God based on faith. What I want is to know Christ, the power of his resurrection and the participation in his sufferings, by being conformed to his death, if only I may attain the resurrection of the dead.

Several aspects of this remarkable paragraph warrant comment. First, Paul uses strong language to describe how he feels about his heritage and his days as a Pharisee ("loss," "rubbish"). It has led some interpreters to the conclusion that he rejects his past, undergoing a 180-degree change that involves turning his back on Judaism. It is significant, however, that the controlling language in this text comes from the world of bookkeeping. What once were valued as assets are now written off as losses. There is no hint that the past is regretted, as if it were sinful and something about which to repent. Even his persecution of the church was the result of religious zeal. Stowers comments, "Paul's narrative no more regards his past Jewish life as worthless than the exalted prerogatives that Christ gave up should be regarded as worthless. Rather, the first pales in comparison with the second" (Stowers 1991, 120).

Of course, Paul's past is reassessed. The verb *ēgeomai* ("count," regard") occurs three times in the paragraph (3:7, 8 [twice]). "Paul characterizes this change in his life as a matter of change in perception—a cognitive shift" (Gaventa 1986, 33). What has occurred is a transformation in the way value is assigned, what matters and what does not matter. The rhetorical effect is to invite the readers to a similar reevaluation of all claims of any kind.

If recognition is at the heart of Paul's transformation, then we should be cautious about too easily applying the word "conversion" to what is described in 3:4-11. The story does not relate a conversion in the sense that Paul changes religions from Judaism to Christianity, as one might "convert" today from being a Methodist to being a Muslim. He still worships the God of Abraham and Sarah and still counts himself a Jew (2 Cor 11:22). In this text, what has been transformed is Paul's *perception* of his past and present.

In addition to the strong language used in 3:7, this passage is highly christocentric in content. The experience of Christ turns out to be the substance of Paul's transformation. Expressions such as "gain Christ," "know Christ," and "be found incorporated into Christ" are frequent throughout the passage, expressing both the cause and goal of Paul's altered perception. Being incorporated into Christ now determines Paul's self-understanding.

This christocentric emphasis sheds light on the translation of the notoriously ambiguous phrase in 3:9 *dia pisteōs christou*. The NRSV renders it "through faith *in* Christ," but also provides a marginal translation "through the faith *of* Christ." Is "Christ" the object of faith ("faith in Christ"), or does the phrase designate Christ's own faith (or faithfulness)? Most modern translations, unlike the KJV, translate it "faith in Christ" with the implication that the faith referred to is a human's trust in Christ.

In recent years, however, the expression has been the topic of much research, and an increasing number of scholars are now inclined to translate the phrase "faith [or faithfulness] of Christ." (Among others, see Hays 1983; Williams 1987, 431-447; and Hooker 1990 "Pistis Christou," 88-100.) Syntactical arguments on either side of the debate tend to be inconclusive, with the result that the fundamental question comes to be whether in this particular context it makes more sense to read Paul as pitting one human activity (doing the stipulations of the law) against another human activity (believing) or to interpret him as pitting a human activity (doing the stipulations of the law) against a divine activity (Christ's faithful obedience). In 3:9, where the contrast is drawn between two kinds of righteousness, the issue is not human works versus human faith, but an identity grounded in the law versus an identity grounded in Christ. In light of the christocentric emphasis of the paragraph (in addition to the avoiding of redundancy with the phrase "based on faith"), the rendering "faith [faithfulness] of Christ" makes more sense. The expression becomes something of a shorthand reference back to the statement in the hymn that Christ "became obedient to the point of death, even death on a cross" (2:8).

Running through the paragraph is an epistemological issue expressed in the phrase "the surpassing value of *knowing* Christ Jesus my Lord" (3:8). How does one *know* Christ? In 3:10-11 the answer comes in an effective chiasm. One knows Christ by knowing

A the power of his resurrection
   B the sharing of his sufferings
   B' by becoming like him in his death,
A' if somehow I may attain the resurrection of the dead.

Knowing Christ is not a matter of acquiring more adequate information about his life nor is it a question of developing a proper attitude toward him. The primary locus of knowledge here is neither the brain nor the emotions. Instead, the knowledge of Christ is spelled out in terms of *participation* in Christ. The present participle ("by becoming like him") suggests continuous conformity to the crucified Christ, confirmed in baptism, and lived out by "constantly bearing in the body the death of Jesus" (2 Cor 4:10). Knowing Christ, then, does not involve merely a single faculty of perception, but the whole person and comes to expression not in books but in the deep engagements of life.

This affirmation of knowing Christ fits with what we have seen to be the broad intent of the letter, namely to mold in the community a practical reasoning that is distinctively Christian, a reasoning that can then result in unity, humility, and courage in moments of oppression. The readers learn from Paul's autobiography that adopting "the mind that was in Christ" entails the conformity of life to Christ's death, in anticipation of the resurrection of the dead.

Behind 3:10 lies the Pauline notion that in his death and resurrection Christ acted as a representative person and that in baptism believers declare their inclusion with Christ in these events (cf. Rom 6:1-11). The life of faith then takes a cruciform shape, particularly when, in obedience to the gospel, the community finds itself beleaguered and under oppression. Such moments become occasions for participation in Christ's sufferings (cf. Gal 6:12-14; 2 Cor 4:7-12).

In light of the Pauline notion of Christ as a representative figure, two readings of 3:10 need to be avoided. First, though mystical language is used in the text, what is being proposed is not a purely meditative reliving of Christ's passion. The focus is rather on a participation with Christ in the midst of real-life sufferings and struggles. Second, the text does not imply that martyrdom is something to be sought on the promise of full and complete knowledge of Christ (so Lohmeyer 1953, 139). Martyrdom probably came for Paul, but it did so as he served the cause of the gospel, not because he sought martyrdom.

Finally, verses 10-11 also reflect the pattern of the Christ-hymn, especially 2:8. As with the examples of Timothy and Epaphroditus, the hymn presents the primary exemplar in a way that generates the language and motifs that recur in the other examples in the letter. Paul does not tell his story in order to share with the readers some otherwise unknown information about his life, or to strengthen the intimate bond between them, or to advertise his own piety. His story is subordinated to the story of Christ. "The 'little story' of Paul's life finds meaning by being related to the 'big story' of which the organizing center is Christ" (Beardslee 1975, 306-307).

Life Between the "Already" and the "Not Yet"
(3:12-14)

The autobiographical section of 3:4-11 is continued in a telling reflection on how Paul understands the present (3:12-14). The mention of "the resurrection of the dead" in 3:11 sparks the disclaimer in 3:12 that the resurrection has already been achieved. Paul has not yet obtained it nor has he reached the goal toward which he is oriented. He has been united with Christ in his death, but he awaits the resurrection of the dead (cf. Rom 6:1-11; 1 Cor 15:20-28). In a play on words, Paul declares that he presses on to "take hold of" that for which he has "been taken hold of" by Christ.

Some interpreters have contended that there is a polemical edge to 3:12, aimed at a group of persons either in Philippi or the surrounding area who assume that they have arrived at the goal, that they already now possess a kind of heaven on earth. It could be that these are the people Paul has in mind when he writes in 3:15 of those who "think differently." Such groups can be found in other Hellenistic congregations (Corinth) and could be in Philippi as well (cf. Koester 1961-62, 317-332; Lincoln 1981, 93-95).

More important than deciding this issue, however, is the recognition of Paul's eschatology in the passage. The "already" that Paul can affirm now is the knowledge of Christ found in sharing his sufferings and in conformity to his death. Christ has already made Paul his own. At the same time, Paul eagerly awaits resurrection with Christ when the knowledge of Christ will be consummated: there is a "not yet" in his faith. "Now I know only in part; then I will know fully, even as I have been fully known" (1 Cor 13:12b). Life in the present is lived between the "already" and the "not yet," between the "now" and the "then."

Following a direct address (actually "brothers and sisters" and not "beloved" [NRSV]), Paul introduces the metaphor of the athlete, which provides the structure for 3:13-14. Between the "already" and the "not yet," the apostle compares himself with a runner whose concentration is focused exclusively on the tape at the end of the race. (It is important to note that the metaphor does not suggest in any way competition. This is not a race in which someone wins and others lose.) What lies behind (what he has already reckoned as "loss") cannot distract him. His orientation is eagerly toward the future—toward the upward calling of God in Christ. The prize is not a surprise, but a confirmation of the divine calling already received and followed in this life (cf. Rom 11:29; 1 Cor 1:26; 7:20). As Barth put it, "He [Paul] is called. To be true to this calling is both his task and his reward" (Barth 1962, 109). The specification of the calling as "upward" anticipates the depiction of the church as a community whose "citizenship is in heaven" (3:20).

Exhortation to Follow Paul's Example
(3:15-17)

In the next section (3:15-17) Paul makes it clear that his story should be read as an example to follow. Modern readers tend to bristle at the arrogance of one who openly says, "Do as I do." But two things have to be kept in mind. In the first place, we should remember the historical setting of the Philippian congregation, as a new community, without clear precedents, whose members needed a variety of models to provide guidance for their faith and life.

Secondly, we should remember the expectation in the ancient world that
pupils would imitate their teachers. Dio Chrysostom, reflecting on the
relation of Socrates to Homer, wrote:

> Whoever really follows anyone surely knows what that person was like, and
> by imitating his acts and words, he tries as best he can to make himself like
> him. But that is precisely, it seems, what the pupil does—by imitating his
> teacher and paying heed to him he tries to acquire his art. (*Discourse* 55. 4,
> 5; cf. De Boer 1962; Kurz 1985, 103-126; Best 1988, 59-72)

While it is clear that Paul invites his audience to read his story as exemplary, it is not so clear what the tone and details of his invitation are. For
example, is there a polemic in these verses (especially 3:15-16)? Do they
assume a group in Philippi that is antagonistic toward Paul's point of view
(or toward whom Paul is antagonistic)? If so, then the statement "God will
reveal this to you" might be read more sharply as "I am confident God will
set you straight on this." Or do the verses address individual readers, providing room for those who are at different places in their personal pilgrimages?
In this case, the text should not be read as coercive of those who differ from
Paul's perspective, but rather as leaving space for God to guide each person
in his or her individual life. Or does the text address the community as a
whole and assume a commonality between writer and readers? "As mature
Christians, let us follow a mature way of reasoning; and if any among you
hold misguided notions, God will help you see the truth about them."

Three brief observations are significant in adjudicating such readings.
First, in his letters Paul regularly uses in an inclusive rather than a partitive
way the Greek relative pronoun *hosoi*, translated "those of us who are" in
3:15. The pronoun does not normally separate individuals within a group,
but addresses them collectively (e.g., Rom 6:3; 8:14; Gal 3:27). Thus it does
not appear that he is distinguishing between mature and immature readers.

Second, the letter as a whole is concerned with the community and its
common life. Nowhere does Paul address the spiritual progress of individual
readers, and it would be strange to find such in 3:15-16. Third, there is
nothing in the letter to suggest that the Philippian community was in any
way sharply divided. It is thus hard to find a polemical edge to these verses.
Instead, the text invites the readers (whom Paul deems to be already
"mature") to share the same reasoning he has advocated in his autobiographical reflections. While there may be differences among them, all are to
continue to live according to what (or better, to whom) they have already
committed themselves. (See further Caird 1976, 143-144.)

Thus far in the letter Paul has pointed to Christ (2:5-11) and, by association, also Timothy and Epaphroditus (2:19-30) as a paradigm for the readers (2:5-11). It is clear from the relevant passages what is exemplary about each. The intent in 3:4-17 is the same as with the others: to develop a moral reasoning in the community that will enable believers to live faithfully in the midst of opposition. (Note the same imperative in 3:15 that is used to introduce the Christ-hymn in 2:5, *phroneite.*)

Paul's story, however, is much longer than the stories of Christ, Timothy, and Epaphroditus. What in his autobiography is to inform the mind of the readers? What precisely is "the example you have in us" (3:17)? Three features of the story stand out. First, knowing Christ has become the center of Paul's life, and it has made a claim on him that has forced a reassessment of all other claims. Second, knowing Christ happens by participation in his sufferings and death, in the expectation of the resurrection of the dead. Third, knowing Christ fully, however, remains a future orientation, a goal to be aimed at and pressed toward. Paul eagerly awaits the resurrection. In other words, it is not his personal experience nor his conduct that readers are invited to imitate, but his perception of what it means to know Christ.

Despite the first person singular language, the invitation to imitation itself turns out to be inclusive in two ways. First, "join in imitating . . .", a highly unusual imperative in Greek, indicates that the imitation is to bind the readers together, to bring them to a common mind. Second, "observe those who live according to the example you have in us" broadens the paradigm to include a number of others, whose stories with Christ parallel Paul's. Paul, Timothy, and Epaphraditus are not the only models to be noted.

A Negative Model: Enemies of the Cross
(3:18-19)

While 3:17 is usually treated in connection with 3:15-16 because of the common subject matter, modern translators have a good reason for beginning a new paragraph at 3:17. The direct address ("brothers and sisters") signals a fresh departure, and 3:18 introduces (*gar*, "for") yet another example for the readers, but one that sharply contrasts with the example of Paul and his companions. In fact, the depiction of the "enemies of the cross" (3:18-19) serves as a dark backdrop both for the autobiography of Paul (3:4-14) and for the ensuing statement of the church in 3:20-21. Castelli goes so far as to say, "The implication is that those who do not join in imitating Paul are enemies of the cross of Christ" (Castelli 1991, 95-96).

The comparison of antithetical models was a rhetorical exercise practiced in Greco-Roman schools. It is a powerful device because, as Hermogenes noted, it has the effect of amplifying both virtuous deeds and misdeeds (cf. Marshall 1987, 53-54). The reactions to Paul's imprisonment in 1:15-18 are good illustrations. Setting the two groups in sharp contrast heightens the selfish ambitions of the one group as well as the good will of the other.

Several qualities characterize this negative model in 3:18-19:

- enemies of the cross
- their end is destruction
- their god is the belly
- their glory is in their shame
- they mind (*phronountes*) earthly things

Since the descriptions are rather imprecise, general in scope and evocative in effect, it is difficult to identify this group with other groups mentioned in this or in other Pauline letters. That Paul has repeatedly told and is telling again the readers about the group may even suggest a location other than Philippi. The label "enemies of the cross" hints at a connection with groups in Corinth (1 Cor 1:10–2:5) or Galatia (Gal 6:12), but either connection is tenuous. No doubt the group has created anguish and frustration for the apostle since he mentions them with "tears." The most particular feature of the description is the statement "their god is the belly"; however, "belly" can be construed as a metonym either for self-indulgence and an unbridled appetite or for the opposite, a preoccupation with regulations about eating and drinking. As in the case with the group in 3:2, the purpose of including the "enemies of the cross" in the letter is not to warn the readers of an imminent threat, but to present a model to be avoided, an example of how not to let their minds be shaped.

The connections with other paradigms in the letter are striking. While this group is depicted as "enemies of the cross," Christ is obedient unto death on the cross (2:8); Epaphroditus comes close to death for the work of Christ (2:30); and Paul seeks to share Christ's sufferings and to be conformed to his death (3:10). But by contrast for this group the end is destruction, whereas Christ's end is universal lordship (2:9-11); and Paul's goal is the upward calling of God in Christ (3:14). Finally, the "mind" of this group is oriented toward earthly things, whereas the community's mind is to be shaped by Christ's story (2:5) and by Paul's story (3:15).

A Positive Model: Heavenly Commonwealth
(3:20-31)

Not only do the "enemies of the cross" function rhetorically as a foil for Paul's story, but they also form the background for the statements about the Christian community in 3:20-21. Whereas they focus on earthly things, "our citizenship is in heaven"; whereas their end is destruction, our end is "the body of his [Christ's] glory." The eschatological depiction of the church stands out against the noneschatological focus of the negative model.

Several features of this eschatological depiction are significant. First, the Greek term rendered "citizenship" or "commonwealth" binds the text closely to 1:27 ("live as citizens worthy of the gospel of Christ"). Both texts are particularly appropriate to a Philippian audience, people who would have cherished their own Roman citizenship. Citizenship in Rome and citizenship in heaven would not be mutually exclusive, but the latter in many circumstances could become subversive of the former. "Heaven" is the locus of citizenship, because the Lord Jesus Christ is there.

Second, the current situation of the community is that it "awaits" the Savior. The Greek verb is used six times in the Pauline letters (Rom 8:19, 23, 25; 1 Cor 1:7; Gal 5:5; Phil 3:20), each time carrying the notion of an eager expectation. The community "awaits" the return of Christ, not in passive resignation, but in engaged and hopeful anticipation.

Third, the coming of Christ will produce a transformation of the body, from humiliation to glory. The motif of bodily continuity but future change is consistent with Paul's extensive discussions in 1 Cor 15:35-57 and 2 Cor 4:16–5:10. And yet here the context is more corporate than individual (despite the NIV, that erroneously translates "body" as if it were plural). A single event is envisioned: the coming of the Savior to earth, not the separate deaths and transformations of individuals.

Fourth, the "conformity" to Christ's death in 3:10 is paralleled in 3:21 by "conformity" to the body of his glory. The link reminds the readers again of the eschatological nature of knowing Christ. In the present ("the body of our humiliation"), such knowledge consists of an active participation in and with the crucified Christ. At Christ's return, however, complete knowledge will involve new life in conformity to his glory.

Fifth, the statement concludes with Christ's universal authority that brings all things into subjection. The parallel with the Christ-hymn is obvious (2:9-11), not only in the submission of all things to Christ but also in the particular titles used in both passages, "Lord Jesus Christ."

Some commentators have found in 3:20-21 a pre-Pauline hymn or creedal fragment of six lines. In 3:21 there are several striking parallel expressions. The term "Savior" occurs only here among the undisputed letters of Paul. In addition, there are numerous linguistic connections between 3:20-21 and the hymn in 2:6-11, suggesting that the letter contains two separate hymns coming from the same tradition or from the same conceptual context in early Christianity. Certainly the linguistic correspondence between the two passages is impressive. Lincoln isolates nine Greek expressions from 3:20-21 that are paralleled in 2:6-11.

But Lincoln makes a persuasive case against the presence of a pre-Pauline hymn in 3:20-21. As we have already seen several times, the language of 2:5-11 is employed widely in the letter, and there is good reason to suppose that in 3:20-21 Paul has drawn on 2:5-11 again. It is more likely that the Christ-hymn serves as a linguistic model for the statement about the church than that the apostle quotes two separate hymns with such strong verbal connections. In drawing from 2:5-11, Paul implies that the pattern of the church's life should reflect the pattern of Christ's career as expressed in the hymn. (For an argument in favor of 3:20-21 as a pre-Pauline hymn, see Reumann 1984, 593-609; for an argument against such a hymn, see Lincoln 1981, 87-89; cf. also Hooker *Adam* 1990, 20-22).

Three Exhortations
(4:1-3)

The larger section (3:1–4:3) closes by returning to specific exhortations that are now undergirded by positive and negative models. The conjunction that introduces the injunctions (*ōste*, "therefore") indicates the close link intended between the models and the exhortations. The latter are not merely tacked on at the end; they spring from the models themselves and from the invitation to the readers to imitate the models.

The first exhortation ("stand firm," 4:1; cf. 1:27) is surrounded by affectionate expressions of Paul's close relationship to the readers, reminiscent of the warm and cordial beginning to the letter (1:3-11). While we have repeatedly referred to the literary and social conventions of friendship, there is no reason to question the sincerity of the language, as if it were merely a formality and without substance. The Philippians' history of contributing materially to the Pauline mission undermines any notion that this is only a paper-friendship (cf. 1:7; 4:10-20; 2 Cor 11:9).

The second exhortation ("to be of the same mind," 4:2) is made to Euodia and Syntyche, two women who apparently have leadership roles within the community. Since the same exhortation has also been given to the larger community (2:2), it is likely that their differences have the potential of leading to a wider division. The intriguing part is what is *not* said about these two church members as well as what is said about them. The text relates nothing about the nature of their differences (whether personal or theological), nor does it suggest that the point of view of one is to be favored over the other (though the letter may address the issues dividing the two without modern readers being able to detect it). They are both treated as responsible persons within the community.

What *is* said about the two women is highly laudable. "They have struggled beside me in the work of the gospel." The athletic metaphor used in 1:27 for the community is now used, specifically in reference to Euodia and Syntyche. They were hands-on workers with the apostle, vulnerable to the same strife and danger, to the same opposition and suffering.

Does this appeal to Euodia and Syntyche to come to a common agreement reveal the real purpose of the letter? Has Paul been building up to this point in order finally to get at a root difficulty in Philippi, namely a conflict between two women that threatens to split the community? Some impressive evidence can be marshaled to argue this case: the unprecedented use of the women's names; the repetition of the unity theme in 1:27; 2:2; and 4:2; the location of the appeal at the end of the body of the letter. And yet 4:2-3 hardly seems to be the climax of the letter. Too many community-oriented issues have been previously addressed (e.g., the renewing of ties of friendship; the need for unity in the face of suffering; the development of a distinctively Christian way of thinking; the working out of the community's "salvation" with fear and trembling; conformity of life to the crucified Christ; the shaping of an identity as a heavenly citizenship). The purpose of the letter can hardly be reduced to this single conflict. One could argue that Euodia and Syntyche had been involved with these larger issues, perhaps as spokespersons for opposite sides, but such a conclusion would at best be speculation. More likely, the women were named because they were leaders, co-workers with Paul, whose differences grieved him and hardly brought honor to the community.

The third exhortation is given to "my loyal companion," who is asked to assist the women in settling their differences (4:3). The direct address is mysterious. Who is this "true comrade"? Is it a person named Syzygos (the transliteration of the Greek word used here)? Is it a reference to the whole congregation (Barth 1962, 120) or to one of Paul's co-workers, such as Timothy (Collange 1979, 143) or Luke (Fee 1995, 394) or Epaphroditus (Lightfoot 1913, 158) or to Paul's wife (so Clement of Alexandria)? Any suggestion is a guess. No doubt Paul's intended audience could decipher the allusion (if it was not a name), even if we cannot.

Echoes of 1:27 can be heard in the language of these exhortations in 4:1-3, bringing to a conclusion the major section of the letter (1:27–4:3). Standing firm, being of one mind, and striving together in the cause of the gospel are the specific ingredients needed in the development of a distinctively Christian mindset in Philippi. As the letter moves to a conclusion, further exhortations will be given to the readers, but they are not so pointedly related (as 1:27–4:3) to the community's responsibility to maintain unity in the presence of fierce opposition.

The Matter of Giving and Receiving

(Philippians 4:4-23)

Following the specific exhortations of 4:2-3, addressed to individuals within the congregation, the Philippian letter comes to an end. Most of the features normally found in the conclusions to the Pauline letters are found in these verses also. Two separate paragraphs of final exhortations (4:4-6, 8-9b), more general than 4:2-3 but still appropriate for the Philippians, are each concluded with a promise of peace (4:7, 9c). Greetings from the writer and those with him to the addressees (4:21-22) are followed by a final benediction (4:23).

What intrudes into this conclusion and immediately grabs the reader's attention is the extensive reflection on the Philippians' gifts to Paul (4:10-20), a section that has vexed interpreters because of both its location in the letter and its tone (so much so that many have taken it to be a separate letter). Following the proposal of recent interpreters, we will argue that the thanksgiving plays a critical role in the letter as a final expression of the friendship between the apostle and the Philippians, now expressed concretely in terms of gifts given and received. When seen in light of the social conventions of the first century, the section turns out not to be a "thankless thanks" but another indication of the warm and intimate ties between writer and readers.

The conclusion of the letter then has the following structure:

final exhortations	(4:4-6)
peace wish	(4:7)
continued exhortations	(4:8-9b)
peace wish	(4:9c)
the matter of giving and receiving	(4:10-20)
greetings	(4:21-22)
benediction	(4:23)

Final Exhortations
(4:4-6)

The first set of exhortations (4:4-6) differs both from those that immediately precede them (4:2-3) and those that follow (4:8-9). They are less specific than the words spoken directly to Euodia, Syntyche, and "loyal companion" and contain a miscellaneous collection of four independent exhortations ("rejoice," "let your gentleness be known," "do not worry," and "let your requests be made known to God") and one affirmation ("the Lord is near"). Except in the latter two exhortations that are juxtaposed with "but," no conjunctions appear to connect the parts of the section. On the other hand, the exhortations that follow in 4:8-9 are much more smoothly linked and rhetorically structured.

Despite their miscellaneous nature, the exhortations in 4:4-6 are very appropriate to the letter that has preceded them. Rejoicing is a note heard repeatedly throughout the letter (1:3, 25; 2:2, 17-18, 28-29; 3:1; 4:1, 4, 10). "Gentleness" (either in the sense of "generosity," "largeness of spirit" or "meekness," "gentle forbearance") is needed by a congregation threatened with possible conflict. Prayer as an antidote to worry is a fitting word for a community undergoing opposition and suffering. The statement made in the midst of the exhortations ("the Lord is near") keeps before the reader the eschatological thrust of the letter.

"Rejoice in the Lord Always"
(4:4)

Three features characterize the repeated emphasis on joy in this letter. First, joy is highly paradoxical. It appears where it is least expected—often amid suffering and trial. Paul explains this paradox in Rom 5:1-5, but it is abundantly clear in Philippians, where the audience is threatened with persecution and the writer is in prison. As Calvin wrote, "It is a rare virtue that when Satan endeavors to irritate us by the bitterness of the cross, so as to make God's name unpleasant to us, we rest in the taste of God's grace alone, so that all annoyances, sorrows, anxieties, and griefs are sweetened" (Calvin 1965, 267).

Second, joy is eschatological. Often used in conjunction with hope (e.g., Rom 12:12; 15:13), joy is "the Christian's relatedness to the future" (Bultmann 1952, 339). As those whose "citizenship is in heaven" (3:20) and for whom "the Lord is near" (4:5), the readers have reason to rejoice.

Third, joy entails mutuality. It is the experience of shared delight and deep pleasure shared between parties (as in 2:17-18). The phrase "in the Lord" (4:1, 2, 4) carries ecclesial as well as christological overtones.

"The Lord Is Near"
(4:5b)

"The Lord is near" (4:5b) provides a theological undergirding for the first paragraph of exhortations. The word "near" is open to either a spatial or a temporal reading. The former would reflect the language of such psalms as 34:18 and145:18 that speak of God's presence to those who are broken-hearted and who call upon God. The context of the letter, with its strong eschatological emphasis, however, makes the temporal reading more proba-ble. The coming of the Lord Jesus Christ, whom the community eagerly awaits (3:20), is not far off, and necessitates the future orientation expressed in the apostle's autobiography ("straining forward to what lies ahead," press-ing on "toward the goal for the prize of the heavenly call of God in Christ Jesus" [3:12-14]).

In light of the imminence of the Lord's coming, members of the com-munity are told that they do not have to bear the burdens of the world and its future alone. In prayer their burdens can be left in divine hands. Heavy anxieties can be countered only by an openness to God, in which believers acknowledge that from beginning to end life is a gift and that gratitude is the appropriate mood for asking and receiving. "Thanksgiving for past benefits is the surest road to confidence in future ones" (Caird 1976, 151).

Peace Wish
(4:7)

The first paragraph of exhortations concludes with the first of the two promises of peace (4:7). A study of the Pauline letters indicates that a peace-wish is a regular feature of the conclusions (Rom 15:33; 2 Cor 13:11; Gal 6:16; Phil 4:7, 9; 1 Thess 5:23). Most likely Paul is following the practice of Semitic letter writing in which the farewell wish ("Shalom") is the most common formula. In Paul's letters it serves to close the correspondence and to express concern for the spiritual well-being of the audience (see Weima 1994, 99-100).

The conventional form of the peace wish, however, should not cause us to miss two claims Paul makes about God's gift of peace. First, it transcends human understanding. In a letter that seeks to shape the practical reasoning of the readers and that in the next verse urges a meditation on certain virtues ("think about these things"), it is a bit surprising to find God's peace depicted as a reality above and beyond human reasoning. Second, the function of God's peace is to "guard your hearts and your minds in Christ Jesus." Like a sentinel who keeps watch at his post, the divine shalom protects both the willing and thinking faculties of God's people. More than a mere convention, this first promise of peace in 4:7 turns out to be a comforting word for a community struggling to work out its own salvation in fear and trembling.

Continued Exhortations
(4:8-9)

Unlike the miscellaneous collection in the first paragraph, the second paragraph of exhortations (4:8-9) is presented in a more eloquent and forceful form.

> whatever is true,
> whatever is honorable,
> whatever is just,
> whatever is pure,
> whatever is lovely,
> whatever is commendable,
> > if there is any virtue and
> > if there is anything worthy of praise,
> > > think about these things. (4:8)

> what things you have learned, and
> > you have received, and
> > you have heard, and
> > you have seen in me,
> > > do these things. (4:9)

In 4:8 six virtues, introduced by a similar "whatever," are listed, followed by two conditional clauses and a present imperative ("think about these things"). In 4:9 four verbs are listed and then followed by a present imperative ("keep on doing these things"). The paralleling of the two imperatives indicates that the two verses should be read together.

The six virtues listed in 4:8 are the stock-in-trade of Hellenistic moralists and in no way represent peculiarly Jewish or Christian virtues. Yet the readers are told to meditate on them, to persist in making them the object of reflection. The writer implicitly recognizes that there is much of value in pagan culture, and the community is urged to learn from it. But in 4:9 Paul calls attention to the distinctively Christian teaching, tradition, spoken word, and example he has set before the readers. Included is another invitation to follow the example of the apostle himself (see the discussion at 3:15-17). Thinking and doing are the complementary activities asked of the audience. The paragraph concludes with another peace wish, this time in more conventional wording (i.e., "the God of peace" rather than "the peace of God").

Giving and Receiving
(4:10-20)

In 4:10-20 Paul acknowledges the gifts given to him by the Philippians, both the most recent one brought by Epaphroditus (4:10) and earlier ones, probably when he was in Corinth (2 Cor 11:7-9), certainly when he was in Thessalonica (4:16). The question is often raised why this expression of thanks comes so late in the letter? The question ignores the fact that the giving of the Philippian congregation has already been acknowledged at the beginning of the letter (1:5-7) and in connection with the return of Epaphroditus (2:25-30). What is said in this section is a follow-up of previous references. Fee rightly argues that instead of being a thoughtless delay of gratitude, the repetition of thanks at the end of the letter is "rhetoric at its best." Readers (or better hearers, since the letter would have been read aloud in the community) would come away remembering Paul's gratitude for "the gifts you sent, a fragrant offering, a sacrifice acceptable and pleasing to God," coupled with the promise of God's rich blessings (4:18-19; Fee 1995, 423).

The tone, as well as the location, of the thanksgiving has also been a cause for concern. The passage has sometimes been read as a begrudging expression of gratitude, since Paul plays down his need (4:11-13) and makes it clear that he did not seek the gifts (4:17). Caird (1976, 152) has suggested that Paul faces a delicate situation. On the one hand, he wants to express his gratitude since he knows the real cost to the Philippians in making the gifts (cf. 2 Cor 8:1-6). On the other hand, if he overdoes the gratitude, they may think he is in worse straits than he is and feel guilty for not helping him sooner or with a more generous gift. With sensitivity, he steers his way through the traps of a "thank-you" note saying enough but not too much, expressing genuine gratitude but not asking for more.

A more likely explanation for the seemingly enigmatic expression of thanks, however, lies in the ancient social conventions of friendship. In the Greco-Roman culture the exchange of gifts was essential to friendship. While it was morally commendable to give without seeking a return, the one who benefited was under a heavy responsibility to reciprocate with the equivalent, if not more than was received. Aristotle even counseled that one ought not to make friends with a person unless he or she were willing to return the friend's favors (*Nicomachean Ethics* 8. xiii. 9).

The language used in Philippians ("no church *shared* with me i*n the matter of giving and receiving*, except you alone," 4:15) is characteristic of a genuine friendship and reflects the close bonds between the two parties. The commercial expression in 4:18 ("I have been paid in full") is Paul's acknowledgment that the Philippians have done more than their share "in the matter of giving and receiving" and that he now has a responsibility to them, a responsibility he will have to entrust to God to discharge (4:19). The mention of God in connection with the satisfying of Paul's obligations to the Philippians is highly appropriate, since their gift to him was "acceptable and pleasing to God" (4:18). Marshall rightly concludes,

> Paul then is drawing upon familiar notions of friendship to acknowledge the recent gift and to express his gratitude. Rather than pointing to tension or embarrassment on Paul's part over the gift, the language implies the opposite. It reflects a warm and lasting relationship. He not only receives the gift gladly as a sign of their continuing concern, but also recalls the mutual exchange of services and affection which they had shared in the past. Though he himself cannot reciprocate in kind, he is confident that God would more than make good the gift out of, and in a manner befitting, his boundless wealth in Christ Jesus. (v. 19) (1987, 163-164; cf. also 1-18)

Two further features of this expression of gratitude need to be noted. First, the passage begins with a return to the theme of joy ("I rejoice," 4:10; cf. 1:4, 25; 2:2, 17-18; 3:1; 4:1, 4). A number of other verbs could have been used to introduce this expression of gratitude. The reiteration of joy, however, reminds the reader of the close relationship between Paul and the Philippians (and the Lord). His delight focuses on the warm and friendly ties that bind him to his partners in ministry, who have repeatedly shared in his mission.

Second, reflecting on his own life, Paul makes the striking comment, "I have learned to be content with whatever I have" (4:11) and follows this with specific examples (4:12). The word translated "content" (*autarkēs*) is widely used by Greek philosophers, particularly the Stoics, to denote a self-sufficiency, an inner freedom not dependent on the ups and downs of life. Seneca wrote, "The wise man is sufficient unto himself for a happy existence" (*Ad Lucilium Epistulae Morales*, ix.13). Whether Paul borrowed the term from the philosophers or whether it was already in common use, in either case it serves to express a remarkable confession of faith. Verse 13 roots Paul's contentment in Christ, rather than in his ability to transcend the vicissitudes he encounters. In turn, the "all things" that can be accomplished in Christ (4:13) do not refer to extraordinary feats, but to the circumstances Paul encounters in the activity of ministry—to plenty and want, prosperity and need.

Greetings
(4:21-22)

The concluding greetings (4:21-22) broaden the ties of friendship beyond Paul and the Philippians. "Every saint in Christ" is greeted, and "the brothers and sisters" with Paul share in sending their regards. Paul includes specifically "those of the imperial household" state officials, soldiers, freed people and slaves, who were attached to the imperial staff at the place of Paul's imprisonment. Whether the reference in 4:22 specifically denotes the socially higher officers or the slaves or some combination of all the groups is impossible to determine. It may be that the special mention of this governmental group is intended to build bridges with similar groups in the Roman colony of Philippi. In any case, the Christian message has begun to reach people around Paul, providing further proof that his imprisonment has in reality turned out for the progress of the gospel (1:12).

1 Thessalonians

Introduction

The Letter

First Thessalonians is a gem often ignored by readers of the New Testament. Overshadowed by the so-called "chief epistles" of Paul (Romans, 1 and 2 Corinthians, and Galatians) with their trenchant theology and their lengthy arguments, 1 Thessalonians represents a remarkable model of pastoral sensitivity and church support. Readers are given a glimpse into an early congregation whose circumstances are much different from that of problem-plagued Corinth or from the struggling communities in the area of Galatia. The believers in Thessalonica have been tested and found trustworthy (1:5); they are commended as an example to others (1:7); they are encouraged to keep on living and loving in the way they have begun (4:9-10).

Furthermore, since 1 Thessalonians is the earliest letter written by Paul, the first theologian of the early church, it represents what Koester has called "an experiment in Christian writing" (Koester 1979, 33-44). To the best of our knowledge, Paul had no Christian predecessor as letter-writer, no model for adapting and transforming the existing patterns of the Greco-Roman letter-form, no established *literary* vocabulary on which to draw. First Thessalonians breaks new ground and becomes the first in a line of letters written by Paul or in his name to sustain and instruct the congregations he has founded.

In an initial reading of the letter one is struck by at least four features. One is Paul's positive and affirming tone in writng to the Thessalonians. Nothing negative is said or implied about the addressees. Paul's attitude is epitomized in his response to the good report brought by Timothy: "How can we thank God enough for you in return for all the joy we feel before our God because of you?" (3:9; NRSV). Second is the clarification Paul gives about his earlier apostolic ministry in Thessalonica, that they did not come to deceive or exploit the Thessalonians (2:1-13). Third are the exhortations throughout the letter, but especially in 4:1-12 (and 5:12-14), to live so as to please God. Finally, there is the attention given to questions raised by the Thessalonians about the return of Jesus and the place of the already deceased in the final ingathering (4:13–5:11).

In light of these impressions, what kind of letter is 1 Thessalonians? Identifying its type is another way of discovering the writer's aim and purpose, a critical step in interpretation. The fact that two documents, somewhat later than Paul, mention as many as twenty-one (*Pseudo Demetrius*) and forty-one (*Pseudo Libanius*) types of epistolary creations, however, makes one cautious in putting a precise label on this first Christian letter. The categories used in designating letters tend to overlap, and many letters are obviously written to achieve more than one objective.

Moreover, many commentators in analyzing the letter prefer to use the categories drawn from ancient rhetoric rather than those of epistolary theory. Questions such as how much epistolary theory was included in the rhetorical instruction in the ancient world and how broadly rhetorical practices were employed in letter writing are widely debated. Both sets of interpreters, however, in making their categorizations are attempting to discover the letter's purpose, what aims it seeks to accomplish. We note three influential proposals.

First, reading 2:1-12 (and particularly reading between the lines) leads to the suspicion that Paul was under attack in Thessalonica from a group insinuating that he was a renegade, and that he "like many a pagan itinerant preacher, was self-deluded, sensual, and deceiving, delivering his message in flattering words as a foil to cover selfish greed and requiring honour to be paid him" (Frame 1912, 90). Thus, according to Frame, the letter (especially chapters 1–3) was written as a defense of Paul's motives and methods in preaching the gospel. It takes the form of an apology (one of the twenty-one types mentioned in *Pseudo Demetrius*), in which Paul reflects on his relations with his readers, their response to his preaching, and the genuineness of both his intentions and actions. Then having argued his case in the first half of the letter, Paul in the final two chapters addresses the difficulties of the weak, the idlers, and the fainthearted in the Thessalonian community. The exhortations, however, are somewhat incidental to the defense, which is the primary reason for writing.

A critique of the letter when understood as an apology can be found in the commentary at 2:1-12. Suffice it here to say that many of the statements that have been read as a defense are typical of ones found in contemporary moral philosophers. Writers, such as Seneca, Epictetus, and Dio Chrysostom, were careful to distinguish themselves from competing charlatans, who addressed their audiences with excessive flattery and sought financial gain. Paul uses conventions and styles similar to those found in the philosophers. He seems not so much to defend himself as to set the apostolic ministry in Thessalonica apart from the efforts of other unscrupulous teachers, who competed for the ears and pocketbooks of the audience.

Second, Malherbe has argued that 1 Thessalonians should be taken as a paraenetic letter (one of the types mentioned in *Pseudo Libanius*). While there is general agreement that chapters 4–5 have a definite function as exhortation, Malherbe has made the case that chapters 1–3 exhibit a number of features characteristic of the paraenetic writings of Greco-Roman moral philosophers. Specifically, in the first half of the letter Paul lays a foundation for the particular advice that comes in the second half. For example, a paraenetic intent can be found in the imitation motif in 1:6; 2:14; in the theme of remembrance of what the readers already know (1:6; 2:1, 5, 9, 11; 3:3); and in Paul's repeated praise of the readers (1:2, 6-8; 3:6-9). Establishing a close relationship between writer and recipients prepares the way for the exhortations that come later (Malherbe 1992, 287-293; 1983, 238-256).

Third, while not opposing Malherbe's designation of 1 Thessalonians as paraenesis or exhortation, Olbricht has offered an analysis of the letter employing an Aristotelian methodology. Aristotle, he suggests, understood rhetoric more as an art than an exact science and never dissuaded others from building on his foundations or from adding fresh categories. In light of his analysis, Olbricht concludes that Thessalonians is a distinctive form of church rhetoric, with a genre he labels *reconfirmational.*

> It might be said that Paul's purpose in the letter was to do precisely what he said he did when he was there "encouraging, comforting, and urging you to lead lives worthy of God" (2:12), which was likewise the reason he sent Timothy "to strengthen and encourage you" (3:2) and the reason behind the charge to the Thessalonians: "Therefore encourage one another and build up each other, just as in fact you are doing" (5:11). (Olbricht 1990, 227; Gaventa follows Olbricht, but prefers the terms "consolidation" or "upbuilding" to "reconfirmation." Gaventa 1998, 5-7)

The proposals of Malherbe and Olbright stand close together. Both reject the notion that the letter is a defense against accusations leveled at the apostle. Both recognize the positive, affirming approach of Paul in addressing his readers (as contrasted with the more confrontational posture Paul takes toward the Galatians). The primary way in which Olbricht has supplemented Malherbe's analysis is in the reminder that Paul's exhortations in the letter are in the service of confirming the Thessalonians and of corroborating the direction in which they are already moving as a Christian community. The parenthetical comment in 4:1 is particularly instructive: "We ask and urge you in the Lord Jesus, that, as you learned from us how you ought to please God (as, in fact, you are doing), you should do so more and more (NRSV)."

Integrity of the Letter

One of the unusual features of 1 Thessalonians is that its appears to contain two prayers of thanksgiving. The conventional one follows the salutation, celebrating the readers' reception of the gospel and their continued faithfulness in the face of persecution (1:2-10). The second comes in a single verse (2:13), repeating in abbreviated form the tenor and content of the first thanksgiving. This has led to the suggestion by several twentieth-century commentators that 1 Thessalonians in fact contains two letters of Paul, written to the same readers at different stages in their development.

Earl Richard contends that 2:13–4:2 is an early missive, beginning with the second thanksgiving (2:13). It is sent shortly after the apostles' departure from Thessalonica (3:17) and reflects a high degree of anxiety about the readers, their vulnerability as a small group living in a pagan environment, and concern for their survival (2:11-19). Timothy is dispatched to Thessalonica and has returned with good news about their faithfulness and their mutual affection for Paul (3:6). This letter of encouragement then is sent, focusing on Paul's desire to be there, his pain at separation, and his acknowledgment that his own work can only be measured by the communities he has founded (2:19). It should be noted that Richard takes 2:14-16 as an interpolation, un-Pauline in origin and reflecting a later generation's misreading of the situation of the Jews (Richard 1995, 11-19).

The second missive (1:1–2:12; 4:3–5:28), is more fully developed, written somewhat later in response to oral reports brought from an unnamed emissary. It contains comments concerning the founding of the community (2:1-12) and the matter of holiness (4:3-8) and answers questions specifically raised with the apostle (4:9-12, 13-18, 5:1-11). According to Richard, this second missive reflects a dynamic and thriving community, which has become a model for other communities in its own missionary activity and hospitality (1:6-9). Enough time has elapsed from the early missive for the Thessalonians to develop a reputation of their own (1:6-9). During the course of the editorial process, the later missive has provided the structure for splicing in the early missive (plus the much later interpolation, 2:14-16) into what we now have as 1 Thessalonians.

Essentially, Richard's composite theory rests on two factors: the presence in the letter of a second thanksgiving (2:13) and the tension between an early period of apostolic anxiety about the Thessalonians and a later period in which they have become a model community. First, regarding 2:13, it is important to recognize that it closely parallels the first thanksgiving (1:2-10). Both are thanksgivings to God for the manner in which the Thessalonians received the gospel, for the fact that God remains at work among them, and for their imitation of other believers. It is likely, as Gaventa notes, that the second thanksgiving simply makes emphatic the first thanksgiving, underscoring Paul's desire to consolidate the faith of the Thessalonians (Gaventa 1998, 34). Moreover, Paul never seems stuck within a rigid pattern of letter writing. In Galatians he entirely omits a prayer of thanksgiving, making it not implausible that he could include two in a single letter to the Thessalonians.

Second, regarding the two stages of development of the community's life, Richard places much emphasis on 2:17–3:13 as an expression of the apostles' anxiety that in turn precipitates the dispatching of Timothy to Thessalonica to discover how the community has held up under pressure. This earlier time of uncertainty is then contrasted with the strong commendation of the readers reflected in the later missive. But Paul's anxious concern for the Thessalonians is an expression of his feelings *prior* to the sending of Timothy (3:1-5) and an explanation of why Timothy was sent. The letter is not written until after Timothy returns, bringing a positive report of the life and witness of the community. Paul rejoices at what he hears from Timothy and says, "We have been encouraged about you through your faith" (3:7). It is hard to find much tension between 3:9 (which comes in the so-called early missive) and the commending statements of 1:6-8 (in the second missive). Without discerning two stages in the life of the Thessalonian community, the composite theory collapses.

Whether 2:14-16 (or some portion of it) with its strong denunciation of the Jews is part of the original letter or a later interpolation has been debated for some time. The commentary acknowledges its un-Pauline character, but does not find the evidence for its addition convincing. See the discussion at 2:1-16.

Structure of the Letter

From beginning to end, 1 Thessalonians reads like an uncommonly warm piece of pastoral support to a congregation heading in the right direction but needing encouragement. While orderly and following a definite plan, the letter nevertheless expresses such a depth of relationship that the debated issues of structure seem less critical than in other letters.

Four liturgical passages stand out and provide clues to the framework of the letter. The first is the prayer of thanksgiving (1:2-10) that comes at the conventional location in Greco-Roman writing and expresses gratitude to God for the steadfastness of the Thessalonians in the face of opposition. Some commentators end the prayer at 1:5 and begin the body of the letter at 1:6; however, the focus of 1:6-10 on the readers argues for its inclusion as part of the prayer. The second prayer of thanksgiving (2:13) reiterates the themes of the first prayer and confirms for the readers their identity as people in whom the gospel is at work.

The other two prayers are expressions of supplication to God and fittingly come at the end of the two major blocks of the letters. In the first of the two (3:11-13), the dominant pronouns are first and second person plurals ("we," "our," and "you"), bringing to conclusion a section in which the focus has been on both the apostles and the Thessalonians. The second supplication (5:23-24), where the primary pronoun is second person ("you," "your"), concludes the section of exhortations given to the readers.

The following is a structural outline of the letter.

I. Opening (1:1-10)
    A. Authors, recipients, and greetings (1:1)
    B. A prayer of thanksgiving (1:2-10)
II. Body (2:1–3:13)
    A. The integrity of the apostles (2:1-12)
    B. The readers as recipients of the gospel (2:13-16)
    C. Pastoral concern for the Thessalonians (2:17–3:10)
        1. Paul's desire to see the Thessalonians (2:17-20)
        2. The sending of Timothy (3:1-5)
        3. Timothy's positive report (3:6-10)
    D. A prayer for love and holiness (3:11-13)
III. Exhortations (4:1–5:24)
    A. Directions for living and pleasing God (4:1-12)
    B. Eschatological encouragement (4:13–5:11)
        1. Comfort concerning those who have died (4:13-18)
        2. Encouragement concerning the coming day of the Lord (5:1-11)

Paul and the Thessalonians

In Paul's day, Thessalonica was the capital of the Roman province of Macedonia in northeastern Greece. The Romans had taken over the area in 167 BCE and made the city a regional headquarters. Travelers could leave Rome on the Via Appian, which led them to the southeast coast of Italy, take a short sea voyage across the Adriatic, land in Apollonia, and follow the Via Egnatia all the way across northern Greece to Byzantium. Thessalonica's location on the Via Egnatia made it a bustling commercial center. Paul no doubt traveled along this road from the Aegean Sea when he came first to Thessalonica.

Piecing together bits of information from Paul's own letters, we can judge that he arrived in the area of Macedonia following an extended sick leave in Galatia (Gal 4:13) and missionary activity in Asia Minor. His first stop was at Philippi (1 Thess 2:2; Phil 4:15-16) and then Thessalonica. Apparently he stayed there for some time, long enough to earn money from his tent making (1 Thess 2:9) and to receive at least two gifts of support from the believers at Philippi (Phil 4:16). Paul with his co-workers (Timothy and Silvanus) preached the message of Christ in Thessalonica, and a certain number of Gentiles accepted the good news, turned from their pagan worship, and formed a community (1 Thess 1:9-10).

From 1 Thessalonians we can determine that a deep, intimate bond was forged between Paul and this early group of believers. Like Philippians, the letter is filled with warm words of affection and high commendations for their faithfulness in the gospel (1:3-8; 2:13, 17-19). And yet when Paul and his co-workers first left Thessalonica he acknowledged that he worried about them. He feared that they might be shaken in their faith. To break with their religious past and embrace a new way entailed social consequences, alienation from family and friends, and harrassment of various sorts. So concerned was Paul that he sent Timothy from Athens back to Thessalonica to offer encouragement and to bring word of their circumstances (3:1-5).

The report Timothy brought was exceedingly positive and became the occ-casion for encouragement to Paul amid his own stress and trials (3:6-7). The letter then is written to the Thessalonians to say all this and to answer specific queries carried back by Timothy.

The picture of Paul's relations with the Thessalonians looks somewhat different if Paul's letters are supplemented by material from the book of Acts (17:1-9). Mention is made in Acts of a synagogue in Thessalonica (where in a three-week period the mission is begun) and of a positive response to Paul's preaching not only by Greeks but also by Jews. Other Jews become jealous of Paul's success and create a scene, leading the town authorities to arrest many of the group and forcing Paul and Silas to make a nighttime departure to Boroea.

Aside from the additional details of Paul's visit, two difficulties emerge when Acts is somehow melded with Paul letters. First, a Jewish group in the church is not hinted at or implied in 1 Thessalonians. The account of their conversion in 1:9-10 would seem to indicate that most members of the community (if not all) were Gentile. Second, Acts specifies that the opposition to Paul's mission is initiated by "jealous" Jews. No such Jewish opposition is implied in the letter. In fact, the identification of the opposition in 2:14 as "your own compatriots" (in contrast to the Jews of Judea) would indicate a non-Jewish opposition.

Since Acts is written well after the time of Paul, a privileged place needs to be given to the letters in reconstructing the historical situation. Paul's per-sonal participation in the events mentioned and the early date of the letter gives priority to his account. Since all commentators do not agree on this principle, attention is given in the commentary to passages where interpreta-tions differ because of a reliance or lack of reliance on Acts.

A Lavish Beginning

(1 Thessalonians 1:1-10)

Paul begins his letters in the traditional Greco-Roman form, with appropriate modifications expressing the Christian conviction with which they are written and adapted to the particular group to whom they are sent. First Thessalonians is no different. It begins with the names of the senders, followed by the names of the recipients, an initial greeting (1:1) and, as readers familiar with Paul's other letters would come to expect, a prayer of thanksgiving (1:2-10).

In light of the openings of other Pauline letters, several features of 1 Thessalonians stand out. First, the designation of multiple authors ("Paul, Silvanus, and Timothy") is not at all unusual for the Pauline corpus (six other letters in the collection of thirteen are co-written); however, with the exception of 2 Thessalonians (which is likely an imitation of 1 Thessalonians), only in 1 Thessalonians is there no title, either for Paul or his co-authors (no "apostle of Jesus Christ," "servant of Christ," or "prisoner of Christ"). Since this is the first of Paul's letters, it is impossible to determine why this letter should come title-less, except that the status of the senders is apparently not questioned in Thessalonica. There is no challenge of apostolic authority; therefore, the names seem sufficient. Paul is the primary author (2:18), but the fairly consistent use of the first person plural pronoun throughout the letter indicates that Silvanus and Timothy have been and remain full partners in the ministry at Thessalonica.

Second, the prayer of thanksgiving is lavish (particularly when something like a second prayer of thanksgiving appears in 2:13-14). God is thanked because of the readers' "work of faith, labor of love, and steadfastness of hope" (1:3); for their ready acceptance of the gospel, confirming their election (1:4-5); for their demonstration of joy amid affliction (1:6); and for the example they set for believers in Macedonia and Achaia, an example that has had effects even beyond Greece (1:6-7). Since the prayers of thanksgiving in other letters often serve the rhetorical function of building bridges to the readers, establishing rapport and creating good will, one might suspect Paul of being excessive in his affirmations about the Thessalonians, of laying the compliments on a bit thick, to prepare the ground for later criticism—except for two things: no sharp critique of the Thessalonians is forthcoming in the letter, and the direction of the thanksgiving is primarily to God for gifts of election and sustenance rather than to the Thessalonians themselves. As with Philippians, the prayer of thanksgiving expresses a genuine appreciation for the readers, an appreciation sustained throughout the letter.

Third, highlighted throughout the prayer is the particular way in which the Thessalonians welcomed the gospel into their midst and the way in which their response had become a topic of conversation among the Christian communities throughout Greece (1:8). Despite "persecution," the gospel was received with joy (1:6). The readers were transformed from pagan worship to the service of God (1:9). While the report is as much about those who brought the message as those who received it, nevertheless the readers have become an "example" to others. Their glad reception of the gospel has paved the way for the apostles to be heard elsewhere.

What can be said about the "persecution" the Thessalonians had undergone? The Greek noun (*thlipsis*) rendered by the NRSV as "persecution," together with its cognate verbal form (*thlibō*), appears four times in 1 Thessalonians (1:6; 3:3, 4, 7). Its literal meaning is "pressing" or "pressure," but it is regularly used in a figurative sense as "oppression, difficulty, affliction." Its range runs the gamut from violent distress caused by war (1 Clem 57:4) and cosmic tribulations (Matt 27:21, 29) to mental anguish (2 Cor 2:4) and labor pains (John 16:21). The context of 1:6 makes it likely that the word signifies the social dislocation and attendant difficulties that accompany one's move from pagan worship to the service of the living God rather than violent and sustained persecution from a particular group. A religious change to a radical monotheism can be paralleled by the grief and isolation experienced by aspiring philosophers whose choice of the philosophic life often entailed leaving friends and normal social relationships. The contemporary moral philosophers warned of "the bitter criticisms," "the scoffing and joking," the taunts and derisive laughter they would receive from former friends as well as the unfriendly (Epictetus, *Discourse* 1.22.18-19; Plutarch, *Progress in Virtue* 78A-C; see Malherbe 1987, 38-39). A similar situation may have attended the believers at Thessalonica as they abandoned the cults of Dionysus or of Serapis and Osiris or of the Cabiri for the Christian community.

There is an interesting interplay in the notion that those who were "imitators" of the apostles and of the Lord have become "an example to all the believers in Macedonia and Achaia" (1:6-7). Those who have themselves followed a model have become the model to be followed by others. How could the word of their conversion have spread so broadly? One can only surmise that the Thessalonians themselves became engaged in a mission and apparently a successful one in which they repeated their own story of what God had done in their midst.

Fourth, the conversion of the Thessalonians celebrated in 1:9-10 is described in such unusual (for Paul) language that some commentators have detected the use of a traditional creedal formula, pre-Pauline in origin. Several of the expressions in these verses are not used elsewhere in the Pauline letters (e.g., "real," "out of heavens," the Greek word *anamenein* for "wait"), and others are employed here in peculiar ways (e.g., "Son" as the figure coming out of heaven; the verb "deliver" in an eschatological context rather than the verb "save"). Moreover, were these verses Paul's own creation, one would expect some statement of Jesus' death by crucifixion, a characteristic designation of Jesus in other Pauline letters. Best proposes that Paul employs an early creedal formula in two three-line stanzas:

> You turned to God from idols
> > to serve the living and real God
> > (and) to wait for his Son out of heaven,
> Whom he raised from the dead,
> > Jesus who delivers us
> > from the approaching wrath.

In each stanza the initial line refers to the past, the second line to the present, and the third line to the future (Best 1972, 81-87). If Best is correct, it is also possible that the formulation, alongside others, was a part of Paul's missionary preaching on his initial visit to Thessalonica, when he called them to abandon their idols for the worship of God. Its relevance, of course, is particularly for Gentiles (who abandon their idols) rather than for Jews.

Often the prayers of thanksgiving in the Pauline letters telegraph important themes to be developed in the body of the letter. While it may be too much to claim that the thanksgiving functions as a table of contents, it nevertheless serves to set the letter's agenda. This is the case with 1 Thessalonians. Four themes emerge in the thanksgiving that are taken up later in the letter.

- The steadfastness and faith of the Thessalonians in the face of difficulties (cf. 1:6; 2:13-16).
- The character of the apostles (cf. 1:5; 2:1-12).
- The familiar triad: faith, love, and hope (cf. 1:3; 5:8).
- The eschatological orientation of the Thessalonian community (cf. 1:9-10; 4:13-5:11).

A further word of explanation is needed on the eschatological orientation of the Thessalonian community. They turned from idols to serve a living and real God and *to await the return of God's Son from heaven*. The Son is then identified as Jesus, whom God raised from the dead and who is to rescue believers from the approaching wrath. The resurrection of Jesus signals not the end of his earthly pilgrimage but the beginning of a new time of waiting, in anticipation of his return and deliverance from "the wrath that is coming." Paul returns to the theme in 4:13–5:11 when he offers comfort to those in the community who have had loved ones die and who wonder about their destiny.

The notion of God's wrath is particularly difficult for modern people. For Paul, it is something more than a mechanical working out of universal laws of justice and something different than a divine emotion (e.g., God's becoming angry just as humans do). Paul uses the word frequently in Romans and 1 Thessalonians (cf. 1:10; 2:16; 5:9) to depict God's stance toward a world that rejects the divine lordship. In Rom 1:17-18 the revelation of God's wrath is the reverse side of the revelation of God's righteousness. It is God's reacting presence in a world over which God remains in charge, even as the world stands in defiance. In 1 Thess 1:10 it is spoken of as an event to occur at the endtime. Ironically, God's wrath is not presented as a threat to the readers to keep them in the straight and narrow way, since, as Paul puts it later in the letter, "God has destined us not for wrath [meaning God's wrath] but for obtaining salvation through our Lord Jesus Christ" (5:9).

What has been accomplished in the first chapter of 1 Thessalonians? Paul has greeted his readers whom he describes as faithful believers, chosen and beloved of God. He particularly recalls with thanksgiving their initial reception of the gospel, how they were transformed from worshiping idols to serving the living God and how their own story of divine grace has become known throughout Macedonia, Achaia, and beyond. In the service of God, they now await the return of Jesus.

At the same time that this remembering of the readers' past has resulted in their commendation, it has also set the ground work for the theme of 2:1-16—the character of the apostles' ministry in Thessalonica. The apostles had been the instruments of the gospel's coming to the Thessalonians, and it had been presented "in power and in the Holy Spirit and with full conviction." In their stay at Thessalonica the apostles had proven to be people of integrity, leading the believers even to imitate them. Now the stage is set for a fuller description of the pastoral work of the apostles.

Integrity of the Apostles

(1 Thessalonians 2:1-16)

The section that begins the body of the letter (2:1-16) follows on a theme introduced in the prayer of thanksgiving: "You know what kind of persons we proved to be among you for your sake" (1:5). Though the verses are somewhat loosely connected, they nevertheless present a coherent picture of the character of the apostles' ministry among the Thessalonians, particularly in light of the vivid familial imagery—"brothers and sisters" (2:1, 9, 14), "infants" (2:7b), "nurse" (2:7b), "father with his children" (2:11). The structure of the section is as follows:

The claim of bold speech	(2:1-2)
Denials and affirmations about the ministry	(2:3-7a)
The apostles' pastoral concern	(2:7b-12)
The Thessalonians' reception of the gospel	(2:13-16)

The Claim of Bold Speech
(2:1-2)

The first claim made about the apostolic ministry is that "we had the courage (*eparrēsiasametha*) in our God to declare to you the gospel of God in spite of great opposition" (2:2). Though the apostles had received harsh treatment in Philippi before coming to Thessalonica, they were not intimidated, but, as the verb *parrēsiazō* suggests, spoke openly and freely. The source of this bold speech is God, who entrusts the apostles with the message of the gospel (2:4). According to the moral philosophers, the appropriate context for such frankness of speech is friendship, and precisely friendship and intimacy are what Paul develops in the ensuing verses with his use of the images of "infants," "nurses," and "fathers" (see Fredrickson 1996, 163-183). To put it in contemporary terms, Paul's pastoral relationship with the Thessalonians is the context for his bold and free preaching of the gospel.

"The great opposition" mentioned in 2:2 is vague. It is possible to read the reference in the light of Paul's visit to Thessalonica described in Acts 17:1-9. The opposition specified there is a group of jealous Jews, who with a band of ruffians managed to have Jason, the host of Paul and Silas, and some other believers detained by city officials. The Greek word translated in the NRSV as "opposition," however, is *agōn*, an image from athletics denoting a race, a contest, a struggle. Its use points to the intense competition for the ears of the Thessalonians. As a speaker, Paul was debating and contesting for the gospel amid competing voices, and he acknowledges that in Thessalonica it was a fierce struggle.

Denials and Affirmations about the Ministry
(2:3-7a)

How are verses 3-7a to be read? A number of commentators have understood this section to be an apology on Paul's part, a defense against allegations made about the apostles' ministry in Thessalonica (often leaning heavily on Acts 17:1-9). Particularly the denials in 2:3-7a are taken to be a response to charges that the apostles' motivations have been less than honest ("our appeal does not spring from deceit or impure motives or trickery;" "we speak not to please mortals;" "we never came with words of flattery or with a pretext for greed; nor did we seek praise from mortals").

Who are these accusers? Frame, who leans heavily on the book of Acts (17:1-9) in interpreting the Thessalonian situation, identifies Paul's opposition as Jews who become jealous of his success in attracting to the gospel other Jews and Gentile God-fearers (Frame 1912, 90). Schmithals identifies the accusers as a group of Gnostic teachers, who have come into Thessalonica and, among other things, have charged that Paul lacks spiritual power in his preaching and operates from greedy and deceitful intentions (Schmithals 1972, 123-218). Marshall, while denying any organized opposition to the apostles at Thessalonica, nevertheless argues that Paul is defending himself "against actual or possible criticisms from outside the church" (Marshall 1983, 61).

The difficulty with taking the passage as an apology, however, is that no particular group can be identified as the critics who are bringing charges against Paul and his colleagues. Frame's heavy dependency on Acts makes his proposal somewhat suspect. Schmithals' suggestion has found few supporters. Marshall's sounds plausible but vague. The letter evidences nothing else that would indicate that a party either within or without the community at Thessalonica was attacking the apostles (see the discussions at 1:6; 2:14; 3:3-

5). As mentioned in connection with 1:6, the other references to persecution seem to indicate not so much violent opposition as the social and religious disruption of believers, when they changed from pagan religions to the worship of a God who demanded total allegiance.

A more likely proposal, made by Malherbe, notes that the section (2:1-12) closely parallels several passages in the contemporary moral philosophers in at least two ways (see Malherbe 1970, 203-217; 1987, 52-60). First, the philosophers recognize that the teacher must model what he or she teaches. Seneca points to the value of a personal mentor:

> The living voice and the intimacy of a common life will help you more than the written word . . . because men put more faith in their eyes than in their ears and because the way is long if one follows precepts, but short and helpful, if one follows patterns. (*Epistle* 6.5-6; cf. 11.8-10; Epictetus, *Discourse* 3.22.38-49)

In like fashion, what Paul does in 2:1-12, with remarkable self-confidence, is to offer himself and his colleagues as paradigms for the Thessalonians. Their manner of ministry has been consistent with their preaching and can continue to serve as an example to the community. In fact, the readers have already become "imitators" of the apostles and of the Lord (1:6).

Second, the moral philosophers are eager not to be confused with charlatans, who pose as teachers, engage in excessive flattery, for selfish interests or monetary gain, and are often intimidated by the sometimes unruly mob. Dio Chrysostom comments that it is not easy to find a person who speaks his mind "without guile" and faces the disorder of the crowds without worry about his reputation and "not for gain" (Dio Chrysostom, *Discourse* 32. 11-12). In like manner, Paul, particularly in 2:3-7a, distinguishes the apostolic ministry in Thessalonica from the practice of unscrupulous teachers. In doing so, he reflects the conventional patterns of the moral philosophers not only in content but also in antithetical style ("not . . . but"). Thus there is no need to read between the lines to find actual or potential allegations against the apostles in order to interpret the section.

The picture of the apostles that emerges from 2:3-7a is one of a group authorized by God and seeking only to please God (and not mortals). Their pastoral and public style coheres with their commission in that they do not resort to deceit or pompous rhetoric, as many charlatans do, nor are they out to fleece the public. The frank and honest voice that they give to the gospel is rooted in their divine authorization.

Rhetorically, this self-presentation serves two purposes. First, content-wise it functions as exhortation. The Thessalonians are to live and engage in their mission in this way, namely with integrity, boldness of speech, not to please mortals but to please God. The text recalls for them this example of a genuine ministry. Second, the passage serves as what Aristotle called an *ethos* method of proof. It establishes the credibility of the writers to be heard so that the ground is laid for further exhortations to be made in the letter. The picture of the apostles as genuine witnesses leads to their "urging and encouraging you and pleading with you to lead a life worthy of God."

The Apostles' Pastoral Concern
(2:7b-12)

In 2:7b-12 the relationship between the apostles and the readers is depicted with the use of familial imagery, connoting tenderness and warmth. The imagery is quite extensive, particularly if one chooses the Greek word *nēpioi* ("infants") instead of *ēpioi* ("gentle") as the reading in 2:7b. The evidence from the ancient manuscripts strongly favors *nēpioi*, but the RSV and NRSV opt for the lesser supported word—no doubt because of the awkwardness of a sentence reading "we were infants among you, like a nurse caring for her children." But such a choice violates a fundamental rule of textual criticism: choose the more difficult reading, the reading that explains how an emenda-tion might have arisen to present a more sensible text. Furthermore, Paul on occasion can use a related but slightly mixed metaphor, such as is done here with "infants" and "nurse" (see Gal 4:19).

The choice of "infants" removes the association of "gentle" with "nurse," but it presents a forceful contrast with the previous statement in 2:7a, which, literally, speaks of the apostles as "able to be a weight (of influence)." Paraphrased: "Instead of being among you as apostles with the authority to make heavy demands, we were among you as infants, like a nurse taking care of her own children." The vulnerability of "infants," combined with the ten-der, loving care of the lactating nurse (providing milk and nurture not to someone else's children but to her own) present a double counterpoint to the picture of demanding apostles (see Gaventa 1991, 193-207).

The images of "infants" and "nurse" (cf. Num 11:12) are then followed by the familiar "brothers and sisters" in 2:9 and "father with his children" in 2:11, reinforcing the sense of family solidarity among the readers (see also "orphans" in 2:17) and depicting a nurturing ministry of pastoral care.

The readers themselves, along with God, are repeatedly called to testify ("you remember" in 2:9, "you are witnesses" in 2:10, and "as you know" in

2:11) to the integrity of the apostles' ministry. Three facets of the ministry are singled out: that the apostles worked hard in order not to be financially dependent on the Thessalonians; that their conduct was "pure, upright, and blameless"; and that their mission was intended to foster among the Thessalonians "a life worthy of God."

Throughout 2:1-12 the phrase that gives unity to the whole is the thrice-repeated "the gospel of God" (2:2, 8, 9). It gives focus to the apostles' work in Thessalonica. It is the message they declared with bold speech and yet not apart from the giving of themselves. Verse 8 summarizes the section: "So deeply do we care for you that we are determined to share with you not only the gospel of God but also our very selves, because you have become very dear (*agapētoi*) to us."

The Thessalonians' Reception of the Gospel
(2:13-16)

In the concluding paragraph of this section (2:13-16) Paul gives thanks for the reception of the gospel by the Thessalonians, repeating a note already sounded in the initial prayer of thanksgiving (1:2-10). What is particularly striking about the Thessalonians' acceptance of the gospel is that they received it "not as a human word but as what it really is, God's word." The statement entails two inferences. First is a commendation of the Thessalonians' powers of discernment. In "the foolishness of preaching" (1 Cor 1:21) they have detected the power and wisdom of God. Second is a claim about the preaching of the apostles: that it conveys the word of God. The same double inference was noted in the initial prayer of thanksgiving: "our message of the gospel came to you not in word only, but also in power and in the Holy Spirit and with full conviction" (1:8). What is reflected is the dynamic at work in the engagement of faithful preaching and attentive listening.

The Thessalonians are still in the forefront in 2:14-16 in the comparison drawn between the suffering they received from their countrymen and what the churches in Judea suffered from the Judeans. The comparison leads to some very unPauline-like comments about the Jews, who are charged with killing Jesus and the prophets, driving them out, with displeasing God, and, in their opposition to everyone, with hindering the Gentile mission. Nowhere else in the Pauline letters is any particular group blamed for the death of Jesus. Paul is more interested in the theological issues at stake in the crucifixion (Rom 3:25; 5:8; 1 Cor 1:21-25; Gal 1:4; 2:20) and in its cosmic scope (1 Cor 2:6-9) than in who, historically, the culprits were. While in

Acts the Jews are often identified as the group responsible for harassing Paul and resisting the mission to the Gentiles, the Pauline letters only on rare occasions speak of non-Christian Jewish opposition (such as 2 Cor 11:24, 26). What is stated in 2:14-16 is likely to come from a Paul frustrated and enraged that a particular group of fellow Jews have not only failed to accept the Messiah, but also have hindered the outreach of the gospel to non-Jews.

Two exegetical comments about 2:14 are appropriate here. First, the Greek term that the NRSV renders as "the Jews" (*hoi Ioudaioi*) can also mean "the Judeans," and since the geographical reference to Judea is already in the text, the latter seems the better choice. Thus the term does not designate all Jews but a particular group, those residing in Judea. Second, the expression "your own compatriots" (or "your own countrymen"), without being specifically racial, surely denotes a gentile group. Since the believing community at Thessalonica is predominantly Gentile (cf. 1:9-10), it would be unnatural to take "compatriots" as a reference to Jews. Only if one reads the passage in light of Acts 17:1-9 could one conclude that the "compatriots," who are opposing the believers at Thessalonica, were Jews.

Verse 16 presents another set of problems. Paul's stance toward his own people, the Jews, is painstakingly laid out in Rom 11:25-32, where their rejection of the Messiah has led to the inclusion of the Gentiles. But because "the gifts and calling of God are irrevocable," the Jews remain God's "beloved," and "all Israel will be saved." Does 2:16 imply a change of mind or at least a development of thought on Paul's part from an early letter such as 1 Thessalonians to a later letter such as Romans?

Answering that question is further complicated by two intractable exegetical problems in 2:16. The first is that the text provides no help in determining whether a (and if so, which) particular historical event is intended as the display of God's wrath in 2:16 (as in Rom 13:4-5; 1 Cor 10:6-12; 11:30-32) or whether the reference is to the eschatological wrath (as in 1:10 and 5:10). The other problem is how to render the concluding Greek phrase (*eis telos*)—as the NRSV does with "at last" (with the footnoted alternatives "completely' or "forever") or with "to the end." Both options are possible.

One position, in line with the argument of Romans, is that God's wrath includes both the divine judgment expressed at the cross and the confirmation at the last judgment (Donfried 1984, 242-253). The language used in 2:16 ("filling up a measure of their sins") is repeatedly found in Jewish apocalyptic literature to reflect an understanding of divine justice. It identifies the level of transgressions to be reached before God's wrath is exercised (Dan 8:19, 23; 9:24; 11:36; 2 Macc 6:12-16). In light of these eschatological associations, verse 16 might be paraphrased: "They have been filling up the complete measure of their sins; but God's wrath has overtaken them in the cross and will overtake them until the end." Concerning the differences in Paul's stance toward the Jews in 1 Thessalonians and in Romans, Donfried then concludes, "1 Thessalonians reports God's attitude of wrath toward the Jews from the death of Jesus until the last day; Romans adds that at the last day God's mercy will be revealed toward them in a mysterious and radically new way" (Donfried 1984, 253).

Another position argues that 2:14-16 is an interpolation added later, probably after 70 CE, when the relationship between Christians and Jews was at a low ebb and when anti-Jewish comments by Gentiles were not unusual. The fact that Paul makes no other charge against the Jews like this one and the fact that several expressions in these verses are rare or nonexistent in the other Pauline letters contribute to the notion that they come from a later hand and have been inserted here (see Pearson 1971, 79-94; and more recently, Richard 1995, 119-127).

The major obstacle to the interpolation theory is that there is no manuscript evidence either for the omission of 2:14-16 or for the transposition of these verses to another location. Moreover, the verses do present a tension with Paul's position in Romans, but not in such a way as to warrant their removal from the letter. Due to the occasional character of Paul's writing, polarities are to be expected rather than avoided. For example, it is not surprising to encounter in Galatians a stress on the temporary nature of the law and its inferiority in relation to the promise, and in Romans to hear that the law is spiritual, holy, just, and good. The peculiar contexts in the communities evoke different emphases from the apostle.

Assuming the integrity of the letter (and however the exegetical problems are decided), what 2:14-16 states is that a group of Gentiles in Thessalonica and a group of Jews in Judea have offered serious opposition to the congregations in each locale and, in doing so, have resisted the apostles' mission to the Gentiles. The action of the Judeans is in line with that of their forebears who killed Jesus and the prophets, and the wrath of God has come upon them. The judgment of one Jew (Paul) about other Jews is not so strange; one finds it throughout the Old Testament and strongly in the Qumran literature. What the text, harsh as it sounds, does not mandate is for a Gentile church, presuming to be the instrument of God's wrath, to engage in reprisals and vindictive actions against Jews. The long and grievous story of anti-Semitism by the church unfortunately testifies to the universalizing and misuse of a text like this.

What we have seen of the intense feeling Paul and his colleagues have for the Thessalonians throughout the early part of the letter is now reaffirmed in 2:17-20 and confirmed by the report Timothy has brought of "the good news of your faith and love" (3:6). It is this reveling in the mutuality of affection that controls the next section.

Personal Relationships

(1 Thessalonians 2:17–3:13)

The picture one often gets of the apostle Paul is that of a crusty curmudgeon, defensive about challenges made to his authority and advocating a tight theological position from which divergences are not tolerated. In Galatians he wages war on a group of Jewish Christian missionaries, who share with him an ecumenical vision but who believe that God reaches out to Gentiles through the law and not apart from it. In the Corinthians letters he at times castigates a less than faithful congregation for moral lapses (1 Cor 5:2) and ridicules them for their arrogance (1 Cor 4:8-10).

First Thessalonians (and also Philippians), however, paints a very different picture of the apostle. Allowing for whatever excess may be attributed to rhetorical flourishes, Paul and his colleagues, Timothy and Silvanus, still come through as caring pastors, capable of deep friendships and genuinely involved in the lives of people in their churches. We have already seen how their initial foray into Thessalonica was not as heavy-handed apostles but as vulnerable infants, as lactating nurses with their own babies, and as fathers concerned about their children's lives (2:7-12).

The same notes of warmth and intimacy mark the section from 2:17 to 3:13. The text relates the apostles' intentions in sending Timothy to Thessalonica as an emissary and the delight experienced when Timothy returns with such a positive report of their faith and life.

The section divides cleanly into three paragraphs.

The pain of separation from the Thessalonians	(2:17-20)
Timothy's visit to Thessalonica and his report	(3:1-10)
A prayer for the opportunity of a return visit,	
for increasing love for one another, and for holiness	(3:11-13)

The Pain of Separation from the Thessalonians
(2:17-20)

Separation from the Thessalonians after the initial visit was hard for Paul. He speaks of longing "with great eagerness" for a chance to see them again, and though he repeatedly tried to return, it had not been possible. He describes the separation with the arresting image of being "made orphans." Like children who have lost their parents, the apostles are deprived of their day-to-day relationship to the believers in Thessalonica. More than simply missing them, Paul expresses a sense of the incompleteness of the family, while he is separated from them.

Then in a profuse display of commendation the readers are called "our hope or joy or crown of boasting before our Lord Jesus at his coming," "our glory and joy." The connection with the return (*parousia*) of Christ indicates the depth of the relationship between the apostles and the Thessalonians. Their quality of life and their steadfastness amid difficulties give him great cause for pride, even evidence in the final day of his own faithful ministry.

In explaining why he had not been able to visit them again, Paul makes an unusual statement, "Satan blocked our way" (2:18). Whether he had a specific incident in mind is difficult to determine. The term "Satan," meaning "adversary," appears seven times in the undisputed Pauline letters and sometimes plays the role of the tempter (1 Cor 7:5; 2 Cor 11:14), who tries to outwit God's people (2 Cor 2:2) but who will soon be crushed (Rom 16:20). In two cases, however, "Satan" clearly is functioning under the authority of God, not so much as an enemy but as an agent. In 1 Cor 5:5 the congregation is directed to hand over to "Satan" the member engaged in incest for the destruction of his flesh. Whatever this entails, it is but a step on the way to the possible salvation of the man's spirit in the final day. In 2 Cor 12:7 Paul's "thorn in the flesh" is described as "a messenger of Satan," which in turn prepares Paul for accepting the sufficiency of divine grace. In like manner, Satan in blockading of Paul's way in 1 Thess 2:18 seems to play less of a tempting role and more the role of a divine agent.

Timothy's Visit to Thessalonica
(3:1-10)

Timothy's visit to Thessalonica is motivated by the apostles' need for contact with the congregation at Thessalonica. At one point (3:2) the text indicates that the decision to send Timothy was made by "we" (Paul, Timothy, and Silvanus); at another point (3:5) Paul claims responsibility himself.

Timothy appears frequently in the letters as an emissary for Paul, going where and when he could not himself go. In Philippians, Timothy is endorsed with high words of praise (Phil 2:19-23). Of all possible candidates to be sent to encourage the believers there, he alone seeks the welfare of the members. "Like a son with a father he has served with me in the work of the gospel" (Phil 2:22). Likewise, with the Thessalonians Timothy is the logical choice since he had been active in the service of the gospel there.

Aside from Paul's own longing for the Thessalonians, what in the context of the church itself spurred the visit? Amid all the tender commendations made about the community at Thessalonica, there remains a persistent worry that things will become too difficult for them to handle. Twice the word "persecutions" (noun and verb) occurs in 3:3-4, but, as we noted in connection with its use in 1:6, it has a broad range of meanings—from the violence of war to mental anguish. The expressions of Paul's concern in 3:3, 5 suggest that the problem the community in Thessalonica faces is not that of violent opposition but the cultural and social estrangement that comes with moving from pagan worship to the worship of God. Paul worries that their circumstances will intimidate them, that they will feel the pressure (root meaning of the noun *thlipsis* translated "persecution"), become discouraged, and give up their commitment to the gospel. Timothy is sent "to strengthen and encourage you for the sake of your faith" (3:2).

Timothy brings a positive word from his visit, that the Thessalonians have remained steadfast through their periods of transition and, as the prayer of thanksgiving indicates, have become an example to others (1:7). Paul is overjoyed and reiterates his desire to pay a return visit to Thessalonica.

The comment that the apostles wish to "restore whatever is lacking in your faith" (3:10) need not be taken specifically to identify an inadequate commitment on the part of the Thessalonians, thus setting a caveat beside the joy the apostles genuinely felt and expressed. They simply are a young congregation facing enormous problems of living as a minority community in the midst of a larger, highly charged religious environment. To remain faithful to the gospel would be no easy task, and Paul acknowledges that help from the apostles might still be needed.

The geographical scenario reflected in this section is difficult to reconstruct, given a certain number of conflicts with the account in Acts 17–18. First Thessalonians provides no record of the apostles' departure after their initial visit to Thessalonica. Eventually the three (Paul, Timothy, and Silvanus) came to Athens, where "we" (Paul, or Paul and Silvanus?) were left alone when Timothy made his return visit to Thessalonica (3:1-2). Is Paul still in Athens when Timothy brings his good report and when the letter is written, or has he moved on? The former would seem more likely, though the latter is not ruled out.

Acts 17:1-15 reports that Paul and Silas (Silvanus) initially left Thessalonica under duress and went to Beroea, where Timothy and Silas were left behind, while Paul traveled alone to Athens. The three colleagues do not get together again until Paul leaves Athens and arrives in Corinth (Acts 18:5). No specific mention is made of Timothy's having been sent by the others to Thessalonica. Assuming the three are present at the writing of the letter, the only location for the writing, according to Acts, would be Corinth. Since Acts was likely written two or three decades after Paul's death, priority has to be given to the Thessalonian information, sketchy as it is.

Prayer for a Return Visit, Love for Others, and Holiness
(3:11-13)

The section ends with a prayer-wish with three petitions: that Paul make a return visit to Thessalonica (3:11), that the readers increase in love (3:12), and that they be strengthened in holiness in order to be blameless at the parousia of Jesus (3:13). All three reflect themes mentioned and developed elsewhere in the letter. For instance, Paul has already indicated that he desired to visit the Thessalonians on more than one occasion, but that "Satan blocked our way" (2:18). Since the reasons for not coming are beyond Paul's control, he prays that God will yet make a visit possible.

The Thessalonians have already been commended for their "labor of love" (1:3), something Paul learned not only from firsthand experience but also from the positive report Timothy brought of their current situation (3:6). His prayer is that their love will increase both within the life of the community and beyond the community ("for all"). Since the letter expresses a marked sensitivity to the social environment in which believers live, particularly in terms of the alienation experienced by new converts (1:6; 3:3-4), this addition of "for all" takes on added significance. It echoes Jesus' teaching to love the enemy as well as the neighbor (Matt 5:43-47). In the next chapter more specific directions are given on how the Christian community should respond to the hostile environment (4:9-12).

Finally, Paul's prayer for the Thessalonians asks that they be strengthened in holiness (*hagiosunē*) "with all his saints (*hagioi*)" Words translated "holiness," "saints," "sanctification" (4:3), and "sanctify" (5:24) all belong to the same family. Rather than building on previous references in the letter (as with "love"), the mention of holiness in 3:13 points forward to an upcoming discussion about its nature in 4:3-8 and to another prayer for God's gift of holiness in 5:23 (*hagiazō*). Two observations are relevant at this point. First, the prayers (3:11-13 and 5:23) echo back and forth in that both mention holiness in an eschatological framework (being blameless at the return of Christ). The association with "blameless" indicates that "holiness" has an ethical dimension. It is the quality of life believers are to live to make them acceptable in the day of divine judgment. But the "holiness" required is a gift of God. It is twice made a petition in prayer because God alone "sanctifies" people, and the second prayer concludes with the affirmation, "The one who calls you is faithful, and he will do this" (5:24).

With 3:11-13 the body of the letter comes to an end. What has been established is the nurturing ministry of the apostles and the amazing strength of the Thessalonians to love one another and live their faith in an environment hostile to the gospel. Paul is overjoyed at the positive news from Timothy that, instead of being discouraged and shaken, they have prospered and their story has been told and retold throughout the land of Greece. The letter encourages them to continue to lead a life worthy of God, to persevere in standing firm.

Though the body of the letter is dotted with general exhortations, it primarily paves the way for a more specific section of exhortations to follow concerning holiness, appropriate living when the Christian community is alienated from the larger society, and eschatology.

Directions for Pleasing God

(1 Thessalonians 4:1-12)

The first three chapters of 1 Thessalonians comprise the body of the letter, and with 4:1 the section of specific exhortations begins. "Finally, brothers and sisters" (some Greek manuscripts make it stronger by adding "then") suggests a decided break, introducing a new section. It soon becomes obvious, however, that the change is not abrupt and the ensuing content not radically different from what we found in the body of the letter. The same positive relationship between writer and readers is nurtured; many words and expressions are repeated. What one discovers is that the divisions between the body of the letter (i.e., its gist, its theology) and the exhortations are not sharp. As noted in the Introduction, some commentators read the entire book as a letter of exhortation. What we are calling "the body" of 1 Thessalonians (2:1-3:13) contains exhortations about leading "a life worthy of God" (2:12), and the section of exhortations (4:1–5:24) contains numerous theological statements: about God's authority (4:9), about Jesus' resurrection and pending return (4:13–5:11), about the salvation for which God has destined the Thessalonians (5:10), and about God the faithful sanctifier (5:23-24). In both sections of the letter, then, theology and ethics are intertwined.

The connection between theology and ethics becomes clear in the first paragraph of the exhortations section. Three times (4:1, 2, 6) the memories of the readers are jogged to recall teachings of the apostles during their first visit to Thessalonica. The initial preaching of the gospel, which led to the conversion of some (1:9-10), was accompanied by instruction about the way the believers were to live. For the apostle, receiving the gospel and embodying the gospel in one's daily relationships cannot be separated.

The section of exhortations is divided into three major units:

Directions for pleasing God   (4:1-12)
Eschatological encouragement   (4:13-5:11)
Directions for the community' s life   (5:12-24)

Structurally, the first section (4:1-12) seems a bit disjointed, perhaps even more so in the Greek text since 4:3-6 is one long, unwieldy sentence. There are two features, however, that provide unity and coherence to the passage. The verbs *parakaleō* ("urge") and *peripateō* ("live" and "behave") appear in the opening (4:1) and closing sentences (4:11-12), linking the beginning and the end; and three times in the space of a few verses some form of the Greek root *hagio* appears: "sanctification" (4:3, *hagiosmos*), "holiness" (4:4, *hagiosmos*), and "Holy Spirit" (4:7, *to pneuma hagion*).

The beginning unit of exhortations can be divided into three sections:

Continue to please God	(4:1-2)
Called in holiness	(4:3-8)
Love one another; live quietly	(4:9-12)

Exhortation to Continue Pleasing God
(4:1-2)

The beginning of the exhortations includes a verb (*parakaleō*), translated in 4:1 as "urge," which becomes in the early Christian vocabulary a standard term for an appeal dealing with the moral or communal life of the congregation (cf. Rom 12:1; 2 Cor 2:8; 6:1; Phil 4:2; Titus 2:6; Jude 3). It carries the note of urgency but in the tone of a request, not of a command. In the letter to Philemon, Paul writes, "Though I am bold enough in Christ to command you to do your duty, yet I would rather appeal (*parakalō*) to you on the basis of love" (Phlm 8-9). His appeal to the Thessalonians, then, is not harsh but sensitive to the situation of his readers (cf. 2:12; 3:2, 7; 4:10, 18; 5:11, 14).

The expression "to live and please God" underscores a fundamental character of the Pauline ethic (4:1). "Pleasing God" has already been used in the letter as a way of describing the apostles' motivation (2:4), and now it comes as an appeal to the readers. Rather than relating human conduct to a legal code or to a particular anthropology or to an understanding of the nature of society, Paul orients human life to God. As Collins comments,

> It is a religious response to the God-Father who has chosen the believer (1:5) as his child. In this respect one can speak of gospel morality as a morality of response or a morality of thanksgiving. God, rather than moral perfection or the human ideal, is the perspective of the believer who endeavors to live in an upright fashion. (Collins 1984, 305)

Generally in the ancient world, morality was more in the purview of philosophy than religion. While philosophers, writing about morals, did provide a theoretical framework, it often had to do with what made for a sane or rational life. In contrast, the initial section of exhortations in 1 Thessalonians (4:1-12) lays a heavy emphasis on God as the reference point for human conduct (see Malherbe 1983, 250-251).

Called in Holiness

(4:3-8)

What does it mean to say that God's will is "your sanctification" (or "your holiness," *hagiasmos*)? The Greek word for "holiness" appears rarely in the Septuagint, but the verb (*hagiazō*) and noun (*hagios*) from which it is derived appear often. To call God "the holy one" is to speak of a quality that sets God apart as supreme and unlike humans (e.g., Isa 6:3; 40:25; Ps 78:41; 89:18). The term then is applied to persons (Lev 11:44-45; 16:5,7) and to places (Isa 48:2; 2 Macc 2:18) that are set aside from their ordinary functions for the service of the holy God. The particular noun used in 4:4 signifies more the process of being made holy than the results.

The manner in which the theme of "holiness" is developed in 4:3-8 is intriguing. Clearly in 4:4-6 "holiness" has to do with abstention from immorality and with living a quality and style of life different from those who do not know God. But 4:7 speaks of God's calling not "to holiness," but "*in* holiness," suggesting that "holiness" is "the state of purity in which believers have been placed and to which they are to be faithful in their behavior" (Richard 1995, 197). Furthermore, God gives the "Holy Spirit" to believers for guidance and strength in their life of faith (4:8). "Holiness" then happens as a result of divine action, and what is depicted in 4:3-6 (abstaining from fornication, controlling the body, not exploiting a brother or sister) is the conduct that is indicative of those being sanctified or made holy by God.

Two exegetical problems in 4:3-6 virtually defy a satisfactory solution. The first can be illustrated by three English translations of 4:4.

(RSV)   "that each one of you know how to take a wife for himself in holiness and honor"

(NRSV) "that each one of you know how to control your own body in holiness and honor"

(NAB)   "each of you guarding his member in sanctity and honor"

Is the Greek noun *skeuos* (literally, "vessel") used metaphorically to signify "wife" or "body" or the male sexual organ? Does the infinitive *ktasthai* retain its more basic meaning "to procure for oneself, to acquire," or can it be stretched to "to gain control over"? Those commentators who agree with the RSV translation appeal to the statements on marriage in 1 Cor 7:2-6 as a parallel to 1 Thess 4:3-6. They argue that the nonexploitation of 4:6 presupposes the widespread notion of sexual property rights, i.e., that sexual relationships with a woman to whom one is not married is an offense against the man (father, brother, or husband) to whom she "belongs."

On the other hand, those commentators who agree with the NRSV rendering of *skeuos* as "body" can cite the weighty evidence that each of the other uses of the word in the Pauline letters refers to people and not specifically to wives (Rom 9:21, 22, 23; 2 Cor 4:7). Moreover, the context tends to support the translation "body" (or even male organ). What 4:3-5 would be saying is that the process of sanctification means that one abstain from fornication (*porneia*, a general word for sexual immorality), which entails having control over one's own body, one's sexuality.

The other problem in the passage is determining what is meant by the phrase "in this matter" (*en to pragmati*). Does the exploitation of a brother or sister specifically relate to the "matter" of fornication (or possibly not offending a fellow believer in acquiring a wife), or does it more generally refer to treating fellow believers nonexploitively? To put it another way, does Paul deal in 4:3-6 with the one issue of sexual conduct (including the acquiring of a wife), or does he deal with two issues—sexual conduct and social justice? *Pragma* ("matter") in itself is generic and draws its meaning from the context in which it appears. In 1 Cor 6:1 it refers to a grievance in the discussion of lawsuits; in Rom 16:2 it denotes the needs Phoebe might have when she arrives at Rome. How one decides the previous issue (whether the acquisition of a wife or the control of the body) in the final analysis is likely to determine how one settles the antecedent of *pragma*. What is at stake in the above exegetical decisions is whether 4:3-6 is primarily an exhortation to proper sexual conduct or a discussion of holiness and the quality of life, both sexual and social, that reflects God's activity in making believers holy. The latter option seems more likely.

However the exegetical problems are solved, the concluding verses of the paragraph (4:6b-8) provide four reasons why the community should give evidence of God's holiness: the reality of divine judgment (4:6b); the character of God's calling "in holiness" (4:7); the danger of rejecting God's authority (4:8); and the gift of the Holy Spirit (4:8). While the mention of God as "an avenger in all these things" (4:6) functions as a warning, it should be read in light of Paul's later conclusion about the plans God has for the readers: "For God has destined us not for wrath but for obtaining salvation through our Lord Jesus Christ" (5:9).

Exhortation to Love Others and Live Quietly
(4:9-12)

The section concludes with another paragraph that on the surface looks disjointed, but in fact makes good sense and has a certain logical movement throughout (4:9-12). That the readers really do not need to hear what is to be written of course heightens their interest in listening, especially when they are told that they have been taught by God. The content of the exhortation is the encouragement to love another, as they have already been doing. But then the character of love is clarified in terms of three infinitives, particularly applicable to the Thessalonian situation: to aspire to live quietly, to attend to one's own affairs, and to work with one's own hands. By doing so, the community can then maintain a good name in the broader society and not have to be dependent on others.

What does it mean to be "taught by God" (4:9)? Though similar expressions are used (e.g., John 6:45), the Greek word *theodidaktoi* itself appears nowhere else in the New Testament. Since there is no hint in the letter at all of a special revelation of God made to the Thessalonians, three inferences are possible, all of which are likely correct. First, there may be some effort to distinguish the experience of the readers from many current philosophers who stressed that one must be self-taught. In contrast, the Thessalonians are "God-taught." Second, the expression may be a way of interpreting all that had happened to the readers in their experience as believers. God is present as teacher in their midst as they have learned to live together as a special people and particularly as they have come to love one another. Third, the Holy Spirit is mentioned in the previous verse (4:8) as God's gift to the community and since the verb in the clause is present tense ("you yourselves *are* taught by God," unlike the NRSV), the continuing ministry of the Spirit as the divine teacher may be inferred (cf. 1 Cor 2:10-16; Gal 5:22).

Not only are the Thessalonians "taught by God" to love, but also their love has moved out beyond the environs of the city to "all the brothers and sisters of Macedonia." As was noted earlier in connection with 1:7-8, they apparently had been engaged in a mission beyond their borders, and in special ways that mission was a demonstration of love. But the particular exhortation "to do so more and more" has specifically to do with their relationships in Thessalonica, to the immediate culture. Living quietly,

minding one's own business, and earning one's own living are not revolu-
tionary imperatives, but they have an appropriate relevance for a small band
of believers like those in Thessalonica. Rather than calming an apocalyptic
excitement in the community, these "urgings" seem more directed to the
social dislocation experienced by the community. Members face upsetting
situations in the confession of their new faith—disruptions in families, alienation from previous support systems, antagonism from the dominant
religious communities (see the comments on 1:6 and 3:3). In the presence of
such hostility Paul calls for a style of living that is civil, decent, and proper
(*euschēmonōs* cf. Rom 13:13; 1 Cor 14:40) and that will command respect
from outsiders. How different from the Epicureans, who claimed to be phil-
anthropists but whose quietism and withdrawal from public life often
incurred the sharp criticism of others for being socially irresponsible (see
Malherbe 1983, 24-28).

As an introduction to the section of the letter called "exhortations," what
has 4:1-12 set out? Four issues come to the forefront. First, readers learn that
the holy life is both a gift of God and a task of the Christian community.
Believers are called "in holiness" and are to reflect "holiness" in the routine of
their daily decisions—in matters such as sexual morality and in the treatment of brothers and sisters. Being set apart and special to God is a calling
worked out in the arena of human existence. Second, the focal point for all
moral decisions is God, not legal codes or human ideals. What the apostles
have instructed the Thessalonians to do and what they are already doing is
"to please God." Third, Paul returns to the theme of love (mentioned earlier
in 1:3-4; 3:6, 12), affirms it as the teaching of God, and urges the readers "to
do so more and more." He has not yet written 1 Corinthians 13, but it is
clear in this initial letter that love for one another binds the community
together and becomes the occasion for witness throughout Macedonia.
Finally, the "more and more" of love is clarified in terms of the wider, often
hostile community. Quiet, unobtrusive lives that are lived above reproach
become a strong witness to the new life found in Christ.

Eschatological Encouragement

(1 Thessalonians 4:13–5:11)

The section of 1 Thessalonians labeled "Exhortations" begins at 4:1 with a definite shift from the body of the letter. The word "Finally [then], brothers and sisters" signals a move from a prayer for the readers' growth in holiness and love to a reminder that they are to live so as to please God. God's will and their holiness are not ethereal issues but have to do with the routine of daily life, such as the way they behave sexually and the manner in which they treat one another (4:1-8).

The three sections of exhortations that follow (4:9-12, 13-28; 5:1-11) are each introduced by the same preposition (*peri*): "concerning love of the brothers and sisters" (4:9); "concerning (NRSV: about) those who have died" (4:13); "concerning the times and seasons" (5:1), indicating a succession of topics probably initiated by the readers themselves. In 1 Corinthians the same preposition is used to respond to issues included in a letter to Paul (1 Cor 7:1, 25; 8:1; 12:1; 16:1). Whether the Thessalonians had written a letter (none is specifically mentioned) or whether the matters were brought to Paul by Timothy (3:6) is difficult to determine. In any case, the issues of these sections grow out of the circumstances of the readers.

The two sections to which we turn now (4:13-18; 5:1-11) are closely connected. Not only are they similarly introduced, but they also have to do with the eschatological anticipation of the community and are concluded with the exhortation to encourage one another (4:18; 5:11). The former section speaks to an urgent pastoral issue in the community, while the latter addresses the more speculative matter of "the times and seasons" (5:1).

Comfort Concerning Those Who Have Died
(4:13-18)

Apparently the first issue grows out of a concern among the Thessalonians who expected that Jesus would return soon. Meanwhile, however, family

members and Christian friends have died. Since the anticipation of the
parousia was a critical element in the gospel they had initially accepted (1:9-
10), they wonder what this means for the deceased. What is their situation
now? Are they disqualified from the final blessings? Will they be at a dis-
advantage because they did not live until Jesus' return? The Thessalonians'
puzzlement had no doubt compounded the process of grieving, and Paul
owes them a response. There is no indication that they are perplexed about
the delay of Jesus' return or that they have embraced a distorted understanding of the resurrection, either Jesus' or their own, or that they have become
totally hopeless. They simply entertain natural questions about members of
the community who have died.

Paul does not chide the Thessalonians for grieving, but insists that they
understand their loss in a manner different from others who have no hope at
all (4:13). Stoics, for example, tended to urge adherents to transcend grief, at
least any outward display of emotion, since reason taught that death was natural for all people. Believers, however, grieve, but at the same time have good
grounds for hope.

The foundation is laid in 4:14 with the reminder that Jesus died and
rose again. Paul repeatedly in his letters anchors the hope for the future in
the reality of Jesus' resurrection. In writing to the Corinthians, he begins
with the received message that Jesus died, was buried, and was raised (1 Cor
15:3-4) and from that moves to counter those in the community who contended that there would be no final resurrection of the dead (15:12-19).
Earlier in the letter one of the reasons given for shunning fornication is the
sanctity of the body, itself important because "God raised the Lord and will
also raise us by his power" (1 Cor 6:14). In 2 Corinthians faith and proclamation rest on the knowledge that "the one who raised the Lord Jesus will
raise us also with Jesus" (2 Cor 4:14). In Romans the Spirit is defined as a
life-giver: "If the Spirit of him who raised Jesus from the dead dwells in you,
he who raised Christ from the dead will give life to your mortal bodies also
through his Spirit" (Rom 8:11). Together these verses indicate that for Paul,
Jesus' resurrection is not primarily the end of his earthly sojourn, the miracle
that brings closure to his historical presence; rather, it is the beginning of the
new age. Jesus' resurrection opens the door on a new future, assuring the
resurrection of the dead.

Furthermore, in each of these verses in 1 and 2 Corinthians and
Romans, the Greek verb used for the raising of Jesus is *egeirō*. In 1 Thess
4:14, however, the verb is *anistēmi*, not normally used by Paul for Jesus' resurrection, suggesting the possibility that he is citing a fragment of a creed or
liturgical formula (further supported by the introductory words "we

believe"). If 4:14 does contain a fragment known and used by the Thessalonians, which also seems plausible, then the basis for Paul's response to the Thessalonians' puzzlement is rooted in the shared worship experience of writer and readers.

Verse 14 contains two grammatical ambiguities that have led to a variety of translations. First, is the prepositional phrase "through Jesus" to be taken as expressing the agent through whom God works to gather together those who have died (so NRSV: "even so, through Jesus, God will bring with him those who have died"), or does it identify those who have died as being Christians (so KJV: "even so them also which sleep in Jesus will God bring with him")? The word order in the Greek text slightly favors the latter alternative (KJV), but it is sufficiently ambiguous to allow the former also (NRSV). Second, does the phrase "with him" denote God or Jesus? The NRSV maintains the ambiguity of the Greek text, whereas the NEB specifies the "with him" as Jesus ("and so it will be for those who died as Christians; God will bring them to life with Jesus"). However the grammatical difficulties are settled, v. 14 begins to set the stage for the apocalyptic scene in depicting a final gathering together of God's people, initiated by God and warranted by Jesus' resurrection.

Verse 15 takes the scenario a step farther by assuring readers that those who are alive at the return of Jesus will not precede those who have died. An early death of friends and loved ones will not mean either that they will be excluded or that they will have to take back seats at the eschatological gathering. In fact, they will be at the front of the line. Verse 15b is a strong negation.

What is implied in the identification of this assurance as "the word of the Lord"? Some interpreters have suggested that Paul is citing a saying of Jesus (as perhaps he does in 1 Cor 7:10) to clinch his point (e.g. Marshall 1983, 125-127). Though it is possible that Paul could have known a saying of Jesus that did not find its way into the written texts, we have no likely candidates in the canonical Gospels. More plausible is the suggestion that Paul underscores his role here as the prophetic messenger who brings the word of God, as did the prophets of Israel in the Old Testament (e.g., Jer 2:1; Hos 1:1; Joel 1:1; Amos 3:1). In specifically calling on divine authority, Paul adds to the reassurance offered to the readers about the deceased in the community. It is the message of God he brings and not merely his opinion.

By using the first person plural pronoun ("we"), is Paul expressing the expectation that he will be among those who are alive at the return of Jesus? The answer appears to be "Yes," though it is difficult to be certain. In letters written later in his career he seems to anticipate his own death (e.g., Phil

1:21-24). As Paul's ministry developed, the expectation of Jesus' return could have been projected farther into the future, making the reality of his own death more imminent. And yet even in 1 Thessalonians he is inclined to leave it an open question: "So whether we are awake or asleep, we may live with him" (5:10).

The picture of the grand gathering at the end is painted in more colorful hues in 4:16-17. The Lord's advent from heaven is signaled by "a cry of command," "the archangel's call," and "the sound of God's trumpet." All three are conventional apocalyptic imagery and, as Gaventa notes, have to do with the issue of power (Gaventa 1998 , 65-67). The "command" (only used here in the New Testament) is that of the military leader often in a time of war. The company of angels (Mark 8:38) and the blast of the "trumpet" (Joel 2:1; Zeph 1:14-16; Zech 9:14; 1 Cor 15:52) are associated with the day of the Lord and signal the arrival of the royal figure. All three images add to the depth of this scene of ingathering and reinforce the notion that the returning Lord comes as the vanquisher of all principalities and powers, the destroyer even of death (1 Cor 15:20-28).

Verses 16-17 reiterate what has been stated in 4:15: that those who have died will arise first, and only then those who are alive at Jesus' return will join them in this great ingathering. The order ("first" and "then") is expressly aimed at the questions raised by the readers about their loved ones. They are reassured that deceased members of the community are not forgotten but will have a prominent place in God's future.

The amazing conclusion of this apocalyptic scenario comes in the words, "and so we will be with the Lord forever" (4:17). The use of the particular preposition "with" (*syn*, and not *meta*), as Best points out, is very significant. Throughout Paul's letters (and not elsewhere in the New Testament) *syn* is used in a series of compound words that speak of suffering, dying, living, and rising "with" Christ (Rom 6:3-11; 8:17; Gal 2:19). The same preposition is also regularly used for eschatological existence with Christ (1 Thess 4:14, 17; 5:10; Phil 1:23; 2 Cor 4:14; 13:4), linking the life with Christ in this world with existence with Christ after death. Put another way, the future life with Christ is a continuation and a consummation of a life with Christ already begun (Best 1972, 200-202). Moreover, since the expressions of life with Christ in the here and now always entail a corporateness (see the connection between Rom 5:12-21 and 6:1-11), the use of *syn* in eschatological contexts such as 1 Thess 4:14, 17 implies the same sense of the community in the final ingathering.

Two final observations on this section are needed here. First, the text paints a picture in conventional apocalyptic colors of the return of Jesus, the rising from the earth of the dead in Christ, and the inclusion of those alive at the time of the return. Word, phrases, and symbols are drawn from the rich linguistic storehouse, already a part of the Jewish and early Christian resources. What makes the picture distinctive, however, is the figure of Christ, already presented in the letter as one risen from the dead, who is to rescue God's people from the coming wrath (1:10). The repeated mention of "the Lord" (4:14, 15, 16, 17) stresses the exalted role Jesus takes in the eschatological ingathering.

Second, the reason for laying out this apocalyptic scenario is given in 4:18: that the Thessalonians in their grief might find comfort (*parakleite*) by repeatedly reminding each other of the returning Lord and the final ingathering. Both those alive at the parousia and those who have died will have their place in the company of God's people. The assurance comes as a prophetic utterance ("by the word of the Lord," 4:15) and thus can be trusted. It provides the consolation that distinguishes the grief of believers from the grief of those who have no hope.

Concerning the Times and Seasons
(5:1-11)

Whereas 4:13-18 is written in response to a concern among readers about the deceased and the place they will have in the final ingathering, 5:1-11 comes in response to questions "concerning the times and seasons." What precisely were those questions? Since we have no other access to the readers than this letter, all we can do is to examine what Paul writes and surmise what questions likely lie behind his response. Unlike many other places in the New Testament, the primary anxiety does not appear to arise from the delay in Jesus' return (as, e.g., in Matt 24:48; 25:5; 2 Pet 3:3-10). The passage (5:1-11) does not argue that Jesus will come, even though his arrival has been postponed for a time.

It is more likely that the Thessalonians were anxious about themselves and whether they would be prepared for and acceptable to Jesus at his advent. Perhaps they could be helped by having a more precise schedule of events leading to his arrival. It is primarily the uncertainties and fears they have about themselves that Paul addresses. The section is structured in such a way that a conventional apocalyptic scenario is affirmed (5:1-3; that the day of the Lord will happen unexpectedly, and that no one will escape it). But then a sharp turn is taken (at 5:4) as the readers are specifically addressed ("brothers and sisters") and are assured that they are children of light and not creatures of the night. The day of the Lord should not sneak up on them.

Furthermore, they are those destined by God for salvation and not condemnation (5:9-10).

"The day of the Lord" (5:2) is a familiar expression used frequently by the prophets as a term for the endtime, when God's purposes will be fulfilled. In Amos 5:18-20 the people who desire the day because they expect it to bring vindication are warned that it is a day of darkness and not light. In Joel 2:31-32 "the day of the Lord" is "great and terrible," but those who call on the Lord will be saved. (cf. Isa 13:6-13; Obad 15; Zech 14:1-21). The early church found the expression useful, particularly in that they understood "the Lord" as a reference to Jesus and then could make his return the centerpiece of the eschatological hope. (For the expression "the day of Christ," see 1 Cor 1:8; 2 Cor 1:14; Phil 1:6, 10; 2:16.)

A frightful scene is depicted in 5:2-3. Just when voices are declaring that it is a time of "peace and security," lulling the people into a false sense of ease and tranquillity (cf. Jer 6:14; 8:11; Ezek 13:10; Mic 3:5), the day of the Lord appears "like a thief in the night," a character who plans his intrusion just at the victim's most vulnerable moment. The Lord's coming is unexpected. And it is sudden, like labor pains overtaking the pregnant woman. "There will be no escape!" (a strong negative in the Greek). Nothing here to relieve the anxieties of the readers.

Then comes the graceful shift: "But you, brothers and sisters, are not in the darkness . . . you are all children of light and children of the day" (5:4-5). An emphatic "you" sets the readers apart from those who will be totally surprised by the arrival of the day of the Lord. The struggling community in Thessalonica with its uncertainty about the final day are reminded of who they are. As children of light, they need not anticipate the endtime as a threat. In 5:5b the pronoun changes from "you" to "we," with the result that Paul and his associates are included among the children of the day. This rather careful distinguishing of believers from "the others" (*hoi loipoi*) is not done in a disparaging way, but seeks to reinforce among the readers their distinctive identity and thereby the positive stance they can take in face of the day of the Lord.

As Collins has noted, this section revolves around three traditional antitheses: light-darkness (day-night), being awake-being asleep, and sobriety-drunkenness (Collins 1984, 166). While the contrasts are forceful and reflect Paul's apocalyptic dualism, words are used in varying ways throughout the passage, and the reader must be alert to the shifts. For example, in 5:5-6 the contrasts are developed with the figurative use of words: two orbs of power antithetical to one another (daylight or night-darkness) and two kinds of behavior appropriate to each orb of power (keeping awake or being asleep). But then in 5:7 "sleep," "night," and "drunk" are used to convey everyday experiences: people usually sleep during the nighttime hours and get drunk at night. Again, "awake" and "asleep" in 5:6 are symbols for preparedness and lack of preparedness, but in 5:10 the same two words are euphemisms for "alive" and "dead." These blurs in meaning are reminders of the imaginative character of apocalyptic language. Much like poetry, the power of its graphic imagery is more evocative than precise.

The affirmations of identity are closely linked in 5:6-8 with two positive injunctions: "stay awake" (*grēgorōmen*) and "be sober" (*nēphōmen*). The former verb is used in the New Testament in both apocalyptic contexts (e.g., Mark 13:34-37; Rev 16:15) and in nonapocalyptic contexts (e.g., Mark 14:38; 1 Cor 16:13; 1 Pet 5:8) to urge readers to a vigilance and alertness to the times and circumstances in which they live. The latter verb carries the notion of self-discipline and self-control, that is, being free from every form of excess, such as drunkenness (e.g., 2 Tim 4:5; 1 Pet 1:13; 4:7; 5:7). Whether there is a third injunction to add to these two is debatable. Some interpreters take the participle in 5:8 as carrying the force of the imperative (so NRSV: "*put on* the breastplate of faith and love, and for a helmet the hope of salvation;" cf. Marshall 1983, 138-139). Other interpreters argue that the aorist tense of the participle refers to the clothing of armor already given to believers at the time of baptism and is thus not an injunction (NEB: "*armed* with faith and love for breastplate and the hope of salvation for helmet," Richard 1995, 254-255). In support of the latter is the allusion to Isa 59:17.

If the readers have been slow to absorb the positive affirmation of their identity in 5:4-5, they will not miss the even more direct words of 5:9-10: "For God has destined us not for wrath but for obtaining salvation through our Lord Jesus Christ, who died for us, so that whether we are awake or asleep, we may live with him." Two reasons are given why the readers need not be anxious about the coming day of the Lord. First, their future is determined by God, who has appointed them for salvation and not punishment. At key points in the letter the language of election (1:4; 3:3) and the language of calling (2:12; 4:7; 5:24) surface to reinforce for the readers that they are a distinct people because of the place they have in God's plan. Second, the death of Jesus makes possible this destiny of salvation, which consists of living "with him." Although no images of the atonement appear here, the simple prepositional phrase "for (*hyper*) us" likely reflects the formula widely used by Paul and inherited from believers before him (1 Cor 15:3; Rom 5:6, 8; 14:15; 2 Cor 5:14) to depict the vicarious character of Christ's death (see Cousar 1990, 55-56). The "for us" is a variation of "for our sins" (1 Cor 15:3; Gal 1:4), "for the ungodly" (Rom 5:6), "for all" (2 Cor 5:14).

Finally, the concluding injunction repeats the exhortation of 4:18 to encourage one another, but adds to it a second verb ("build up each other"). Later, in the letters to the Corinthians the verb (*oikodomeo*) is repeatedly used in an ecclesial sense for the strengthening of the church. Whether in the matter of eating meat offered to idols (1 Cor 8:1, 10; 10:23) or in worship (1 Cor 14:4, 17) or in leadership (2 Cor 10:8; 12:19; 13:10), the purpose of every activity is the building up of the church. So the talk of " times and the seasons" aims not to be a threat or to create needless anxiety but to be encouragement and edification for the community.

Directions for Communal Life; Closing

(1 Thessalonians 5:12-28)

The letter moves toward a conclusion with a series of exhortations, a prayer for the holiness of the readers, and some of the conventional (and not so conventional) features of a letter closing. Following the specific response to the eschatological concerns of the Thessalonians in 4:13–5:11, the ending may seem like a winding-down. On the surface the injunctions are so general and universal that unfortunately they are often treated like trite moralisms, and yet they comprise an integral piece of the nurturing of the congregation. Directed not at a specified group but to the whole readership, they underscore the caretaking responsibilities of each member of the community, responsibilities that are remarkable when one considers that this congregation is hardly a year old and lives and worships without official leadership.

The section is structured as follows:

I. Exhortations for community life (5:12-22)
   A. Acknowledge and show honor to those who work among you (5:12-13)
   B. Take responsibility for the more marginal members (5:14)
   C. Do good rather than evil (5:15)
   D. Rejoice, pray, and give thanks (5:16-18)
   E. Be open to the Spirit; test the prophetic utterances (5:19-22)
II. A prayer for holiness (5:23-24)
III. The closing (5:25-28)
   A. Request for prayer (5:25)
   B. Greet with a holy kiss (5:26)
   C. Autobiographical adjuration (5:27)
   D. Benediction (5:28)

Exhortations for Community Life
(5:12-22)

It is difficult to determine exactly how indigenous leadership developed among the early congregations of believers and how individuals moved from fulfilling functions to occupying "offices" in the community. In the undisputed letters of Paul the only mention of local leaders is the reference in Phil 1:1 to "bishops and deacons" (perhaps rendered as "overseers, who are servants"). In 1 Corinthians lists are provided to designate the gifts of leadership given by God to the church (1 Cor 12:411, 28-31; cf. Rom 12:6-8), but these can hardly be called offices. Only with the later Pastoral Letters does one discover defined positions (bishops and deacons), with qualifications specified for each office (1 Tim 3:1-12). This does not mean, however, that the early congregations were without leadership.

The initial exhortations of this section (5:12-13) speak of acknowledging and honoring leaders within the congregation. Determining whether the three activities listed designate three types of leaders or whether they characterize three activities performed by a single group of leaders is uncertain. In either case, the activities have to do with "laboring among you" (an often used expression for faithful service; cf. 1:3; 3:5; Rom 16:6, 12; 1 Cor 15:10; 16:16; Phil 2:16), with "having charge of you" (perhaps better translated as "showing care for you"), and with "admonishing you." Though no local polity has developed this early, persons engaged in pastoral activities for the community are to be esteemed "very highly because of their work."

The second set of injunctions is directed at the care for those on the margins of the community, particularly three groups. The first group is called in the NRSV (and the RSV) "the idlers," though this translation is heavily dependent on reading 1 Thessalonians in light of the situation of 2 Thessalonians, where people refused to work and were living on the support of the community (3:6-12). Here the more general meaning of "the disorderly" seems a better choice. As Malherbe notes, "Idleness may be one way in which such a disposition is expressed, but by referring rather to some people as disorderly, Paul draws attention to what he finds particularly disturbing—the social dimension of their disruptive behavior" (1987, 92). The other two groups ("the fainthearted" and "the weak") are less definable. The "fainthearted" may be an allusion to those perplexed about members of the community who had died and were dying prior to the return of Jesus (in 4:13-18). The Greek word translated "weak" does not appear elsewhere in Thessalonians but has a wide range of meanings in the Pauline letters, designating the sick (1 Cor 11:30), the feeble and less important (1 Cor 4:10;

11:22), the morally weak (Rom 5:6), and those "weak in faith" (1 Cor 9:22). Since none of these meanings resonates with what we know of the Thessalonian situation, it is better to leave the word in its general sense. The verbs "admonish," "encourage," and "help," together with the admonition "be patient to all," suggest a pastoral sensitivity to the groups on these margins.

The single injunction in 5:15 is reminiscent of a similar verse in Romans: "Do not repay anyone evil for evil, but take thought for what is noble in the sight of all" (12:17). The law of retaliation is expressly rejected in several places in the New Testament (Matt 5:38-48; Luke 6:27-36; 1 Pet 3:9), though here the alternative to do good is given a broad and inclusive interpretation (*"always* seek to do good to one another and to *all"*).

Verses 16-18 include three brief and familiar injunctions—rejoice, pray, and give thanks. Because of the word order in the Greek, however, stress is actually placed on the condition under which each is to be observed. They might be translated: "Always rejoice; without ceasing pray; in all circumstances give thanks." The exhortations are given to initial readers who, though new to the faith, had already experienced hostility and opposition (1:6; 2:14). The "always," "without ceasing," and "in all circumstances" take account of the situations when rejoicing and praying and giving thanks have not and do not come easily, yet even in unpleasant contexts the imperatives are rooted in the will of God and contribute to the nurture of one another within the congregation.

The three final injunctions (5:20-22) call the community to be open to the work of the Spirit, not to reject the prophetic utterances that the Spirit evokes, but to discern everything according to the criterion of what is good. Whether or not there has been a quenching of the Spirit and a suspicion about prophetic activity within the Thessalonian community is impossible to tell. In the initial prayer of thanksgiving Paul commends their reception of the Spirit (1:5-6) and throughout seems to assume the Spirit's presence in their midst (4:8). Nothing else in the letter hints at either a conflict or a spiritual inadequacy among the readers. It seems somewhat speculative, therefore, to suggest that the community in reaction to unbridled prophecies about the last days has grown distrustful of all prophetic speech and that these injunctions address such a predicament (so Richard 1995, 283, who comments, "The final topic of his paraenesis alerts the reader that it is the Spirit and the function of pneumatic gifts which motivate Paul from start to finish in writing to the Thessalonians about their community's situation.")

What is the purpose of such injunctions when they are apparently not directed at a specific target group? Sampley has suggested that maxims were widely used by speakers and writers in the ancient world and that in crafting pithy maxims a rhetorician could add to his credibility and ethos. By their nature, maxims "call for involvement and self-application. They invite the reader or hearer to engage them, to try them on to see how life would look if one lived in accord with them." They demand active participation, but because they are general in character they leave much to the determination of the individual. "Hold fast to what is good; abstain from every form of evil" (5:21b-22) does not define what good or evil is, but points believers to what they ought to aim for in life. "Such moral counsel resembles guidelines more than casuistry, and goals more than particular steps along the way" (Sampley 1991, 94-98). 1 Thess 5:12-22 and Rom 12:14-21 are two occasions where Paul teaches by using maxims.

A Prayer for Holiness
(5:23-24)

The prayer offered at the conclusion of the section of exhortations in many ways resembles a prayer made earlier in the letter (3:11-13). Both contain a plea for holiness, and both have an eschatological focus ("at the coming of our Lord Jesus"). They echo back and forth over the call to holiness in 4:4-8, which specifies the sexual and social conduct appropriate for those who serve the holy God.

Three features of this second prayer stand out. First, the emphatic way in which God is mentioned ("May the God of peace himself . . .") and the use of the aorist infinitive of the verb "to make holy" or "to sanctify" indicate that the stress is placed on the eschatological status of believers as holy rather than on their ethical progress. It is not simply that God is asked to inspire and sustain believers in their growth in this life (as in 3:11-13); rather, God is asked to present them completely holy at the time of judgment. Second, the unusual mention of "spirit and soul and body" points to the totality of the person who is made holy (cf. Deut 6:5; Matt 22:37). It reinforces the notion of 4:4-8 that holiness has to do with sexual and social matters more than with something strictly religious. Third, the description of God as "the one who calls you" (1:4; 2:12; 4:7) and the affirmation that God is reliable and will do what has been promised (5:24) provide a reassurance to those who may be anxious about the final day. The certainty that they in fact will be holy, sound, and blameless rests on a faithful God and not on their progress or lack of progress in the life of holiness.

Closing
(5:25-28)

Of the four components of the closing to the letter, three are conventional and appear in other Pauline letters. Requests for prayer (5:25) can be found in the closings of Romans (15:30) and Philemon (22) and at earlier locations in other letters (2 Cor 1:11; Phil 1:19). The greeting with a holy kiss (5:26) is more frequent (Rom 16:16; 1 Cor 16:20; 2 Cor 13:12). While it expressed the friendship and conviviality between members, the kiss may also contain the element of reconciliation, reflected in Old Testament stories, such as that between Esau and Jacob (Gen 33:4) and between Joseph and his brothers (Gen 45:15), and in Jesus' parables (Luke 15:20). The grace benediction (5:28) appears in the conclusion of each of Paul's letters (Rom 16:20; 1 Cor 16:23; 2 Cor 13:13; Gal 6:18; Phil 4:23; Phlm 25).

The unconventional feature of the closing is the sharp autobiographical statement in 5:27: "I solemnly command you by the Lord that this letter be read to all of them." The very strong Greek verb rendered "I solemnly command" (*enorkizō*) occurs only here in the New Testament and could be translated "I adjure you by the Lord" or "I want you to swear by the Lord." Why this unusual command? The switch to the first person is in itself not strange. Paul on occasion takes the pen from the amanuensis and adds a final word in his own handwriting (1 Cor 16:21; Gal 6:11). He wants to insist that the letter be read, no doubt publicly, "to all the brothers and sisters." The situation of unity, goodwill, and faithfulness among the Thessalonians can only be fostered by such a open address to the congregation, where each member has access to the text and where none—even the disorderly, the fainthearted, and the weak (5:14)—are excluded. Since the letter seeks to commend and encourage readers, to reassure them of their place and their loved ones' place in the final gathering of God's people, it is a word to be heard by all.

Reading the New Testament Series

Available

Reading Matthew
by David E. Garland

Reading Mark
by Sharyn E. Dowd

Reading Luke (revised)
by Charles H. Talbert

Reading John
by Charles H. Talbert

Reading Acts
by Charles H. Talbert

Reading Romans
by Luke Timothy Johnson

Reading 1 and 2 Corinthians (revised)
by Charles H. Talbert

Reading Colossians, Ephesians, and 2 Thessalonians
by Bonnie Thurston

Reading 1 Peter, Jude, and 2 Peter
by Earl Richard

Reading Galatians, Philippians, and 1 Thessalonians
by Charles B. Cousar

Reading Hebrews and James
by Marie Isaacs

Forthcoming

Reading 1 and 2 Timothy, Titus, and Philemon
by Marion L. Soards

Reading Revelation
by Joseph Trafton